IN SEARCH OF
GHOSTS

IN SEARCH OF
GHOSTS

DARREN W. RITSON

First published in 2007 by Grosvenor House Publishing

Amberley Publishing Plc
Cirencester Road, Chalford,
Stroud, Gloucestershire, GL6 8PE

www.amberley-books.com

British Library Cataloguing in Publication Data.
A catalogue record for this book is available from the British Library.

ISBN 978 1 8486 8121 7

Typesetting and Origination by Diagraf (www.diagraf.net)
Printed in Great Britain

I WOULD LIKE TO DEDICATE THIS BOOK TO MY PARTNER OF 13 YEARS
JAYNE WATSON AND OUR DAUGHTER ABBEY MAY RITSON.
I WOULD ALSO LIKE TO DEDICATE THIS BOOK TO ALL THOSE WHO
HAVE CARRIED OUT SERIOUS PSYCHICAL RESEARCH.

Visit the official website of Darren W. Ritson and Michael J. Hallowell
http://mikehallowell.com/wraithscape/

ACKNOWLEDGMENTS

Let me begin by thanking The North East Ghost Research Team and our patron Mike Hallowell. My thanks go to James Tate for accompanying me to the Village of Borley. Without him it never would have been possible. Thanks to the villagers of Borley for talking to me and being so understanding. Thanks to Catherine and Beverley from The Jolly Sailor pub near Sunderland, and Cheryl Booth, Elaine Hollis, June Thompson and Chris Wood from the Thurcroft Miners Institute in Rotherham. My thanks also go to Rob Irons and the staff at Inveraray Jail in Argyllshire. To the staff and guides at Blackpool pleasure beach and thanks to RDF Media and Channel Four Television for a great experience. Thanks also to all the staff at Chillingham Castle. My gratitude goes to Steve and Sue Amphlett from the Plough Inn at Wigglesworth for their kindness and hospitality. To Corrina Orde and all the staff at the Schooner Hotel, the English Heritage guide at Warkworth castle along with the Jedburgh castle gaol staff, Jedburgh council, and the haunted northeast paranormal group. My appreciation goes to the owners of the anonymous haunted house, which has been featured herein, to Darren Homes and Trudy Barker, the owners of the Mcorville arms in Hartlepool. Thanks go to Dave Wood for the help with the Woodchester Mansion chapter, to Nicky Sewell and the PSI team along with the staff at Woodchester Mansion. Thanks also go to John Humphries of the Ancient Ram Inn at Wotton-Under-Edge for his hospitality and kindness during my visit. My gratitude also must go to Paul Wray – the owner of the City Hotel in Durham city centre for his hospitality during our investigation there. Thanks go to the National Trust and the staff at Washington Old Hall and also to Cindy and Colin Nunn from API (Anomalous Phenomena Investigations) for allowing me access to investigate the Grange at Hurworth.

My gratitude goes to each and every one of you who spoke to me and told me their ghostly tales in Devon, London, Norfolk, North Wales, Ayrshire, The Scottish Highlands, Edinburgh, Derby and York. My thanks also go to TAPS (The Answers People Seek), the northeast ghost hunters, and GHOST (Ghost and Hauntings Overnight Surveillance Team) for the Investigations I have attended with them as a team member. A massive thank you to Paul Adams, co-founder of the Harry Price website for writing the chapter about the great man himself. It is indeed an honour to have your writing as part of this work. A huge thank you to 'The Exorcist' Ralph Keeton and his girlfriend Nikki Austwicke and thanks also go to medium Peter Crawford for organising the event in which we met for the first time. Many thanks to David Wells and Richard Felix – sharing the stage at the many charity events we have publicly spoken at, and to work alongside you both at these events was indeed a huge honour and I look forward to seeing you both again sometime soon. I must also add that I am very much indebted to Peter Underwood FRSA and Guy Lyon Playfair. They have both played a big part in my life recently in regards to my research and my investigating. I thank you for the time you have taken to speak to me and guide me in my quest. My gratitude must also go to G.P. Taylor, best selling author, television presenter, and ghost hunter for writing the foreword to this book. Your kind words to me are the best a writer could ask for. To Mike Hallowell for writing the afterword and to everyone else I have spoken to during the entirety of my travels across the UK I say thank you. Finally to my mother and father for all your support and last but not least, my partner Jayne Watson for her patience and understanding, and our daughter Abbey May Ritson, who brings so much light into my life. I love you both.

CONTENTS PAGE

FOREWORD

For the last thirty years I have searched for the hidden meaning of the Universe. At the age of six I had a near death experience when I fell into a river. From that day I have been convinced that death is not the end of human life and something fantastic is beyond. In my search for the truth I have encountered many strange things and witnessed events beyond the realm of human understanding. The task of finding out about such things is not the work of theologians alone. Scientific evidence is greatly needed. It is no use taking the story of a witness as fact, many a ghost story I have investigated has turned out to be little more than over active imaginations or local rumour.

I am convinced in the presence of a spirit world that sometimes collides with our own. But this is not to be investigated with hocus-pocus or half-baked notions and superstitions. The subject of the paranormal needs rigorous investigation and I cannot recommend Darren W. Ritson highly enough.

I first came into contact with Darren after I presented a television programme on the paranormal called *G.P. Taylor's Uninvited Guests* for ITV. I had the pleasure of reading this manuscript and seeing his work first hand. I was impressed by his scientific approach to the subject and his refusal to accept the fact on face value. He has the courage to investigate, even if this means disproving a supernatural presence. If the truth is out there then Darren will try to find it.

Darren is a real ghost hunter and knows his subject matter and this book reflects all those years of research. It is a real must for anyone wanting to know about the paranormal. There are those who write about the subject without going out in the field and spending long hours waiting and wondering. This book is the culmination of many hours work often in cold and lonely environments. Ghost hunting and paranormal research often attracts the weird and the wonderful that use unscrupulous techniques and have wacky ideas. Darren presents evidence based on the science of paranormal investigation and not drawn from the imagination. This is one of the *best* books on the subject and well worth a read.

G.P. Taylor

Author of the New York Times best seller Shadowmancer. *His other books include* Wormwood, Tersias *and the* Curse of Salamander Street. *He is a lecturer on the occult and the paranormal and an Anglican Priest.*

INTRODUCTION

The United Kingdom is a very haunted isle indeed, a magnificent landmass in which shades of the past and spectres of long-gone days lurk in almost every corner. There isn't a city that does not claim to have a ghost or two tucked away in its ancient (and even newer) buildings. Side streets, back alleys, the nooks and crannies of our villages and towns, parks and woodlands also have their fair share of phantoms and apparitions aimlessly roaming around, trapped between the two worlds for evermore trying to find eternal rest or simply move on to the next plane of existence. Ghost hunters from far and wide visit the UK on a regular basis to investigate our wonderful 'haunted heritage' and more often than not they are not disappointed in what they find.

Let us not forget the vast amount of cities and urban areas we have that are haunted, combined with the splendour of our countryside, national parks, and areas of outstanding beauty that have also had a macabre and bloody history, it is no wonder that scores of ghosts are said to haunt this breathtaking terrain. Ancient battlefields adorn the land and literally hundreds of castles, stately homes and old fortresses still stand today, with a fiery magnificence and an air of grandeur as a reminder of our turbulent days gone by. With ghosts being seen, reported, and investigated almost everyday is it any wonder that the UK is reputed to be one of the most haunted countries in the world. In this book, I have endeavoured to report on some of the many overnight investigations I have had the great pleasure of attending at some of the most paranormally active locations in and around the UK. Some of these investigations reported herein are my own, and others are from when I have been a guest of other research teams.

Similar to the investigations in my first book *Ghost Hunter, True Life Encounters from the North East*, this book takes a look at some of the venues around our wonderfully haunted country and details their histories, the ghost stories and legends that are attached to the venues, and goes into the results ascertained on these investigations of which some of these real-life happenings were truly terrifying indeed. I have also endeavoured to keep the write-ups as real as they can be and no embellishment or elaboration has been used in order to hype up the accounts. What you read is what actually happened!

For me personally, ghost hunting and investigating strange happenings, is not just about spending time overnight in haunted hotels, castles, pubs, mansions, and other such locales tracking down denizens of the other world with all our ghost hunting tools of the trade etc, although doing this is extremely rewarding. But for me it is also about talking to witnesses, meeting people and visiting venues, if only for an hour or two, to hear of the ghostly encounters they have had in their respective properties and venues. From the beautiful Ayrshire on the west coast of Scotland, to Edinburgh to York to Norfolk, from North Wales to London to Derby to the captivating county that is Devon, I have visited and sought out the haunted houses and pubs and other troubled venues and spoke to many witnesses and heard their first hand accounts of ghostly goings on and strange paranormal activity. The people I spoke to and interviewed were all down to earth, level headed and responsible people who held down good jobs and careers with no reason to invent or manufacture stories of such a nature, why would they? The vast amount of people on my travels that I have had the pleasure of talking to all genuinely believe that they have had a paranormal or ghostly experience and they most certainly cant all be wrong, can they? I don't think they are.

I have been in the ghost hunting game for over twenty years now after a lifelong interest in the subject, and for many years I have spoke to witnesses and interviewed people who all claim to have either seen ghosts, felt ghosts, or had a paranormal experience. After a while you get a certain feeling from those you talk to and it is not hard to establish when someone is blatantly making up stories. But it does happen. I can say with all sincerity that I truly believe all of the witnesses that I have spoken to on my journey across the UK and that is why I have chosen to include them in this volume. I hope you, the reader, will enjoy reading about them as much as I have enjoyed listening to them, compiling them, and putting them into a readable format for us all to have the benefit of. They are wonderful accounts of ghost stories and true life encounters that should be documented and most certainly never forgotten.

Like most dedicated researchers, the money I have invested into my travels and ghost hunting does not bare thinking about and probably runs into thousands of pounds. The time I have spent on trains, buses, and long car journeys getting to these places is almost infinite and yet I still continue to pursue and investigate the unknown. It's a passion, it's a way of life, and it's my dream. I am also very fortunate to have a very understanding partner (who has sometimes accompanied me on my trips).

I would also like to point out that although I would like to say I have travelled the length and breadth of the country in search of these ghost stories and investigations I have not! What is covered in this book does not even begin to scratch the surface of this haunted isle – not by a long shot. There are tens of thousands of haunted venues, locales, in which the ghost hunter could visit, and to cover these in one book would be almost impossible. However, as a part time ghost hunter and full time office worker (the mortgage needs paying) I do deem myself fortunate enough to have at least visited a relatively small, but manageable range of these haunted hot spots and investigate, report, interview, and write up all my findings and present them to you, the reader, in this book. But watch this space, with many more areas to visit, places to go and people to talk to I am sure that my ghost hunting around the UK is only just beginning.

CHAPTER ONE

HARRY PRICE
PRINCE OF POLTERGEISTS

by Paul Adams

This book is concerned with the investigation of modern cases of spontaneous phenomena and nearly a century and a quarter after the establishment of the first organisation dedicated to the study of the paranormal – the Society for Psychical Research in Cambridge in 1882 – it shows what is continuing to be carried out at a grass roots level – the collection and examination of evidence of an unseen world which is literally all around us. But if we were to turn the clock back to the time of the founding of the SPR, or even later to say the opening decades of the twentieth century, then Darren W. Ritson and his team would find themselves in a paranormal scene totally different to the one that you will be reading about in this volume, a field of investigation that today very few psychical researchers have had hands-on experience of. This is simply because the first half century of organised scientific psychical research was dominated by the investigation of spiritualistic and mediumistic phenomena and the arena for those investigations was the shadowy world of the séance room. Beginning with D.D. Home, the great and inevitably notorious names of physical mediums such as Florence Cook, Eusapia Palladino, Martha Beraud (Eva C.), the Schneider brothers, Franek Kluski and 'Margery' Crandon chart the course taken by the leading psychical researchers of the day from the last quarter of the nineteenth-century through to the early 1930s.

Haunted houses weren't exactly forgotten during this time and several important cases stand out – one of the SPR's founders Frederick W.H. Myers investigated the classic Cheltenham haunting soon after the Society had been established and the SPR itself organised what in effect was the first systematic investigation of an alleged haunting when it rented Ballechin House in Scotland for three months during the early part of 1897 – but with the fuelling of the spiritualist movement through the slaughter of the Great War giving rise to countless families desperate to establish contact with their lost loved ones, the investigation of the paranormal became a search for psychic truth amongst what became in effect the organised fraud of phoney mediums and crank psychics.

At this time the most prominent paranormal investigators were drawn from the ranks of the more open-minded sections of the international scientific establishment – university-educated doctors, physicists and psychologists they included Baron von Schrenck-Notzing from Munich; Dr Hereward Carrington in America; Drs Gustav Geley and Eugene Osty in France; while in England, newcomer Dr Eric Dingwall was starting to make his mark as one of the twentieth century's leading psychical researchers. The discoveries and research of the day were communicated through the peer-reviewed journals of institutions such as the American Society for Psychical Research, the *Institut Métapsychique* in France and the SPR in England. Not surprisingly, little of this actually filtered through to the proverbial man in the street, the general public at large having to make do with the headlines and sensationalism of the national press together with the editorials of the spiritualist newspapers that conveyed sincere yet obviously biased accounts of investigations into the claims of psychics and mediums. Psychical research had yet to obtain a hero who would be able to present the subject at just such a level.

All this changed in June 1920 when Harry Price was elected a member of the Society for Psychical Research and began in earnest his controversial career in organised paranormal investigation. Price was a Londoner and since he first became prominent in the popularising of psychical research in the 1920s and 1930s he has become a seminal figure in the field of modern day ghost hunting. Paranormal investigators of today, even though they may know little about Price himself are following the procedures that he used to bring the scientific study of ghosts and abnormal phenomena firmly into the public eye over fifty years ago. Harry Price was forty when he made the decision to take an active role in international psychical research and felt that he had a lot to offer on several levels. For many years he had taken a practical interest in conjuring and magicians' tricks and when these techniques, which he himself mastered on an amateur but nevertheless competent level, were applied to the marvellous claims of the many mediums who were operating at the time, he was able to demonstrate that much of their phenomena were in fact cheap but effective parlour tricks designed to relieve the credulous and the desperate in search of their departed relatives and friends of their money. Price was also an avid bibliophile and had amassed an impressive collection of books and pamphlets on conjuring and the occult in the years leading up to his joining the ranks of the SPR, which he offered on loan to the Society. As a collection of rare and important reference material it has never been equalled and survives to this day as one of the most frequently consulted Special Collections at the University of London Library to whom Price eventually bequeathed all his effects and papers in 1937 after what was to be one of the most exciting, eventful and ultimately controversial careers in paranormal investigation ever.

As a person Harry Price was an incredible dichotomy – a talented amateur sci-entist and a prankster; a serious investigator and a showman; a talented technical author and a sensational journalist. Although he quickly proved through his expo-sure of the fraudulent 'spirit' photographer William Hope that he was a force to be reckoned with, he was unable to accept the confines of the organisation and the personalities of the scene in which he had become a prominent part and, after five years of operating in the shadow of the SPR with whom he had an uneasy relation-ship for the rest of his life, he felt the need to reorganize British psychical research on his own terms and in January 1926 opened his own institution dedicated to the study of the unknown, the National Laboratory of Psychical Research which in various incarnations survived continuously as a rival organisation to the SPR for a period of twelve years before being closed permanently on the outbreak of war in 1939. As the Honorary Director, Price found he had the control to present his work in the way he felt was to his best advantage and using his good relations with the editors of several of the national newspapers of the day soon began his popular education of the masses, showing the public what was being done to dis-cover the truth behind the mysteries of the séance room and the haunted house.

Today, Harry Price is known first and foremost as a ghost hunter and although he himself acknowledged this as is made clear by the title of his 1936 book *Confessions of a Ghost Hunter*, the truth is that the investigation of spontaneous cases of pure haunting made up only a small part of his overall career in psychical research. Despite taking part in the first live broadcast from a haunted house dec-ades before programmes such as *Most Haunted Live* made the event commonplace and although his most famous and controversial case is that of Borley Rectory, 'the most haunted house in England' which through his sixteen year association and two full length books he made world famous, the two main areas of paranormal study that occupied Price between 1920 and the time of his death in March 1948 were physical mediumship and poltergeist phenomena. As has been mentioned previously, he was committed to the investigation of the former through the pre-vailing trends of the day, while with the latter, by his own admission he was drawn to study the *Poltergeister* simply because they attracted him so much. Harry Price himself had much in common with these "mischievous 'entities'" as he liked to call them.

Over the years Price had countless sittings with spiritualists who claimed to be able to contact the dead or psychics apparently possessing remarkable paranor-mal powers. He became notorious as an investigator who was able to see through much of the deception to the point that many mediums would not sit for him or allow him to be present at their séances. Among the fakers whom he exposed were Jean Guzik whose materialised séance room animals were nothing but the medium's own hand inside a sock painted with 'eyes' in phosphorescent paint; Pasquale Erto, the 'luminous man of Naples' whom Price discovered was able to glow in the dark only by rubbing iron filings between his buttocks; Helen Duncan who ran screaming into the street during a sitting at the National Laboratory after Price had requested he X-ray her to disprove the theory that her material-ised spirit forms were nothing but regurgitated cheesecloth and rubber gloves; 'Margery' Crandon who fooled many people, brought about major divisions within the American Society for Psychical Research and wrangled with Houdini; and there were many others. On the other side of the coin were what continue to be looked at as impressive and genuine cases of physical mediumship – Stella Cranshaw, a young English nurse that Price met on a train and who was able to lower the temperature of the séance room and produce impressive PK effects; the Austrian Rudi Schneider whom Price brought to London for several series of sittings between 1929 and 1932 and who produced a impressive array of phenom-ena including materialised limbs, cold breezes and the movement of objects. Price met and examined them all.

In 1945, Price published *Poltergeist Over England*, an extended work of 160,000 words, the longest of his many books and which took him two years to write. It was a history of poltergeist phenomena both ancient and modern and could well be described, as a summing up of all that Harry Price found fascinating about the subject. When he first approached the task, Price found that he had so much mate-rial at his disposal that he could have written a dozen books, so therefore he made the decision to publish detailed accounts of all the famous English cases – Cock Lane, Hinton Ampner, Tedworth Drummer and the Wesley case are all there – as well as including some outstanding foreign cases such as the moving coffins in the haunted vault of Christ Church in Barbados where they merited inclusion. In his presentation of his material, the principle of selection used by Price was one of excluding totally fraudulent cases and including only such cases as might, more or less, be considered as being genuine, which resulted in a wider variety of polter-geist cases collected in one book than had ever been presented before and as such, despite later books on the subject, Price's book remains an impressive and useful reference work.

Price personally investigated many cases of alleged poltergeist phenomena during the course of his career in psychical research. A Scottish case in Fifeshire which he described as 'Poltergeist Manor' where furniture and ornaments were overturned and thrown about and several mysterious fires were started occupied him in the immediate years leading up to his death and this was one case about which he hoped but never succeeded in writing a full-length report; but his adventures with the 'entities' had begun many years before. In early 1929 he visited a house in Eland Road in Lavender Hill, London where the owners were reporting striking and startling phenomena. This has become known as the 'Battersea Poltergeist' and caused a sensation at the time with mounted police being drafted in at the height of the disturbances to keep crowds of sight seers away from the 'mystery house' where moving furniture, apported objects and projectiles such as pieces of coal and red-hot cinders were making headlines. Price visited the house several times and was present when objects moved mysteriously, apparently when no one was near them.

Three years earlier in 1926, Price took part in an investigation of the Romanian peasant girl Eleonore Zugun who became known as the 'Devil girl' or 'poltergeist girl'. After visiting Eleonore in Vienna where she was the ward of the Countess Wassilko-Serecki, a titled lady interested in psychical research, and where he witnessed several impressive manifestations including the movement of objects and the appearance of scratches and bite-marks on the girl's arms and face, caused so it was said by a possessing spirit or demon, Price brought the girl to London in September 1926 and carried out observations at his newly opened National Laboratory. Price was rewarded for his efforts with several incidents of what he considered true poltergeist phenomena, which included the movement of a coin totally unaided and the movement of objects apparently from one room to another without human agency.

Like the poltergeist phenomena he himself studied, Price enjoyed playing tricks and was thought to have, on occasions, helped out the ghosts if it resulted in good copy for his reporter friends and increased column inches in the papers about himself and his activities. Controversial amongst his colleagues in the field of psychical research during his lifetime due to his love of the limelight, this critical attention continues to this day and as an individual he continues to arouse interest and comment. However, several leading figures in modern day paranormal research including former *Most Haunted* investigator Phil Wyman, arch sceptic Prof Richard Wiseman and ghost hunter supremo Peter Underwood (who corresponded with Price on several haunted house cases shortly before Price's death) acknowledge him as a leading and influential character. In his 1978 book *A Dictionary of the Supernatural*, Underwood gives a concise review of Harry Price's activities and finishes his entry with a very fair comment on the man himself when he says:

> An informed but impartial estimate of the character of Harry Price suggests that he was neither a totally dedicated, saintly, much-wronged scientific researcher, nor an out-and-out fraud on whose views or whose word no reasonable person could ever rely. He was a mixture of the two, and he possessed a genuine and very knowledgeable enthusiasm for all facts of psychic research, mysteries and the unknown, and devoted much of his time, energy, money, gifts and ingenuity to these interests. On the other hand, there is evidence that, where his personal self-esteem was involved, he was capable of the most extraordinary double-dealing, spite and intrigue.

Several of Price's cases and Borley Rectory in particular, has been the subject of much critical study in the years since his death, as has Price's own personal reputation. Recent studies have uncovered much about Price the man that will of course be used by his critics to dismiss his work and the achievements obtained during his lifetime, but although as a person he was indeed a shrewd, complicated and at times calculating individual, his writings and adventures provide a legacy that continues to inspire to this day.

More information about Harry Price including detailed accounts of his many cases, a comprehensive bibliography of his books and writings and the latest news about things connected with his life and times can be found at the Harry Price Website, www.harryprice.co.uk which was set up in December 2004 by Paul Adams and Eddie Brazil.

CHAPTER TWO

IN SEARCH OF THE BORLEY NUN, BORLEY VILLAGE, ESSEX

One glorious summer not so long ago I embarked on what was to be one of the best and most memorable field trips away visiting haunted sites. I had visited many haunted sites across the country and undertaken many investigations but now, after wanting to visit this village for most of my life I was on my way to see the site of 'the most haunted house in England', Borley Rectory.

The village itself lies on the top of a windswept ridge in the Stour valley and is in a desolate part of the country. In Borley village there is the former rectory site (as the building was demolished in 1944) and its stable cottage which still stands, Borley church and its gravestones, Borley Place, the farm which stood adjacent to the rectory and the cottage and the road that runs straight through the village and out the other side. Surrounded by acres of lush fields, trees and countryside there is no post office or village shops, that is how small and desolate the village of Borley is. The Borley Rectory haunting is one the most famous cases in the history of psychical research, and according to the investigators of the day (and some investigators of today) it is one of the best-authenticated cases of ghost and poltergeist activity and psychic disturbance ever documented in Britain, maybe the world. The ghost hunter who conducted the whole Borley investigation was the great Harry Price (1881–1948) whom you have just read about in the previous chapter who was unfortunately accused of fraud, elaboration and fabrication by his critics although nothing was ever proved. However it was not until *after* the death of Harry Price when his critics attacked him and attempted to tear his good work and name to shreds with these accusations of fraudulent behaviour.

As pointed out by many people over the years, the critics failed to realise that Harry Price was involved in the case from June 1929 until his death in 1948 and phenomena had been reported years *before* Price's involvement with Borley

Rectory. Even *after* his untimely death reports still came in of ghostly happenings at the village and its neighbouring church. (The most recent being the sighting of the infamous "Borley Nun" in the 1970s). Over the 76 years Borley Rectory stood, it was subjected to all kinds of phenomena and terrifying disturbances. These included the phantom nun walking the Borley garden, Hall Lane, and the Churchyard, a ghostly coach and horses was heard and seen thundering along the old rectory drive, raps and knocks were heard coming from within the old rectory, objects were violently thrown around, a malevolent and physically abusive invisible entity attacked one of the residents between 1930-1935, doors were often heard and seen slamming on their own, the doors also locked on their own and their keys were pushed out of the keyholes. Ghostly voices and mutterings were heard, while footfalls in empty rooms were witnessed too. Unexplained lights in the rectory windows were seen, along with strange and vile smells being reported by many. There were cold spots, mysterious bell ringing throughout the rectory even after the bell wires had been disconnected and objects appeared and disappeared in different areas of the rectory. Pencil writings appeared on the inner rectory walls and a number of unexplained fires started inside the rectory, the last one in 1939 ultimately destroyed it. Those outlined here are the vast majority of phenomena that was reported since the rectory was built in 1863 by many hundreds of independent witnesses including all the incumbents, and their families and friends.

As previously mentioned the rectory itself is long gone and no trace remains. However, Borley church opposite the rectory site, and the village itself has always had a reputation for being haunted and this was one of my reasons for paying my visit. Of course I wanted to see the actual site the rectory once stood upon and visit all the places in and around Borley that once played a part in this magnificent saga, and who knows, I may just run into the Borley Nun who is still believed to haunt the churchyard, and Hall Lane.

Day one of our trip and I got up in the morning to find the weather was dull, overcast, but warm. I gathered up my cameras and my bags and dug out my tent in which my friend and myself would be sleeping in over the next few nights. At 7.30 a.m. James arrived at my house. We loaded up the car, planned our route for the trip but not before heading off to the local greasy spoon to fill our empty bellies with some pre-journey sustenance. By 8 a.m. we were heading southbound on the A1 motorway and after seven hours of driving we arrived at Sudbury in Suffolk. Sudbury lies just one and a half miles from our destination but we needed to get our priorities right so we called into the local tourist information centre and found ourselves a nearby campsite on the Bures road called Willowmere.

We subsequently set up camp and sorted ourselves out before embarking on the last leg of our long journey. This last leg would take us to Borley village. The easiest way to Borley is by going down Borley Road after leaving Sudbury until you reach The Rodbridge picnic area; this is the area where the Borley gallows once stood. Then cross the River Stour as you leave Suffolk and enter Essex on the other side of the river. Then take a sharp left on to Hall Lane and soon you will come across Borley village hall on your right hand side (which until the end of the last century was the home of the Waldergraves of Borley. Sir Edward Waldergrave of Borley was arrested here on charges of heresy, and later died in the Tower of London). Follow the road past Borley Hall and up Hall Lane on a slow and steady incline and before you know it you have reached the village of Borley. On the left hand side near the top of the Lane is a belt of trees and some modern bungalows where between 1863 and 1944 stood the worlds most famous haunted house, Borley Rectory.

At 3.30 p.m we set off from the campsite for Borley village and you cannot imagine what I was feeling at that point, I was eager and very excited to get there as I had longed to see the place for so many years and I wondered what it was like to be there for real. Now I was only 10 minutes away but that 10 minute journey would seem like a lifetime. For those who have studied the Borley story and are influenced by the late Harry Price (as I am) you will know exactly what I am talking about. I guess it was like the anticipation you would feel if you were going to see some world famous tourist attraction like Mount Fuji in Japan or the pyramids in Egypt. Borley village was the same for me as it is the mecca for ghost enthusiasts all over the world. After I had seen Borley in magazines and read so much about the place in ghost books, (including Harry Price's two books on the Borley haunting) I would soon be there.

We arrived at the village and subsequently pulled over in the small man-made lay-by at the side of the road, which had obviously been made by other cars that had been visiting the area. It was on the corner of Hall Lane opposite the stable cottage; the only standing appendage left of the former rectory establishment. To our front right stood the beautiful picturesque Borley church which dates from the fifteenth century with its famous stone entrance porch and clipped yew trees in the graveyard. As I was walking around in the graveyard taking my photographs I was simultaneously searching for the graves of the some of the Bull family members. Henry Dawson Ellis Bull built Borley Rectory in 1863 and when he died in 1892 his son Henry Foyster Bull took over from him as Rector of Borley until his own death in 1927, (coincidentally both men (father and son) died in the blue room which was the most haunted room in the house, at the rear of the rectory) and these were the was gravestones I was looking for. My search proved fruitful as I soon found the grave of the Reverend Henry Foyster Bull and his sister Caroline Elisabeth Harden. I then photographed these graves for my records and after having a good look around while taking some shots of Borley church and some other graves, I turned my attention to the stable cottage or the old coach-house.

Standing on the corner of Hall Lane right next to where the rectory once stood, the old coach-house was once used as a cottage where the Bull family employees lived and worked (coach drivers and servants) It is incredible to think that the fire that had ripped through the rectory on the night of 27 February 1939 did not even remotely damage the stable cottage. How this building did not catch fire is a miracle to say the least, as it was only a few yards away. I subsequently started to take some photographs of what is left of the former rectory buildings, again for my records. As the house is privately owned, I knocked on the door to see if I could gain permission to take a walk around the back of the cottage. I did not get an answer so I proceeded to walk around anyway in the hope that the owners might be around the back; I guess my luck was in. When I walked around the back of the coach-house, in what were the old horse stables, was the gentleman who now lived in the coach-house. These old stables had been converted into garages, sheds and a little workshop. I introduced myself and asked him if it would be possible to take some shots of the old rectory site and have a browse around. He very kindly agreed.

I saw what would have been the side of the rectory, which would have housed the kitchens. Through the trees and over the new driveway which runs straight through what would have been the rectory, I could make out the first of the bungalows which were built in the 1980s after the site had stood derelict for nearly 40 years. This bungalow was built on the spot of the tennis lawn and garden that stood directly in front of the rectory and it indicates roughly where the famous nun's walk began. (The nun's walk was a section of the Borley garden where this famous phantom was mostly seen and now stands at the rear of the bungalow, which is again privately owned). This view of the rectory site also gave me an indication of how big the rectory actually was.

Later on his wife came home and I was introduced to her. We had a good old chat about the history of the rectory although she made it clear that she thought the whole "ghost thing" as she put it, was all nonsense. She also told me that she thought Borley Rectory was demolished in 1942 and not 1944 (I would take Harry Price's word on that one). After our conversation we said our goodbyes and left by the old rectory gateway, which is now the road into their property. I was now headed to see the bungalows, which now occupy the site of the actual rectory gardens and the famous rectory drive where the phantom coach and horses were seen on a number of occasions.

There was not really much to see as nothing at all remains of the rectory so it was left down to my imagination as to where things were. I then photographed the bungalows and their drives for my records. I then took a walk around the corner to visit another building that fits into the Borley story. This building, Borley Place, was often mistaken for the old rectory and it was home to the Bulls for many years before the rectory was built. Borley Place was built in the seventeenth century and it stands alongside the parish church and opposite the farmyard. It is sometimes known as Borley Manor. It too was photographed for posterity. So that was most of Borley village covered and what a place it is – I was in awe.

One lady who lived in Borley couldn't quite believe we had travelled so far to see this village. I said, "I bet some people would have come even further to see this famous haunted little village". (They have come from all over the world).

"Have you seen her yet then?" she asked, obviously referring to the Borley Nun, and I said, "Not yet but I will keep my fingers crossed and my eyes open". She too did not believe a word of the story as she said she read a book called *We Faked the Ghosts of Borley* and she said it was locals who had nothing better to do with their time. Each and everyone to their own!

It was now 5.45 p.m. and we were to leave the village and head a mile or so down the road to Borley Green. This is a beautiful little hamlet with thatched cottages and a huge village lawn and to my right stood Borley Lodge. It was here at Borley Green on the night of the great fire in 1939, Captain William Hart Gregson sent his sons to phone for the Sudbury fire brigade. As Borley Green was the nearest location with a telephone you can imagine that by the time they ran from the rectory, phoned for help, and then waited for the fire brigade, the house was well and truly up in flames and out of control. A terrible shame indeed as this was the beginning of the end of Borley Rectory.

James and myself then left Borley Green and we drove back through Borley, and off to a tiny village called Liston. Liston is a village with immense significance to the Borley story. Again another small village with just a church, a couple of houses and a small rectory. It was here at Liston rectory where Harry Price and his secretary Lucy Kaye would stay during the investigations of Borley Rectory, as he became good friends with the [then] rector of Borley and Liston, Alfred Clifford Henning who was the rector between 1936 and his death in 1955. (By this time no one would take up the post of Rector of Borley alone due to the fearsome and dreaded reputation this old red brick monstrosity had, so the two parishes of Borley and Liston were combined and the rector of both villages lived at Liston).

I will now turn attention to the parish churchyard of Liston, as in the graveyard there is a small plot of land, a plot of land in which some bones (part of a skull and the left jaw mandible) were buried in the 1940s. Harry Price found them while he was excavating the cellars at Borley Rectory in the 1940s (after the rectory had burned down in 1939). They were believed by Harry Price to be that of a French woman called Marie Lairre. Harry Price believed she was the Borley Nun. During one of the many séances held at Borley Rectory it was determined that a fire would burn down the building and the remains of a young woman would be found buried in the cellars. True to the spirits' word this is exactly what happened. When the bones were discovered they were boxed up in a casket and a Christian burial took place in the hope it would stop the Borley Nun haunting the area. It did not. I located the spot of this unmarked grave and duly paid my respects. It is surreal to think that I was actually standing at the graveside of the person whose spirit was believed to be the most famous ghost in history, the Borley Nun.

The last location on our agenda was another little village nearby called Pentlow. At Pentlow we found what was the actual birthplace and home of the builder of Borley Rectory, the Reverend Henry Dawson Ellis Bull who was born in 1833.

This was the first of the two Bull rectories (Borley Rectory being number two) and it was the original Bull family home. It stood behind a copse of trees and has a huge curved pathway with large gates at the roadside. I photographed this magnificent rectory for posterity and then we left, as time was getting on. We needed to head back to the campsite and get changed to go for a well-deserved pint.

After a good night's sleep we ventured back up to the village of Borley for another look around and I took more photographs. This time I had a wander around the bottom of the belt of trees and around the back and found my way into the old Borley Gardens. Looking up the old gardens I could see a bungalow. This bungalow would have been in the area right at the bottom of the long Victorian gardens and where four sisters of the Bull family all saw the phantom nun on a crystal clear day on 28 July 1900. When one of the Bull sisters approached her, she simply vanished into thin air. Since most of this small village had been covered the day before we decided to have a drive to the coast for the day and return later at dusk. Dusk was soon upon us and the idea was for me to have a look around in the dark. I got some great photographs of Borley church while the sun sank behind it but it seemed to take forever for it to get really dark.

When it did get dark my companion drove off and left me to explore the graveyard and rectory corner on my own, it was great to be there, walking around the area hoping to get a glimpse of the nun but alas I did not. It was now starting to get really dark and foreboding in the graveyard and I was starting to wonder if James was going to come back for me! I was on my own and by now my heart was seriously pounding and I could feel myself becoming more and more nervous. I was at the site of the most famously haunted village ever and it was so surreal. After about 45 minutes I worked out where James was and was quite relieved he had not actually left me. He was waiting in the car down Hall Lane next to the gardens. Time was getting on and out of respect for the villagers and the locals we decided to call it a night before it got too late. Although I wanted to stay longer I did not want to cause any alarm; another marvellous day drawing to a close, and lots more drink, food and a few games of pool to come. We headed back to the tent and got ready to go out.

Day three of our visit and it was our last. We got up at 6 a.m. and went to the showers, got ready, and then got our bags packed up, took down the tent and packed it away. We headed off for a full English breakfast before we headed home. It was our second feed at this restaurant and the owner recognised us from the first visit and asked where we were from. We told him we had come down from Newcastle to visit Borley and all the relevant places of interest relating to the Borley story. He then said that he wasn't sure or not if there was anything behind the Borley haunting but he knew someone who did, his brother.

This is what he told us, "A lot of people think Borley is a weird kind of place and think it is haunted, and ok some people don't, but what happened to my brother up there he will never forget and it convinced him it was a well and truly haunted place up at the rectory corner. He was driving on his way to work through Borley village as he did every day, but one morning he had seen a man standing at the side of the road near where Borley Rectory once stood, and he was trying to thumb a lift. Being the kind soul he was, he pulled over and let this person into the car and no sooner had he pulled away he turned to speak to his passenger and lo and behold he was gone, he had vanished completely. My brother is a sensible man and does not lie and this shook him up for a good while. Apparently this has been reported again since my brother had this experience and he now fully believes that Borley to this day is most definitely haunted. He never uses that route to work anymore and will not go anywhere near the corner up at Borley".

He told us this account of his brothers while we were tucking in to our breakfast and what a great story it was to round off our trip, we had spoken to believers and sceptics alike and we had a very packed and full weekend. We saw everything we wanted to see and had done every thing we wanted to do. We ate up and hit the road and came home.

CHAPTER THREE

LONDON GHOSTS

London, the capital of England and the largest city in the UK is without question one of the most historical and almost certainly the most haunted city in the country. Many a time I have been sitting on the train, thundering down the east coast main line heading to one of my favourite haunts for one reason or another. During my many visits to the capital I stayed in the north London suburb of Muswell Hill and enjoyed the hospitality of my second cousin, Christine, who always insists on giving me a tour of the great city every time I venture down there. Past trips have included visiting the famous Budokwai Judo Centre in South Kensington, where I would train, practice, and fight with some of the best Judoka (practitioners) of the art, and competing in the London Marathon.

Other trips to London have included stop-overs on my way, and on my return from Japan which of course was part of a holiday of a lifetime, general relaxing weekends away, and not forgetting hunting down some of London's most active ghosts. A ghost hunter cannot visit this incredibly spiritually troubled city without visiting some of its haunted heritage and of course I am no different. London is a place where I had always wanted to go to track down its resident phantoms, or at least visit some of the areas in which ghosts are said to reside.

London has some of the most famous ghosts in history and one of the most active areas has to be the Tower of London. The Tower of London is said to be haunted by over two-dozen active spirits including Anne Boleyn, Catherine Howard, Lady Jane Grey, Guy Fawkes, Sir Walter Raleigh, and the two Princes that were killed in the tower. Other ghosts include a number of grey and white ladies, King Henry VI, Thomas Becket and rumour has it that a ghostly troop of soldiers has been seen marching through the grounds of the tower. The Tower of London does indeed have a sombre and uneasy feel to it and when one ventures inside you cannot help but feel for the prisoners that were once held, and executed here.

During my visit there a few years ago I chatted with one of the guides who informed me that only a week prior to my visit the alleged ghost of a woman had been alledgedly seen on the battlements and the description fitted that of Anne Boleyn. I was informed that the lady who witnessed the apparition saw it in broad daylight and was dumbfounded to see it disappear right before her eyes. I was also told this same apparition has been seen on countless occasions by other witnesses and has always been seen in this particular area. Whether it was Anne Boleyn or not no one knows but it was very interesting indeed to hear of the story. Of course I ventured over to where she was seen in the hope that I would catch a glimpse of her but unfortunately, I did not.

During cousin Christine's tours of London she took me to a place where she thought there might just be another ghost or two. It was a fascinating museum which takes the visitor back in time to the Second World War with original exhibits, rooms and passageways that have remained untouched since Sir Winston Churchill graced the quarters with his presence at the 'centre for operation' just after becoming Prime Minister in 1940. Known as the Cabinet War Rooms, this huge underground bunker, which is situated at Westminster in Central London, was used by Sir Winston Churchill and his cabinet to direct the Second World War. There are many rooms at the museum and all these rooms were vital for the operations that ran from there between 1940 (when Churchill decided to use the bunker) and the end of the war in 1945.

The famous map room that was the hub of the operation closed down its operations on 16 August 1945 (the day after VJ Day) and it is incredible to think that it was left exactly how we see it today. Every map, book, all the charts, diagrams and plans that were used for the war have remained untouched since 1945.

Some other rooms include the actual cabinet room, in which Churchill and his war cabinet would meet and discuss the conflict, Churchill's bedroom, where he would stay on particularly bad nights during the Blitz, (which incidentally is the German word for lightening) as it was too dangerous for him to return to Number 10, and the transatlantic telephone room where he would be able to communicate with the United States. There is also the Churchill Museum which is housed at the Cabinet War Rooms and is a permanent exhibition dedicated to the man himself.

So, I wondered if indeed there were any ghosts. I had never visited before nor had I ever heard of any accounts of any strange or paranormal activity from this location, until I got there! Upon arrival to this underground museum I found that the long, dark, gloomy and resonant corridors did indeed have a foreboding feeling and one could not help but think that the former war PM may still walk here. When I asked one of the staff members about any potential ghosts I was informed that although he had not witnessed anything personally, he had indeed heard one or two accounts.

He told me that strange and unexplained footfalls had been heard on occasions in the empty corridors, often followed by an ice-cold blast of air and a drop in temperature. Another strange occurrence, which was relayed to me, was of the frequent reporting of a mysterious smell of cigar smoke near the actual bedroom of Winston Churchill! Now it does not take a genius to work out that if indeed these reports are true, and cigar smoke has been smelt in what is normally a non-smoking building, it could well be the ghost of Churchill himself as he was renowned for smoking cigars. It is indeed thought provoking. My time at the Cabinet War Rooms proved rather invaluable to say the least and I heard some fascinating ghost encounters. Deep down I was hoping to experience something paranormal myself but unfortunately I did not. What I did experience was a fantastic step back in time to the early 1940s and a glimpse of World War Two history.

Another one of my 'must visit' sites was the world famous Highgate Cemetery, which is situated on Swains Lane in Highgate, north London. Highgate Cemetery was opened in 1839 and takes up nearly 40 acres of land with almost 170,000 people buried under the 50,000 headstones (including Charles Dickens and Karl Marx). Classed as 'an outstanding and historical Grade II listed park' this Victorian burial ground is split into two sections with many grade I and II listed buildings and mausoleums situated within. It truly is a magnificent and enchanting place and it is no wonder that the cemetery at Highgate was the most fashionable place of rest for most Victorians.

On our way into London city centre on the bus we were fortunate enough to ride past the cemetery's west gate. Needless to say when I realised where we were, I jumped off the bus and found my way in to have a good look around. There are many legends and ghost stories attached to Highgate Cemetery and when you step inside the grounds, and venture down the long overgrown, and overhanging tree festooned pathways, you soon forget about the hustle and bustle of London. City life is left well behind you although you are only a stones throw away from it and you become enveloped in the eerie stillness and deadly silence of this macabre and chilling graveyard. Many ghosts are said to reside at Highgate Cemetery including the ghost of an insane woman who has been seen franticly searching the area. Some say she is looking for the children she so brutally murdered when she was alive. Another ghost is believed to be that of an unknown man dressed in black garb and is said to do nothing but sit and stare looking ever so forlorn. The ghost of a man in a black hat has been seen on numerous occasions standing in Swains Lane and when approached or neared to, simply vanishes into thin air.

However the most infamous ghost or legend associated with the cemetery is known as the Highgate Vampire. Surprisingly this legend only dates back to the early 1970s and was carried on into the 1980s after a spate of alleged vampire sightings were reported. My impressions and my gut instinct led me to believe that this alleged vampire is probably nothing more than a myth or at most, a ghost sighting. However some people believe there are records that show a body was indeed brought from Europe to be buried at Highgate after the dead man in question was accused of vampirism. He is alleged to have killed his victims and drunk their blood.

Whether or not this is true who can say for sure? But the story of a body being brought to the UK from Europe followed by a spate of vampire sightings and an unoccupied coffin does indeed ring an all too familiar bell. In regards to ghosts, perhaps Highgate Cemetery is indeed haunted by a spectre or two, as there is a peculiar and eerie feel to the place and you can't help but feel that eyes are following you every which way you turn. But vampires leaving their coffins and walking the night, terrorising the locals and drinking the blood of their victims? I think we can safely say that this is a classic myth and should be best left in the realms of folklore.

Another venue worth a visit if you are ever in the capital is the Theatre Royal on Drury Lane in Covent Garden. This theatre (designed by Christopher Wren) is said to be one of the most haunted theatres in the world and the building we see today is said to be the fourth theatre that has been built on this spot. Harry Price investigated the theatre back in the 1920s and to follow in his footsteps at this beautiful theatre was indeed an honour. Although I was only there for an hour or two it is a few hours I will not forget and during my short time there I was able to chat with one or two of the staff and they recited their famous ghost stories to me. The first ghost I was told about was that of the famous comedian and clown Joseph Grimaldi. Joey (as he was known) died at an old age after a life long exertion of literally clowning around after his wrecked and decrepit body could take no more. It is said that he haunts the stage area of the theatre and if he feels that actors of today are not giving 100% during their performances, he gives them a friendly kick up the backside!

Another ghost is said to be that of an actor called Charles Macklin. He, I was told, appears back stage in a corridor where he once murdered a fellow actor by the name of Hallum. It is rather odd to hear that the actual murderer rather than his victim is the residing ghost as usually it is the victims that return to haunt! He is said to have been seen a number of times by staff over the years and his presence does indeed scare people quite a lot. By far the most famous ghost sighting here at Drury Lane is said to be that of a spectre known as the grey man. Quite often he is seen dressed in old costume and wearing a tricorn hat. By his side there hangs a sword and he is believed to be the ghost of a man who was murdered here over 200 years ago. His skeleton was allegedly found here in one of the walls with a sword sticking through his ribcage. No one knows exactly who he is. A quick tour of the theatre was offered which I duly accepted but because there was work to be done and the doors were opening soon for the evening's performance it did not last as long as I had hoped. Nevertheless it was a privilege to be allowed in for the short time that I had. We said our thanks and goodbyes and we made our way out of the theatre.

For my last venue in this wonderful city I wish to tell the reader about one of the most foreboding places in all of London at night.

During the day this place is wonderful and serene and is a fabulous area to come and visit to relax and get away from the everyday hustle and bustle of busy London life. There is nearly 800 acres of woodland, ponds, fields, hedgerows and it is known as Hampstead Heath. Hampstead Heath is rumoured to be haunted by Charles Dickens who spent many years of his life walking there, and of course the legendary highwayman Dick Turpin. Part of the land was owned by the manor of Hampstead and the rest was owned by Kenwood House, which I also visited when I was in London and which I will elaborate on now.

Kenwood House is a fine example of an English stately home in the centre of London and was originally built in 1640. Tucked away in this lovely corner of Hampstead Heath this beautiful white walled manor is now in the hands of English Heritage and is a beautiful and serene place to come and visit. Back in the early 1700s Kenwood House was almost burned to the ground and was subsequently re-designed and rebuilt by the famous architect Robert Adam between 1764 and 1779 (the same Robert Adam who rebuilt Culzean Castle). Festooned upon the walls within this great mansion are classic works of Rembrandt, Turner, Vermeer, and Gainsborough and they were awe-inspiring to see and I was told that Constable's famous painting 'Hampstead Heath with Pond and Bathers' is on display here only yards from where it was originally painted.

During my visit I was of course intrigued to hear of any alleged ghosts that may walk the corridors or rooms of this elegant house. Perhaps a ghost may linger in the magnificent library, or saunter down the splendid staircase that leads to the upper levels. All I had to do was ask a guide and that is exactly what I did and I was subsequently told they could neither confirm nor deny any ghost stories. However I did ask another guide who informed me that he did hear of one account of a lady that is said to walk down one of the corridors and disappear at the bottom. Who she is, I was told, no one knows.

London, an enormous city with an abundance of haunted sites with an incredible history has hardly been touched in regards to my visits and I dare say there are hundreds if not thousands more fantastic ghost ridden buildings and locales ready for investigation and exploration. Hampton Court Palace, infamous Whitechapel where the notorious 'Jack The Ripper' butchered his innocent victims in 1888, the Ramsgate public house in Wapping, where the cruel pitiless Judge Jeffries was arrested, Aldwych tube station, The Grand Station Hotel that stands in St Pancras near Kings Cross, the Famous Grenadier pub, Belgravia, Berkeley Square, Ham House, the list goes on and on and it is only a matter of time before I return there to visit, in order to seek out the ghost stories, legends, and some ancient myths of old London town.

CHAPTER FOUR

CASE STUDY

INVERARAY JAIL, ARGYLLSHIRE, SCOTLAND

On a beautiful autumn day a few years ago, the North East Ghost Research team headed up to Argyllshire on the west coast of Scotland to the little Scottish town of Inveraray. Here was the venue for investigation, Inveraray Jail. The jail lies about ten miles south of Oban and is said to be one of the most haunted prisons in Scotland. The building itself has two prisons within its tall walls. The new prison was built in 1848, and the earlier block dates back to 1820. The old courtroom, which is also built on site, was started in 1816 and was completed in 1820. All three locations in the past have been subject to ghostly goings on and there is indeed a history of paranormal phenomena. We had been there once before with The British Paranormal Alliance and found the place to be quite interesting indeed. What would this old prison throw at us on our next visit? It was not long before we found out.

We arrived at the jail at 9.30 p.m. on the day in question and the sub-manager Rob Irons let us in. After a tour of the prison for the team members and team guests who were not with us on our first visit, we carried out some preliminary baseline checks to determine room temperatures, electromagnetic field readings, and a search for any draughts or squeaky floorboards that may be mistaken for ghostly phenomena during the course of the actual investigation. During the walk around we also placed some trigger objects down in the hope of encouraging any spirit interaction. We placed down a flour tray with a crucifix firmly planted in it on the old prison landing, a very large key was drawn around and left in one of the cells in the new prison, and we also left some motion sensors in the courtroom. After determining all the baseline readings and setting up our experiments we were ready to begin.

On arrival in the courtroom we measured the temperature once more and it had risen by 3 degrees since our baseline reading. We got settled in and spent the next

10 to 15 minutes sitting in total silence. I took some digital stills and captured a few orbs but as the room had not quite settled yet, I came to the conclusion that these orbs were merely dust particles still floating in the air. At 10.50 p.m. we all heard four loud but distant bangs coming from inside the building somewhere. As all other groups were inside their locations (old and new prisons) it ruled them out. On inspection we found nothing out of place and all was fine: our first mystery of the night. At 10.55 p.m. our team psychic Suzanne McKay thought she heard the sound of muttering and mumbling and then said her ears seemed to be muffled. She said she got the letter "R" given to her but could not determine what this meant. At 11 p.m. I called out to the atmosphere in an attempt to communicate with any residing spirits and a few knocks and taps were heard and recorded on tape. Suzanne picked up on a presence standing behind her and described it as strong, but not nasty. Suzanne at this point is in the centre of the courtroom facing the judge and sitting at the back. She said this area felt uncomfortable. She also got the impression that at each door to the courtroom there was a man standing guard (like doormen). "Do you want to be a charity case?" are the words Suzanne said she was given. Again what it meant no one knows, yet!

At this point my attention turned to some movement to my rear left. I turned and there was nothing there but I got the feeling there was. I then felt the top of my head being touched! So I called out and said, "please do that again only elsewhere on my body", and sure enough the side of my face was gently stroked. Rob, getting quite excited by now, told us that in the exact place where Suzanne sensed the energy behind her and where I saw movement behind me is the same place in the courtroom where on other investigations psychics and mediums have picked up and sensed the same phenomena. So we now know that two separate independent groups are coming up with the same experiences and evidence that corresponds with each other.

This is what we like and it does indeed help build a case to show something strange may indeed be going on. At 11.30 p.m. we called out again to the atmosphere and recorded it on a dictation machine. The name "Murray" came to Suzanne and when asked if the name Murray corresponds to the letter "R" picked up earlier, she could not say. It would indeed be interesting if there was an R. Murray, or a Murray R. connected somehow to the building. Unfortunately, the other team, who observed and investigated the courtroom at different times during the investigation, picked up nothing in the way of paranormal activity. Nothing was felt, sensed or photographed in this location. Apart from the first group's findings, this location was very quiet. But that is ghost hunting!

We ventured into the old jail block and entered cell 9. Both Suzanne and myself felt very apprehensive indeed. Suzanne picked up on past experiences people have had in this block and said people have heard voices and seen shadows flitting about. (Rob again verifies this is indeed what has happened before, and told us the story about his name being called out while in there alone one morning, the prison was not open and he was the only person on the site). Suzanne then picked up on footsteps scurrying about then stopping, and then she heard the sound of a breath! (It was not Rob, nor was it I). The name "John McKenzie" was picked up by Suzanne and he was described as bald headed, with sunken eyes and very smelly indeed. She also felt his wife was also held in the jail. I ventured along the corridor and explored this level on my own. As I was looking into the end cell on the right hand side, I thought I saw a cat inside the cell. When I asked Rob about any animals that would have been kept in the prison for any reason, he told me the prisons always had a resident cat to keep the numbers of rats and mice down (not commonly known by all accounts). Had I seen a spirit cat in one of the cells? One thing is for sure; there were not any real cats around! The rest of this vigil proved fruitless with nothing else recorded or documented.

While team two were in this location during the course of the investigation a male figure was picked up by Glenn Hall (the other psychic on our team). He said he was a chubby man, with a big ginger beard and was about 6 foot tall. Odd lights were caught on the night vision video camera and everyone heard the distinct sound of keys being rattled coming from along the passageway. This occurred twice in a short space of time. When moving around the old jail they claimed to hear a rustling noise and they reported being followed around by a sweet smell, wherever they ventured this smell accompanied them. Upon leaving the cells after the vigil, they all again heard the noise of movement coming from within. This I feel is a good witness testimony as it was all seen, felt, and heard by not one witness, but all three!

Team three in the old cellblock proved rather interesting too as quite as lot of strange activity was recorded and witnessed, again by more than one investigator. Now what ties in with team one's reports is the sound of footsteps which were heard by a member of team three. (Earlier on Suzanne said that footsteps were heard in this cellblock). Other auditory phenomena were heard too, such as the sound of water dripping, and a whistling sound. More light anomalies were caught on a night vision video camera before it was swiftly drained of battery energy and all members of this team had the feelings of being watched. Two investigators heard the sound of a girl child sighing so they decided to leave some sweets around the area as a trigger object. They were not touched, however since one investigator said the spirit touched his hand (as if to hold it) they decided to put a sweet on the palm of their hands and ask the spirits to take the sweet. On three different occasions with all the members of this group trying it, the sweet on the palm of the hand was moved slowly along the hand by an unseen force. However since the video camera's batteries had mysteriously been drained of energy, it was not recorded on tape. No EMF or temperature anomalies were recorded.

We then staked out the new prison block and on entering the location I set my dictation machine recording while we sat in cell 10. We called out to the atmosphere to see if we could communicate with any of the spirits that may be in there but to no avail. Amazingly Suzanne picked up on the fact that any visiting dogs would not under any circumstances enter cell 10. (Rob verified this and he told us this is exactly what has happened in the past). Suzanne sensed the name "Thacker". I then tried to dowse with a crystal pendulum but no results were ascertained this way. I then had a funny experience. When I was sitting on the stool I closed my eyes for a split second or two only to feel my head moving forward rather quickly (although it did not really move at all). This made me open my eyes and come around so to speak and then at that point I felt quite unwell and nauseous, I expressed the fact (out loud) that I thought it was just me, and this experience was not attributed to any spirits – or so I thought – and then suddenly I was blasted in the face with the strong smell of burnt matches or sulphur. A sudden pain in the right side of my head then occurred for 30 seconds before dispersing. Was this spiritual drainage? Some would say so – perhaps it was. We then left cell 10, leaving the dictation machines recording until the tape ran out. Downstairs all we heard was a loud clicking noise, which we couldn't decide if it was normal or paranormal although no explanation was established.

Team two, when in the New Jail reported some odd phenomena too. On the second floor of the jail, the feeling of strangulation was picked up by Glenn Hall and another investigator's throat felt tight at the same time. They concluded a possible rape and murder of a young girl may have taken place but dowsing with a crystal indicated that the girl died elsewhere. Glenn detected the letter "C" and then he gots the name Catherine. More strange lights were caught on camera and the sound of a cell door was heard closing. (This phenomenon was also recorded in the same area on a dictation machine the last time we were there with Mark Webb from ITV's *Haunted Homes*). A female investigator then saw a shadow in the corridor, and at the same time all the group heard shuffling.

Team Three's turn in the New Jail and motion sensors were locked off in an area that was not being investigated. Once they were set they headed to another section of the new prison and waited. Rod dowsing was interesting as the name Catherine Douglas was identified as one of the spirits. (See Team Two's findings above). Catherine was only a young girl aged between 7 and 11 years old and had blonde messy hair and was wearing a white dress. While Claire Smith was in alleged contact via the dowsing rods she asked the girl if she could produce any other phenomena. Noises and bumps were heard along with sensations of being touched and pushed around. When she was asked to walk through the locked off motion sensors everyone heard a voice saying "Ohh Kaaay" (a long drawn out OK). But the motion sensors did not go off. The sound of a girl's voice was then heard by an investigator saying "Maggie" and this was allegedly Catherine's mother. A guest investigator then took over on the dowsing rods and they moved to cell 10.

At the time when the rods started to move, someone heard movement in the corridor. The guest investigator picked up on Catherine once more and asked her to come closer to him, he then went cold and got very emotional and almost started to cry. They then asked for the spirit girl to touch a certain investigator, he too felt emotional and wanted to cry! This also happened to Claire. It was then claimed that the spirit girl sat on the hammock and the hammock actually started to move back and forth with no one near it. The guest investigators hand was then held by something cold and it grabbed his fingers and tugged upon them gently. He then got another name "Christine" or "Christina" and when he asked the other girl how old she was, the rods become stuck between 7 and 8 years old. After an emotional and very good vigil the stint came to an end and it all happened in Cell 10. They headed back to base for a well-deserved break. When Rob was told about the names he was interested in the Christina or Christine connection. He informed us about a murder victim called Christian (a young girl) and she matched the description of the daughter of a prisoner called Archibald McClellan who he had been murdered. She was 7 years old, nearly 8!

Could this have been the ghost of the murder victim? We may never know for sure. But to pick on a young girl with the same description and get a name and age so close to what her name and age was, was very mysterious indeed. It seemed a bit of the jail's secrecy was unfolding itself to us. It was an amazing occurrence indeed. It had got to 3 a.m. and at this point in the investigation we lost a few key investigators as these people were driving us home after the investigation. Sleep was imperative as we were heading straight home when we had finished at 7 a.m. We too were tired so we had an extended break to recover for a while. We resumed the investigation at 5 a.m.

From 5 a.m. until 5.45 a.m. we sat in the old prison. I sat in one of the cells on my own for a while and we all agreed it was quiet so we headed back to the court-room to investigate further.

Sitting in the courtroom for a while we decided to sit in silence to see if we could pick up any noises or auditory phenomena. A few taps and knocks were heard and incredibly when another of our guest investigators sat in the middle of the circle at the back, she felt someone was standing behind her and she also heard the shuffling of feet. (Suzanne sensed this in our first vigil and this is what Rob verified to us. Now it had happened again to someone else who knew absolutely nothing about these incidences). Suzanne then picked up on a girl called Sally. Sally was close by and standing behind Suzanne and was asking for some help. As Suzanne turned to Sally and held out her hand, Karen Smith (no relation to Claire) saw her.

She said she was a shadow type figure and she was glowing blue with a white aura blending in with the blue. She described how her hair was long and untidy with a fringe across her forehead and that's all she could describe before she took a few paces back and vanished. Karen then became upset and literally cried her heart out with emotion. Rob (the guide) was witness to all this as we were and we all found it very moving indeed.

Suzanne called out to Sally and asked her to make herself known again. I heard 5 taps right at my feet, *tap, tap, tap, tap, tap*! in quick succession. Myself and Suzanne both saw a bright light move across the room, it was incredible. Suzanne had said that Sally was 8 years old and was very confused. She wanted to know why her twin sister had died. Sally is in no way connected to the jail personally but perhaps a family member is. Maybe Archibald McClellan! Wouldn't it be incredible if a Sally could be found in the local records and she did indeed have a twin sister? It would be more incredible if either Catherine Douglas, or Christian turned out to be the other twin.

A fantastic investigation was had by all and it was well worth the 500 mile round trip to do it. Lots of fascinating phenomena was witnessed by all and by the guide too. As always there are more questions that arise than ones we can try to answer and the questions that come up are very interesting ones indeed and if we can seek out and discover the connections between these people it would truly be amazing. So who is Sally? And what does she really want? Could Christian be the twin to Sally, or is that Catherine? Are there any records of twins in the local records and archives? All these girls in question have one thing in common. They are all young girls between the ages of 7 and 11 years old. One is connected to the jail and the others are not. Could one of these be the daughter of Archibald McClellan? She was not linked to the jail, but her father was! It's a tantalising thought. Could all the other phenomena recorded on the investigation be real genuine phenomena too? I ask myself the same question as there was indeed quite a lot documented. Could some of this evidence be misinterpretation on the part of the investigators? Maybe, maybe not as a lot of the recorded experiences tie in with other accounts, accounts which our team knew nothing about. Even if some of the phenomena recorded were indeed misinterpretation, it still leaves a lot which has not been.

Having said that I believe our team do not misinterpret phenomena, as they go through the usual checklist when something odd does indeed happen. If they cannot find a natural explanation for something, it goes down on the notes and is documented. Granted there was a lot of phenomena recorded on the night in question, some of the documented evidence we feel comes from the residual energy, the echoes from the past whether they are visual images or auditory and this is what people usually pick up on and they will always be there. Some evidence is documented from the active spirits, spirits who are actively moving around and causing disturbances within the premises. They are also picked up on by people, but more so the psychic people who have the gift. A lot was picked up and recorded but we have to remember it is indeed a very haunted prison. Our work there is far from over.

During my time up in beautiful Argyllshire I also visited the delightfully picturesque and truly amazing Inveraray Castle. Inveraray Castle is situated on the other side of this wonderful small town and takes only 5 minutes to walk there from the jail. The castle, home to the Duke of Argyle, was built in 1789 after many years of planning and design and is also the home to a ghost or two. The area around the castle is very much haunted too, with a ghostly battle once being re-enacted over the castle grounds. It was said to have just 'faded away' in front of the three men that witnessed it back in the late 1700s.

Another phantom that is said to haunt the area is that of a ghost ship with 3 spectral figures on it and is believed to sail up Loch Fyne. It then advances overland in the direction of the castle, disappearing before it reaches it. The castle itself is said to be home to a poltergeist-like ghost that wreaks havoc in the Green Library. The sound of smashing and crashing and dragging of furniture is often heard in here but nothing is ever found to be out of place. The most famous ghost, however, is that of the phantom harp player. The sound of beautiful harp music is said to be heard reverberating around the castle and emanates from the Blue Room. The harper, a man believed to be called 'Montrose' is sometimes seen in the castle too. It is believed he was hanged on the Grassmarket Gallows in Edinburgh.

CHAPTER FIVE

CASE STUDY

IN SEARCH OF CLOGGY, THE SPECTRE OF THE BLACKPOOL GHOST TRAIN

William G. Bean founded the Blackpool Pleasure Beach in 1896 and to this day it attracts about 8 million people every year and it is one of the most famous and biggest fun parks in Europe, with over 125 rides and tourist attractions including one of the biggest roller coasters in the world. During a twelve-month stint on the North East Ghost Research Team I had the opportunity to visit Blackpool and conduct an investigation at the Pleasure Beach. The venue was the infamous haunted ghost train. This ghost train is reputed to be haunted by a man who has been seen and heard clumping around the tracks with his clog boots on. He is believed to be the builder of the ride back in 1930 and after his death, as he loved his ride so much, it is said that he never left it.

Cloggy, as he is known, is said to follow the workers and staff around the train tracks and touches them and breathes in their faces, giving them a terrifying and unexpected shock. Visitors to the park have reported many spooky goings on whilst being on the ride, leading people to believe that there may be more than just one ghost residing there. A few years ago a well-known television company and ghost-hunting programme visited the site and conducted an investigation and as far as I am aware, we are the only other investigative team that have been allowed access to investigate the hauntings. We were also being filmed for a Channel Four Television documentary and this is why we think access to the ride was given to us.

On the night in question we were shown to the ghost train by two of the Pleasure Beach attendants and by this time the Pleasure Beach was totally deserted. We went inside and walked around the whole ghost train with the lights on so we could familiarise ourselves with it. As we were walking around the film crew were getting some footage for the show and deep down we were all waiting to see if

Cloggy would make his appearance. The television crew told us that they themselves were absolutely terrified knowing soon we were to turn off the lights and
seek out Cloggy. It was not long before we finished our walk around and we were
getting out our ghost hunting equipment ready for the investigation. We then split
into two groups and our group went to one end of the ghost train while the other
group went to the opposite end to minimise any noise pollution we might be making as the ghost train is all long, thin passageways and is very echoey indeed. The
slightest noises made normally would be amplified and the acoustic sounds of the
ride would be phenomenal. We would have to be extra careful not to misinterpret
any normal noises for paranormal activity.

The investigation commenced at 10.40 p.m. On walking through what can only
be described as a pitch-black tunnel, a very loud noise disturbed us. It sounded
like a pump or a generator noise, which continued for several minutes before
abruptly stopping. The other group contacted us via walkie-talkie to say that they
were also aware of this noise. Eventually, we found an area to carry out our first
vigil. An investigator proceeded to call out to the atmosphere in the hope we got
a response. A presence was then felt to the right of us, so a photograph was taken
and a light anomaly was caught! After a while, we all felt that the presence was no
longer with us, so we decided it was time to move to another area.

We decided to do our second vigil of the night in an area where the trigger
objects were placed. Again we made ourselves comfortable and proceeded with
the normal questions. After what seemed like a few minutes, the same noise that
we had heard previously began, only this time it started off faintly and slowly
built momentum until it was very loud. I have to say it sounded very much like
the mechanics of the ride were being activated. Again, after some time the noise
ceased. We were later informed all the rides had been switched off and no power
whatsoever could have turned the rides on. So what was the noise we all heard?

In other vigils we had some more odd experiences. We witnessed one of the rides
internal side doors opening and slamming closed. There were no draughts; winds
or breezes recorded anywhere so that possibility was immediately discounted. This
had all the television crew's hearts racing. We were used to phenomena such as
this, but they had no idea what to expect. It was rather funny in retrospect. I then
called out to the atmosphere and we all heard knocks and bumps emanating from
the walls and ceiling. Mysterious lights were caught on my digital still camera and
a great light in movement was caught on night vision video camera. As previously
mentioned, we heard what sounded like the ghost train ride or generator starting
up and then cutting out again after 2 to 3 seconds. Very odd to say the least.

After our first set of vigils we re-grouped for a break and it was then decided we
should try a séance. By this time the Channel Four film crew had all the shots and
footage needed for the programme, so they departed and waited for us to finish
the investigation. The team found a suitable spot in the ghost train, formed a circle
and held hands and proceeded with the séance. After a short while we all noticed a

drop in the temperature and one or two of us began to shiver with the cold. "Cloggy," I said. "Are you with us tonight?" The area seemed to become even colder. "Give us a sign to indicate your presence, please." At this point a door next to us began to shake and rattle as if someone was trying the handle to gain access. There was no one behind the door. "Thank you, can you give us another sign please?" Nothing. "Come on Cloggy! We know you are here, give us another sign please." I then felt a tap on the shoulder and my blood ran cold. "Let us hear your footsteps please, that is what you are known for isn't it? We are here with the utmost respect for you and we mean no harm. We are just interested in you and we want to prove you are real." At this moment we were all astounded to hear the clump of footfalls emanating and echoing from along the dark passageway. "Who is there?" someone called out. No answer. "Hello! Hello! Is anyone there?" Still no answer. By now the footfalls had ceased.

The circle was closed down and an immediate check of the area showed that no one was on the ghost train except us. All the television crew were outside and the ride was deserted! Had the television crew been filming at this point we may have just recorded the phantom footsteps that are so often heard coming from around this infamous haunted theme park ride. It was now 3 a.m. and it was time to wrap up the investigation. We were on the ghost train for about 5 hours and we all experienced some good phenomena and concluded there is indeed a ghostly presence residing within. So the next time you holiday in Blackpool and decide to go on the ghost train, beware! If something touches you or you hear strange noises just ask yourself, it's just part the ride, isn't it?

CHAPTER SIX

MY ENDEAVOURS IN DEVON

The beautiful county of Devon in England's southwest has to be one of the most enchanting and captivating districts in the whole of the British Isles. Its valleys and hillsides, festooned with rivers, fields and woodlands stretch as far as the eye can see and old lonely country roads adorn the land leading the weary traveller to many a wonderful old village and town. Devon gets its name from the word *Dumnonii* which means "the man who lives in the valley". It was a Roman word, which was given to a Celtic tribe that resided there when the Romans invaded around AD 50. For the next 25 years the Romans occupied *Dumnonii* or Devon, and stationed themselves at Exeter where traces of their occupation can be seen today.

Devon, famous for its clotted cream, beautiful old thatched cottages and cider has long been the land of aesthetic beauty and charm but this was not always the case. Like the vast majority of the UK, Devon has had its fair share of misfortune and misery, as during the middle ages the great plague swept across the British Isles and Devon suffered terribly with the loss of thousands of lives. Plague pits were in abundance and the dead were discarded wherever and however possible. In the 1600s Devon also saw the coldest winter recorded in history with rivers freezing over and the ice-cold snowstorms battered the lands again resulting in the loss of many human lives. Many a battle and invasion has occurred here on Devonshire land with the raids from the Vikings and the Normans, and not forgetting the many civil wars that have occurred in days gone by resulting in the bloodshed of many thousands.

Is it any wonder that Devon is also famous for its tales of ghosts, wraiths, apparitions and echoes of the past that have so often been seen and heard by the Devonshire folk and visitors alike on many occasions. Devon is rich in history, full of legends, and tales of witches and folklore. Many roads and lanes in Devon are said to be haunted by ghosts and spectres and they are all, to a certain extent frightening should you ever come across one. By far the most sinister and alarming accounts of all the haunted roads in Devon is said to be on the B3212 between Two Bridges and Postbridge in Dartmoor. For unknown reasons motorists and bikers have had their steering wheels and handlebars violently wrenched and turned by what can only be described as a ghostly pair of hairy hands. Sometimes these hands encompass the motorists' often resulting in bad road traffic accidents and even deaths.

The accounts of these happenings became so horrific at one time; no one would venture down the road in case they became the latest victims of the Hairy Hands of Dartmoor. Eventually the local authorities altered the dip of the road in an attempt to put a stop to the accidents. The Hairy Hands of Dartmoor is indeed an unorthodox, but very famous haunting indeed and it is believed the ghost responsible must be a bitter victim of a bad crash in this spot many years ago. It has been a few years since any reports have come in of hairy hands or accidents in that vicinity, the last report being in 1989 but still, you can't be too sure. If you ever venture down the B3212 while visiting Devon, be on your guard.

Another very famous legend in Devon concerns the Devil himself and it is known as The Devil's Footprints. One night in February 1855 between midnight and 6 a.m heavy snowfall covered the countryside and small villages of southern Devon. When the Devonshire people woke up in the morning and ventured outside, they were surprised and bewildered to see hoof like footprints in what would have otherwise been untouched snow. These hoofprints were rather sinister looking to say the least as there were only two of them as though created by a biped (rather than if it had been an animal). The hoofprints were eight inches apart and were seen in perfectly straight lines across towns, villages, fields, roads and were even seen going up walls and across the rooftops. They went through some solid walls and came out at the other side, and they even bridged a two mile gap across the River Exe and continued on the other side as though whatever it was walked across the water!

No one knew where they came from and how they appeared. It seems very unlikely that a practical joker could have been responsible as who would be prepared to walk hundreds of miles across the countryside during the night and in the cold snow? The thought is absurd. Other theories included escaped kangaroos from a nearby zoo, or badgers, swans or racoons looking for food but most theories and ideas did not seem to fit and made no sense. It was then suggested that the devil had walked the face of the earth and was searching for sinners and a lot of superstitious people believed this was to be the case as no other explanation could be found. To this day the hoofprints remain a mystery. But who knows, one day, sometime soon, when we are all tucked up and cosy in our beds, the Devil, if it was he, may return once more and walk among us.

It was these types of ghost stories and fabulous legends that inspired me to visit Devon and seek out some of the amazing true life encounters that have occurred here. I stayed in a beautiful hotel in Bideford in north Devon but was disappointed to hear that our hotel had no ghost stories attached to it. However, I did learn that Bideford was the home to Temperance Lloyd, Susannah Edwards and Mary Trembles who were known as The Devon Witches. In 1682 these three alleged witches were tried, and executed at Heavitree in Exeter for witchcraft. A fourth witch, Alice Molland was hung in 1685 and these were the last witches ever to be hung in England. A commemorative plaque to these four women hangs outside Exeter castle, which I also visited on my journey around Devon.

During my stay in Devon I visited the enchanting Chambercombe Manor in Ilfracombe. A beautiful manor house that dates back to the eleventh century and set in a secluded wooded valley this house has a rich, varied, and macabre history. The house has eight bedrooms, a great hall, a chapel and a priest hole or two but only a couple of the rooms lays claim to a ghost. It is believed that a former tenant of the house back in the mid 1800s was making some repairs to the roof of the house when he stumbled across a blocked-up room. Upon later inspection they discovered that the dusty unused room was in fact another chamber linking Lady Jane Grey's room (a former tenant of the manor) with the neighbouring one. To their sheer horror, they discovered the skeleton of a woman lying on a bed. It is believed that this dead woman is responsible for some of the ghostly goings on that has been reported here over the years, although the ghost is not believed to be that of Lady Jane Grey herself.

Along with ghostly moans emanating from the discovered chamber, other ghosts have been reported here too with apparitions of children being reported on an upper level of the house, and a spirit man has been seen to disappear in front of witnesses. It is also alleged that children complain about a stern looking woman who stares at them while visiting the manor, however the parents are always oblivious to this woman. Could she be the ghost of the woman found in the blocked-off chamber? This thought does indeed occur and is a tantalising thought.

During my visit to Chambercombe Manor I was fortunate enough to have spoken to a guide who relayed these ghost stories and legends to me. Upon entering the house you do indeed get a certain feel to it and like a lot of historical houses and museums, you are transported back in time when you venture inside. The smell, the feel, and with the ambience of the whole place, it is not hard to imagine that ghosts do indeed reside within these ancient walls. I spoke to the guide about bringing our team down from the northeast of England to investigate the property and was told this could be a possibility.

Devon is also famous for its unspoiled beaches, long sands and coastal villages. Lynton and Lynmouth on the edge of Exmoor National Park are the epitome of such villages in north Devon with Lynton being perched high on the cliff tops commanding spectacular views across the sea and along the Devon coastline, and

Lynmouth, which nestles at the foot of the cliffs and is more or less on beach level. In August 1952 tragedy struck Lynmouth after weeks of torrential rainfall. A surge of water (90 tonnes) flooded down from the burst riverbanks of Exmoor devastating the little village below with a terrible flood. Houses and buildings were demolished and swept away resulting in the deaths of 34 people and the injury of many others.

During my visit to Lynmouth and its twin town Lynton, I visited the memorial hall, which was built to commemorate the dead after the 1952 floods. The whole area has a sad and sombre feel to it and one could not help wondering if indeed the area may still hold echoes and recordings of the traumatic events of yesteryear. While sitting in one of the many beautiful seaside pubs Lynmouth has, I got chatting to an old local chap who could still remember the tragedy. He told me that for a short while after the disaster, he was awoken at night by the sounds of the rushing water, the boulders crashing down the steep valley, and the cries for help. An echo of the night of 15 August 1952? Or just a recurring dream? He could not specify. Whether it be real or not certainly proves interesting indeed.

While in Devon I also managed to visit the historic town of Exeter where I visited a number of ancient and historic pubs and haunted sites. One of which was the Ship Inn. The Ship Inn is a sixteenth century pub with a maritime theme. It has oak beams across the ceiling and is decked out with old wooden furniture and has an abundance of nautical features festooned upon its walls. Old sea maps, pictures of sloops and schooners, an old ship steering wheel hangs from the wall, along with other sea faring memorabilia. Over a pint of bitter I asked the staff if they had any ghost stories they could relate to me. I was more than happy with their reply.

I was informed about an invisible presence that often opens and closes doors inside the inn. Glasses are moved around and smashed when no one is in the bar area and to my utter delight, I was told of an apparition that had been seen standing in the bar dressed in what could only be described to me as seafaring attire. When approached the apparition is said to disappear. The interesting thing about this pub is that it is reputed to be the one time favourite drinking tavern of Sir Francis Drake! Could it have been his ghost that has been seen here in the bar? The thought did cross my mind!

From Exeter, through Newton Abbot, on to Totnes near Torbay where not far away stands the haunting ruin of Berry Pomroy castle. Standing near the River Dart in southern Devon this beautiful and haunted castle remains. The Pomeroy family first occupied this land back in the eleventh century and apart from Edward Seymour, Duke of Somerset, (who owned the castle in the sixteenth century) it had always been in the Pomeroy family. After the Seymours took over the castle, they embarked on a massive restoration and re-development of the castle and transformed it into one of the most prestigious stately homes and castles in the south-west of England. During the seventeenth century the castle was abandoned and was left to deteriorate and decline into the ruined state it is in today when the Seymour family seat relocated to Wiltshire. Berry Pomeroy is still in the ownership of the Seymour's. The ghost of Lady Margaret Pomeroy is said to haunt the dungeon area walking aimlessly around. Those who see her, I was informed, are said to feel quite unwell and a sense of depression and fear envelopes the eyewitness. Her sister allegedly imprisoned her out of sheer jealousy, as Lady Margaret was far more beautiful and influential than she was. She kept her captive for nearly twenty years before eventually starving her to death. It is no wonder she remains to this day, seeking revenge on her older sister.

Another famous resident of the castle, I was told, is that of the Lady in Blue. Seen on frequent occasions over the years, this ghost is said to haunt the entire castle trying to lure men to their deaths. She is said to be seen with a blue gown and hood over her head and sightings of her date back to the 1800s. It is rumoured that she suffocated her child out of hatred and at times, the child's wails and tormented cries can still be heard reverberating around the ruins. Whatever the truth behind these tales, you cannot deny Berry Pomeroy has a certain feel to it. However, should you visit the castle be careful what mementoes you decide to bring home with you. It is said that they are often returned quickly due to the sense of an unwelcome presence that has followed you home. I chose not to bring anything home with me ... just in case!

During my stay in wonderful Devon, I was lucky enough to visit a vast array of haunted places across the county and I heard many wonderful ghost stories and legends from the locals. Perhaps another volume outlining the others is possible. It certainly seems that there are more than enough tales to make this happen. In the meanwhile I must close this chapter by saying that Devon is a well and truly wonderful and most enchanting place to visit in search of ghosts. I had a fabulous time there and I will certainly be returning in the future to continue my research.

CHAPTER SEVEN

CASE STUDY

CHILLINGHAM CASTLE, NEAR THE SCOTTISH BORDER

Chillingham Castle is situated in the wonderful windswept Cheviot Hills of Northumberland 12–15 miles north-west of Alnwick. It is right on the borders of England and Scotland and is reputed to be one of the most haunted castles in Europe. It is said to be haunted by Lady Mary Berkeley who roams the castle looking for her long lost love who had ran off with her sister and never returned. Indeed on dark cold nights they say you can hear her cries of anguish emanating from within the castle walls and others have felt her long dress as she has brushed past them in various locations in the castle. The swishing of this dress has also been heard when no one is present.

Another spectre seen in the castle is that of the Radiant Boy or Blue Boy. During renovations of the castle a wall was knocked down and a skeleton of a young boy was found along with some blue fabric. It is said that the phantom of this ghost is often seen around midnight glowing blue. The Grey Lady is said to haunt the topiary gardens, which are situated to the side of the castle, and disembodied muttering is often heard coming from the empty library. By far the most haunted area in Chillingham Castle is without doubt the Grey Room. I have investigated Chillingham Castle on four occasions now (once with television medium David Wells) and it is our stay over in the Grey Apartment I wish to tell the reader about.

On the day in question we arrived at Chillingham Castle. It was autumn and the leaves were strewn all over the land. The sun was beginning to shine through the haze and clouds that had previously enveloped the desolate area in which Chillingham Castle stands. At 12.30 p.m. we were shown to our apartment. It had a very large living area with a huge log fire, a passageway, and two very big bedrooms. We sat down around the huge dining table and had some of our sandwiches and a cup of tea before we left the apartment and explored the castle grounds. Before we ventured out we set the audiocassette machine recording in the hope we would pick up something paranormal. We also set up a trigger object experiment using a coaster and a coin. We went out for approximately 45 minutes.

After our scout about outside we came back to the apartment. The tape recording had finished and the trigger objects we had placed down earlier on had not moved at all. When we came back to the main Grey Room area it was noted that a weird smell had filled the room. My colleague thought it was a burning smell but another investigator and myself couldn't quite put our fingers on what we thought it was although we could indeed smell something which was not normal, and had not been there previously. A minute or two later, the smell vanished. Could it have been our first paranormal occurrence of the day? At 4 p.m. an investigator thought she heard the door handle rattling from one of the bedrooms but unfortunately no one else heard this noise. We then decided to set up some more trigger objects and leave the tape recording once more and we went out again for another walk around.

On our return to the apartment an investigator decided to view some footage of what he had just recorded while the room was vacant. Whilst looking through the viewfinder he saw what he described as a brilliant white ball-bearing type of light anomaly with a huge trail behind it and it shot across the screen in a matter of seconds. At about 6 p.m. one of the investigative team decided to take some photographs with his 35mm camera in the apartment and the most extraordinary thing occurred. He noticed that when he faced one way the camera worked perfectly and the flash went off, whereas when he tried to take a photo the other way up the apartment his camera jammed and the flash refused to work! This happened about four or five times in succession and he brought it to our attention. I asked him to try it again so he did, and once again facing one way the camera worked perfectly, and when he tried facing the other way, again the camera refused to work! I asked him to leave the room, go outside and try the camera there and it worked just fine. There was nothing wrong with his camera.

By now it was pitch black outside so we turned out the apartment lights and took a stroll around. I was taking some photographs when all of a sudden the door to the living area behind us creaked loudly and slammed closed. No one was near it at the time as we were all close by in a group near the other doorway to the bedrooms. On inspecting the door for faults we found nothing wrong with it and when we left the door open it would not close on its own. Things were beginning to happen and with over fifteen hours left in the apartment, who knows what type of night we were in for. It was now 6.30 p.m. and we decided to light the huge log fire as it was getting quite cold and we sat and relaxed for a while in the main living area. As we sat there in the dimly lit room the fire burned furiously and the flames rose high with the wood crackling at the same time, emanating an eerie orange glow across all present. It was like a step back in time and it is one of my most memorable moments as a ghost hunter. To spend the night sitting around a roaring log fire in the most haunted room in what is Britain's most haunted castle is something I will never forget. It added ambience to this already atmospheric scenario.

We then set up our infrared night vision video camera while partaking in a little chit-chat and upon looking back on it later we found nothing of any great interest. At 7 p.m. we went for another walk giving us another chance to set the audiocassette recording again as well as leaving the infrared night vision video camera on the tripod as a lock off while we were out the room. We came back some time later and found one of the cupboard doors had opened fully even though it was closed properly when we went out, we had double checked before we left. We then sat in bedroom two for about 15 minutes in the dark and nothing happened so we moved into bedroom one for a further 15 minutes and again nothing happened. We then moved back into the main living area and started the fire up again as it had died down and then recorded some footage with the night vision camera. I sat at the camera while looking through the viewfinder and decided to try and communicate with any of the Grey Apartment ghosts or spirits. After asking for signs I was given some of the strangest light anomalies I have seen to date. I asked three times and got three good responses.

We then went out again for a late night walk around the castle grounds and into the topiary gardens where the Grey Lady is said to walk. When we were out at the front of the castle we noticed that the light was on in bedroom one and we were all 100% certain that just before we came out we had turned them off. Then, whilst standing in the courtyard as we were looking around in the dark and taking photos in the torture chamber, came 5-6 tremendously loud bangs, or raps. It sounded at first as though they were coming from the small stairwell leading up to our room, but when we looked up at our room from the courtyard, the side window was wide open and it was clear that the bangs or raps were coming from bedroom two of the grey. When we went out for our walk, that window was closed. Again, four people can verify this. We ran up the stairs to see if any one was around to make the noises and there was nobody anywhere. We went into the room in question where the window was open and I closed it. Upon looking in bedroom one we found that the light that we had seen on while being outside was off once more. It was very strange to say the least.

We also found the bread bin lid had been moved from its original position when we returned to the main grey area. At this point (I have to be honest) we were all getting quite unnerved. We had goose-bumps all over, and I felt an ice-cold rush of fear run over my head and down my body all over and it was amazing. However we remained calm and cracked on with our investigating. At 1.50 a.m. we set the video camera recording and sat around the fire. After about 10 minutes we all heard three beeps and we wondered what it could be. On checking the video camera we found it had been turned off. I tried to switch it back on and it wouldn't work so I then decided to check the plug in case it was faulty and lo and behold I found the plug had been switched off at the wall. We can all testify to this as no one went near the wall socket. We switched it back on and continued the recording but to no avail. We sat up for a further hour or so before calling it a night. We retired to the beds and had good undisturbed sleep (which is a shame as I would have liked to have awoken to see Lady Mary Berkeley standing over my bed!)

After our investigation at the Grey Apartment and castle grounds I concluded that at Chillingham Castle, strange unexplained things do occur. The ghost, or ghosts of the Grey Apartment, I would consider, being of the friendly sort and being somewhat playful and mischievous and this is based on the actual experiences and the phenomena we all witnessed during the course of the investigation. If you ever visit Chillingham Castle and decide to stay over, I suggest this apartment if you have the stomach for it.

CHAPTER EIGHT

CASE STUDY

THE PLOUGH INN, NORTH YORKSHIRE

For this investigation I headed off to Wigglesworth near Skipton in beautiful north Yorkshire where we were to investigate the Plough Inn Bar and Hotel. Situated in the lush countryside of the Yorkshire Dales, this very friendly family run eighteenth century former coaching inn is said to be haunted by a number of ghosts and spirits. This two star rated building has nine well-appointed en-suite rooms, a bar with a lounge and an open log fire, a huge conservatory restaurant, oak panelled dinning rooms and it was all ours to investigate as there were no guests or paying customers on the premises. This investigation was a first for this establishment, as it had never before been investigated and as I was a member of another ghost hunting unit called The Answers People Seek (which have now disbanded), it was a privilege and an honour for us.

The Plough Inn was built in the early 1700s and was originally one of the farm buildings that belonged to the Wigglesworth estate. The [then] farmer's wife is said to have began selling her own special brew ale from her kitchen to the locals, which of course went down really well with the villagers as you might expect. In around 1750 as the farming industry and trade declined the Plough Inn was established and it became a local drinking hole and coaching inn. Since those days the Plough Inn has gone from strength to strength and has evolved into the beautiful building we see today.

However back in March 1945 disaster struck in the early hours of the morning with a horrendous outbreak of fire resulting in the loss of two lives. The landlady and a domestic servant perished in the flames and it is said that the servant girl can be seen and heard as she scurries around the premises still trying to escape the burning building. She has also been sensed on a number of occasions with the occasional guests and staff reporting feelings of shortness of breath or generally finding it hard to breathe. This seemed to happen in the area where the dead girl had been found. The owner also informed me on our visit that it is not just the building itself that is subject to hauntings. Reports of a phantom horse and cart has been seen and heard clip clopping and rumbling down this once lonely country road that runs past the inn.

We arrived at the premises 10 p.m. after a long but enjoyable journey down and once we were all there we were taken on a tour of the building. As a researcher, report writer and data collator for the team I felt it was my duty to keep the information I had ascertained from the rest of the team, especially the team psychics in order to give the mediums a chance of picking up on any alleged ghosts. I also requested that the lady giving the tour should keep it basic and not give anything away regarding the history and ghosts. This she did. She then showed us around the building indicating where we could go and what the areas were called. And that was it.

The first strange occurrence happened during this tour. When we reached the top of one of the stairwells situated within the building, an investigator claimed to have felt a strange feeling of unease and pointed out that they did not like that area at all. This turned out to be the same area where the servant girl was found and where other people had reported the same thing. We then proceeded to the attic and I subsequently swept the area with my electromagnetic field meter as part of the initial baseline recordings. To my astonishment the meter showed a very high EMF reading of about 8 or 9 milligaus. Normally a reading between 3 and 7 is deemed as interesting and indeed unorthodox but the reading of 9 is astonishing. It must also be noted that in the precise area of the anomaly there were no cables for about a metre in all directions, so to me that does indeed indicate an actual EMF anomaly as the reader has to be approximately one foot away from light or electric cables to get a reading from them. This anomaly subsequently vanished after a few minutes and it is one of the most interesting EMF anomalies I have witnessed on investigations to date.

At 11.45 p.m. we separated into our groups for the investigation and we headed into our first locations for the evening's ghost hunt. Location one for us was the attic and we all clambered up the steep stairwell and into the black void that was housed on the upper level. The room was packed with boxes, cases, and paperwork and there was barely room to swing a cat. We found ourselves a spot in which to sit and began our observations. The EMF meter anomaly was detected once more where it was previously recorded and an investigator informed me they had sensed someone on the stairwell, about halfway up. It was an unkempt thin and gaunt old man with a moustache and a long dark coat. He was waving a stick around and seemed to be upset about something. He was a heavy breather and stuttered when he tried to speak. I was told that the investigator sensed the name Bob or Bill.

Everyone in this location witnessed other phenomena as knocks and bumps were heard emanating from within the attic area although everyone present was sitting perfectly still. Then out of nowhere the sound of a guttural breath was heard and recorded which would have sent chills down the spines of the most sceptical of people. Other documented phenomena included the feelings of being touched, and an immense cold draught or breeze was felt by myself. However the cause of this could have been due to a possible aperture somewhere within the roof. Although we tried to locate one we could not. A very interesting first vigil especially in regards to some of the information that was picked up on and at 1 a.m. we had our first break.

Location two saw us investigating rooms 1,2,11 and 12 along with the conservatory area. At 1.15 a.m. we ventured into the conservatory area first and made ourselves comfortable. At 1.20 a.m. all members of the group saw a flash of light. It seemed to come from inside the conservatory but we couldn't tell if it was a light anomaly or a flash from someone else's camera. I did indeed have a look around and could find no one nearby taking snaps in other locations. When I was checking the area out looking for the source of the light flash I felt a very cold area near the door, I mentioned this to another investigator and she came down to look into it. At this point I thought I felt someone or something touch or rub the back of my upper leg. I turned around and no one was behind me. Rather odd indeed!

Then the other investigator claimed she had felt her leg being touched. Could there have been a hands on touchy-feely type of ghost in there with us? It seemed to be the case. Whom it was we could not determine but it was odd to say the least. We then left this area and headed to Room 11. On our way there an investigator reported that her torch failed to work along with the rest of the group reporting feelings of nausea and chest pains. Paranormal or paranoia?

While sitting in room 11 an investigator got a mental picture of a hooded figure (possibly a monk) pacing back and forth and then stopping to stare out the window.

It was at this point that the other investigator in our group told us she also thought she saw a hooded figure (or a figure with a hat on) standing at the bottom of the bed and she came up with the date 1562. What is interesting is that later research showed that no holy or monastic building had been built here or anywhere near this site, which would eliminate the monk theory. Furthermore, additional research showed that this wing of the building had not been built until fairly recently and this puzzled me to a certain extent. Still, with investigations like these you always end up with more questions than answers, the further thought occurs that the investigators who sensed these people were wrong! It seemed all quiet in this room and everything was still, so we ventured into room 12. This vigil also proved fruitless and nothing at all of any interest was reported, felt or experienced. Rooms 1 and 2 also provided no results.

At 2.30 a.m. we ventured off to location three, which was the magnificent oak panelled dining rooms and adjoining kitchens. A relatively quiet vigil was had in here, which was disappointing because for some reason I thought if we were going to get any good phenomena, we would get it in there. One or two minor occurrences such as the odd feeling of being touched and the occasional light anomaly was photographed but if one is honest you would put that down to dust particles hanging in the air, and the feelings of being touched down to tiredness and imagination. However one curious incident did occur at about 3.15 a.m.

The door to the kitchen rattled and then opened much to our surprise and upon inspecting the door and the area for potential draughts we found no cause for this to have happened. It was now 3.30 a.m and a few of the investigators headed off home leaving just one or two of us to finish the investigation. At 4 a.m it was decided that we should venture back to the attic for more investigation. We sat up there for about 20-25 minutes in the pitch black to no avail. Whatever was there previously, now seemed to have gone. We came back down stairs and had another break after which, myself and Suzanne McKay returned to the panelled dining room.

We sat in there for about an hour and half way through the vigil another investigator joined us. We sat in silence and just waited and observed but nothing happened, it was very quiet indeed. We set up a video camera and my dictation machine to see if we could pick up any paranormal activity while the three of us tried a séance. Nothing happened during our attempt at this and nothing was picked up on my dictation machine. The video footage also recorded nothing of interest. It seemed the investigation was quieting down. At 5.30 a.m. we had one last patrol around the whole premises but things were really starting to slow right down, and we were all getting really tired. We walked around the whole establishment visiting all the locations that we had previously staked out and ended up at the top of the stairs near the door to the attic but found nothing. We then called it a night.

In summary The Plough Inn at Wigglesworth, for me personally, proved to be quite interesting in the respect that some interesting data was picked up by the psychics team which does indeed fit in with the establishment's history and ghosts. To visit a fabulous old haunted inn such as this was indeed an honour and a privilege and it adds to the many growing investigation sites in the UK that I have had the pleasure of staying overnight in to investigate. We were told by the owners we could come back any time to re-investigate and I hope we get the chance to do so. If you are considering a short holiday or even a nice weekend away in the country, visit the Plough Inn in Yorkshire. It is a wonderful, enchanting and captivating place.

CHAPTER NINE

AN AYR OF MYSTERY

Scotland is a country with some of the most fantastic scenery in the UK. Beautiful mountains and craggy glens festoon the national parks and woodlands and bodies of water known as Lochs provide Scotland with some the most beautiful and picturesque tourist attractions in the UK, with Loch Ness being one of the most famous. The landscape is adorned with wonderful old stately homes, magnificent castles, ruined fortresses and boasts the highest peak in the whole of the country, Ben Nevis, which is situated in the western Grampians and rises over Fort William to an impressive 1344 metres, which is 4409 feet.

Earlier on in this volume I took the reader to the beautiful village of Inveraray high on the west coast of Scotland where we investigated their old haunted jail and looked at the ghosts of Inveraray Castle. Now I wish to discuss my visit to the south-west coast of Scotland where I stayed for a while in beautiful Ayrshire. During my time in wonderful "Robbie Burns country" I had the opportunity to visit many reputedly haunted and historical places including the cottage where Robbie Burns was born. Robbie's father William Burns built Burns Cottage in 1757 and on 25 January 1759 the Scottish poet Robert Burns was born. It is a simple old clay and straw construction, it is painted white with a thatched roof and when you venture inside you are automatically transported back in time. "No reports of any ghosts, as far as I am aware" I was told when I asked the cottage guide. "But who knows?" Whether it is haunted or not, Burns Cottage is most certainly worth a visit.

For my time in Ayrshire I was located about four miles south of the Scottish town of Ayr and our accommodation gave us magnificent views across Firth of Clyde to the delightful Isle of Aaron, which lay on the horizon. From where we were staying, clear and beautiful views up and down the Ayrshire coastline were there to be enjoyed and enjoyed they were. Looking north up the coast one day during my visit, I was overjoyed to see what looked like a ruined castle or tower standing dramatically on a cliff top. I subsequently ventured across to explore this old ruin and found myself having the most unorthodox experience.

As I was walking along the golden sandy beaches, which led up to the foot of the cliffs to which this castle ruin was perched, I suddenly became aware of the sound of horses' hooves galloping along the bay and across the sands behind me. I turned around and found I was the only person on the beach! Where had these sounds come from? Could they have been carried on the wind from some distant place? Or, could I have been subconsciously tuning in and picking up these sounds from the past? Whatever it was it was quite astonishing. I approached the foot of the cliff and found a steep but manageable path that lead to the top. The castle was a gaunt ruin, which stood alone, and was perched right on the cliff edge.

Later research told me that this castle is called Greenan Castle and it was built by the Clan Kennedy in around 1600. The towering keep that remains today is only a small section of what once stood there on what was originally the site of another castle of which no trace remains of the original edifice. Beside this present tower there are faint traces of what is believed to be a courtyard and stables. It is said that one morning Sir Thomas Kennedy of Culzean and his servant mounted their horses from there with the plan to ride to Edinburgh. Unfortunately they were ambushed and brutally murdered by a large gang not long into their journey. By all accounts it was a revenge murder as Sir Thomas Kennedy had fought and been killed in the battle of Brockloch near Maybole in 1601.

Located about two miles south down the coast stands another ruined castle called Dunure Castle. Dunure Castle was the original home to the Clan Kennedy which was once the most powerful family in south-west Scotland. It is believed that in 1570 a kidnap took place and a horrendous torture occurred there. Gilbert Kennedy the forth Earl of Cassillis is said to have kidnapped Alan Stuart, the abbott of Crossraguel, and had him roasted over a fire to make him sign away his land to the Kennedys. (This story was relayed to me while visiting Culzean Castle which the Clan Kennedy also built and owned). This event took place in the Black Vault of Dunure castle and it is said that on dark cold nights when the blustery wind blows throughout the ruin, you can still hear Stuart's screams of agony echoing through the dark night, and they are said to be carried on the wind to the nearby harbour where all can hear them. Of course what makes this story so odd, is that his torturer did not actually kill Stuart during the roasting. When he eventually signed over his land he was set free and by all accounts he outlived his captor, Gilbert Kennedy.

When chatting with the some of the locals on my visit to Dunure, this same tale was relayed to me. It seems that one or two of the villagers I spoke to believe they had heard the ghostly wails emanating from the castle ruins. I was also informed that at one time, no one would venture near the ruined castle after darkness had fallen. A local businessman and shop proprietor who has asked to remain anonymous told me that although he was not sure if there was any truth in the alleged haunting and was quite sceptical, he too had experienced something odd while visiting the ruins.

He went on to say; "I was standing on the iron stairwell which has been built over the original stone stairs in order to preserve them, when all of a sudden I felt and heard (but could not see) someone coming down the stairs. As whatever it was passed me, I could clearly feel them, as they brushed passed! The sound of their footsteps passed me and continued to the bottom of the stone stairs where upon they ceased altogether. I was quite sceptical up to this point in my life but now I am convinced there is something in it. "Ghosts are real," he told me "and something happened that day I will not forget in a very long time, I am not sceptical anymore!"

I thanked him for telling me his account and said my goodbyes. The following morning, I rose from my bed and got my supplies for the day ahead, and made my way into Ayr town centre. I was on my way to Culzean Castle. Culzean Castle lies approximately 12 miles south of Ayr and is one of the finest examples of cliff top strongholds I have ever seen. Standing magnificently on its cliftop domain, Culzean Castle (pronounced Cull-Ian) was rebuilt in 1777 by Robert Adam for David Kennedy, the tenth Earl of Cassillis and is one of the most famous Clan Kennedy castles in the whole of Scotland. It is now cared for and looked after by the NTS (National Trust for Scotland) and is reputedly haunted by a number of active ghosts one of which is an unidentified phantom that has been seen on many occasions on the magnificent Oval staircase in the form of white mist.

Legend also has it that the ghost of a piper can be heard playing his pipes, more often than not coming from a stretch of road within the castle grounds called 'Pipers Brae'. It is said that these pipes can be heard on the eve of a family wedding. Other ghosts include the spirit of an unknown female that is said to reside in the most active area of the castle, the Earl's bedroom, along with another ghost lady that has been seen elsewhere in the castle wearing a ball gown. The cavernous passages and smugglers tunnels that are hidden deep beneath the castle in the cliffs are also said to be haunted by the ghosts of the smugglers who once frequented this area; a plethora of ghosts all waiting to be explored.

On the day of my visit, dark thunderous looking grey clouds filled the sky above as though some horrendous storm was brewing. I arrived at 10 a.m. and made my way down the mile long thoroughfare that leads from the main road to the castle. The clouds then broke and the rain began to fall and I managed to find some good shelter under one of the many trees that adorn the side of the long drive towards the castle. The rain was relentless and it looked like it was in for the day so I carried on trundling down the road until I reached the old stone archway. Here I could see the castle in all its glory through the arch so I made my way through and approached the main entrance. Soaked through to the skin I opened the door, stepped inside and introduced myself to the National Trust officials who were waiting to receive their visitors for the day. It seemed I was the first one to visit and I immediately informed them of why I was there.

"Oh, are you ghost hunting? Well you have come to the right place then. Our guides will be more than happy to tell you all about all our resident ghosts."

With that I proceeded to take my tour of the castle. I crossed the main entrance foyer and through the armoury room where there are literally hundreds of old fashioned pistols and guns hanging on the walls. I continued on through a long and magnificent drawing room type of area and before I knew it I found myself at the foot of the beautiful oval staircase. It is here that people have reported seeing a weird mist floating aimlessly on the staircase. I stopped and asked the castle guide if anyone knew who this presence was and I was informed that it may have been one of the Kennedys but which one he could not say.

If I have to be honest though, I would put this down to a generalisation as I dare say a Kennedy family member would be a prime suspect for any alleged ghosts that walk this castle as they did live here for many years and are connected to the castle. I then asked if anything had been seen recently and was subsequently told, as far he was aware, it had not. After my request to take a photograph of the staircase for my records (which was allowed), I moved on into the round room, which leads the visitor into a small area before one ventures into the earl's bedroom. As I walked in to the bedroom I felt an oppressive atmosphere and I was not sure if this room was going to welcome me. As strange as it may sound, I turned to have a chat with another of the guides who I thought was standing behind me only to find no one there! Had I sensed a presence in the earl's bedroom?

A minute or so later I did hear a guide enter the round room so I ventured through and asked her to come into the earl's bedroom. I told her about what I had just experienced (or rather what I thought I had experienced) and was told that it happens all the time. "This is one of the most active rooms in the castle," she told me. She went on to tell me that not so long ago a visiting tourist entered this room and suddenly became ice cold and very apprehensive. Suddenly she started to cry out, "Who is the woman? Who is the woman who has been killed here?" and only after they took her out of the room and settled her down could they make some sense of what had happened.

Apparently, after this lady had calmed down she told the castle staff that as she entered the earl's bedroom she felt a person standing really close behind her although she knew no one was there. She then heard a female voice whisper in her ear. It simply said, "I was killed in here". Needless to say this is why she was so terribly disturbed by her visit to Culzean. One cannot help but wonder if this ghost lady in the earl's bedroom and the other unknown lady in the ball gown that has so often been seen could be one and the same! I thanked the castle guide for relaying this amazing story to me and made my way through the castle and it was not long before I had completed my tour of the interior of Culzean. After exploring the smugglers' caves and taking a look at Piper's Brae, I decided it was time to return to my lodgings.

My trip to the south-west coast of Scotland proved very interesting indeed and I managed to visit a whole variety of haunted and historic buildings. I returned home with many interesting ghost stories after speaking to many different people. During the compilation of this book I endeavoured to cover what parts of Scotland I could (given that I work full time) and what is talked about in this volume barely scratches the surface of this wonderfully haunted and picturesque country. It is my future goal to venture further and explore some more of historic Scotland in the years to come of which my findings may well be published in future volumes. However, you can read on for interesting chapters on the ghosts of Edinburgh, the Scottish Highlands, and an amazing overnight case study in Roxburghshire.

CHAPTER TEN

THE MOST HAUNTED HOTEL
IN BRITAIN

THE SCHOONER, NEAR
ALNWICK

The Schooner Hotel is located on the Northumbrian coastline just a few miles south-east of Alnwick. Formerly a coaching inn, this 32 roomed hotel is claimed to be the most haunted hotel in Britain. No one knows exactly when this now listed building was built but it is said to date to around the 1600s. The village of Alnmouth where this particular hotel is situated has a controversial and historical past as the Germans once bombed it during the Second World War. On 8 November 1941 two bombs hit the village, one in Argyle Street, and the other in a street not far away resulting in the deaths of many civilian people, while three houses were completely demolished.

On 6 September 1940, a spitfire from the 610 squadron based at Acklington crashed on the beach in Alnmouth. Flying officer C.H. Bacon was killed instantly. Going back even further, in the thirteenth century Alnmouth was hit by the plague and was described by John Wesley, as "a place of all kinds of wickedness". The hotel too has a macabre and historical past, with stories of mass murders, suicides, smugglers and all kinds of mysteries dating back from its 400-year history. The Schooner has also had its fair share of famous faces staying there such as Charles Dickens, Basil Rathbone, Douglas Bader, King George III and John Wesley, the founder of Methodism.

The Schooner Hotel has become one of the best known haunted hotels in the country and it is well known for its ghostly inhabitants and paranormal activity. Paranormal investigators from all over the UK visit the hotel in their droves in the hope of uncovering some of the Schooner's macabre history and to try to unearth some of its sordid secrets. With tales of murder, suicide, tragedy, lost love, lies, deceit, smugglers and alleged rapes it is no wonder the Schooner Hotel claims to have so many resident ghosts. I will now take you through *some* of the ghost stories and legends that have been associated with this magnificent 400-year-old coaching inn.

A FAMILY IS MASSACRED

One of the most famous ghost stories relating to the Schooner Hotel is that of the family massacre that allegedly took place a few hundred years ago. Rooms 28,29 and 30 at the top of the hotel are said to be the oldest part, and the most active area in the hotel although when the massacre took place there it is believed that these rooms were all one big room and this is where the family resided. It is said that on one dark winter's night 'William' came home after a night in the local taverns and for some unknown reason, brutally killed his wife and children. Contrary to what people may think it is the ghost of William who is said to haunt this upper section of the hotel rather than his butchered family.

However the sounds of a woman crying and the screams and wails of tormented children have often been reported over the years by staff and guests alike in other parts of the hotel. Could these sounds be attributed to William's murder victims? William is not only reported to haunt rooms 28,29 and 30 but is said to be seen and felt all around this hotel. His evil presence has been felt in Room 7 resulting in paying guests fleeing from the room in absolute terror. Room 4 of the hotel is also believed to be one of William's haunts, and the room is always strangely freezing cold. This is known as the Cold Room. Mention William to locals and hotel staff and the sheer thought of this evil man sends shivers down their spines.

25 DECEMBER 1806

Christmas Day in 1806 saw the worst storms in living memory. As the winds howled and the rains lashed down a small family were crowded around the fire in what is now the Schooner Hotel's chase bar. They were anxiously waiting for their father to return home from a fishing trip out in the North Sea. One of the daughters was lying asleep in her mother's lap when suddenly a number of fishermen burst into the room holding the lifeless body of their father. The mother quickly stood up to see her husband, forgetting that her sleeping child was on her lap. The child subsequently fell on to the fire hitting her head upon the hearth. She was pulled out of the fire all burnt and charred, choking on her own blood and later died due to her injuries. She was only six years old.

On countless occasions the ghost of a small girl has been seen and heard in this area. One lady said while she was sitting in the restaurant adjacent to the chase bar she heard the sound of a young girl coming from the bar. Knowing the bar was empty at the time, she ventured over to see who the girl was with. When she looked in, the sound of the girl abruptly ceased and there was no sign of her. Another witness claimed while she was sitting in the bar having a drink, a young girl ran in, looked at her and then simply vanished in front of her.

PARSON JOHN SMYTH

September is said to a busy time for the active spirits at the Schooner. Legend has it, that in 1742 the Schooner began to brew its own special ale and a cask of this special ale was given to the local Parson John Smyth. As he fumbled to open the cask, the tap is said to have fired off and hit him on the head killing him instantaneously. The tap was returned to the Schooner Hotel and was never used again.

Locals believe that should they use the cursed tap again, and it is returned to the cask, the parson's blood will flow from it. It is said during the month of September the ghost of the parson walks the corridors of the Schooner Hotel holding the offending tap above his head for all to see.

A SAD AND TRAGIC END

A sorry tale of a young lady who took her own life and sacrificed the life of her unborn child is often relayed to visitors of the hotel and village. It had been a month or so since Eleanor had heard from husband Jack, who had been working overseas and she was desperate to hear from him. She would wait by the harbour for hours on end, day after day in the hope that her beloved husband would return home to be with her and settle down with her and the unborn child she was carrying. As the days went on she became more worried and eventually she became really ill.

The owners of the Schooner kindly took her in as she had no family in the area and began to look after and care for her until her husband came home. Early one morning she was woken up and was informed that her husband had been lost at sea some time ago and would never return to her. Totally devastated at the fact she would not see her husband again, combined with the fact she would have to bring up her unborn child on her own, she fled to her room and killed herself along with her unborn child. She knifed herself in the stomach and as she lay bleeding to death, her blood spilled across the bed and on to the floor. Her blood curdling cries were heard by all but it was too late when they got there; she, and her unborn child were dead. Her body was burnt and her ashes were scattered on the nearby beach and Jack's body was never found. The sad ghost of Eleanor has been reported wondering around the hotel still waiting for the return of her dear husband. On some occasions, her spine-chilling screams can still be heard echoing around the premises, making the blood run cold of those who hear them.

The Others

The Schooner Hotel is also said to be haunted by a number of other spectres and visitors from the other side. These include a lady who walks the corridors of the hotel tapping and knocking on the walls and doors. Another woman who was brutally beaten and strangled to death is said to haunt the second floor of the hotel. A man in an RAF uniform is said to appear, glide down the corridors of rooms 15–19 and disappear at the end of the hall but the most sinister apparition seen was along by room 20.

Two employees of the hotel were doing their rounds one morning when out of room 20 came a black figure. It flew out of the room and into the fire exit door opposite creating a loud bang as it hit the door. It then, to their utter horror came padding down the corridor towards them. They dropped everything and ran in total, absolute terror. These eyewitnesses were very shaken up to say the least.

The North East Ghost Research Team Investigations

Our ghost hunting team has been lucky enough to investigate this wonderful hotel on a number of occasions and each time, we were not disappointed. Of course many of the paranormal happenings experienced on these investigations were not paranormal at all and rational explanations were indeed found. However there has been some amazing ghostly goings on which our team were at a loss to explain. Trigger objects that we had placed down in room 17 had moved a good few inches off the line. With the object being locked off and in a controlled room, with no draughts, we can only conclude it was down to the playful ghost that is said to reside within.

On other occasions we have witnessed a door opening slowly and then banging shut very abruptly, giving myself and another investigator a bit of a fright to say the least. Massive temperature drops have been recorded in room 4 and room 28, and in room 7 one night the lights flickered violently and then we all heard the sound of a massive thump as if someone had jumped on the floor. Footsteps were heard in the room and they seemed to exit where the door is and then the footsteps continued down the corridor outside the room and away. Everyone was accounted for, either sitting on the beds or the chairs, and the whole experience was frightening, yet very interesting indeed.

Of course other north-east based teams have investigated the hotel too and the results of their investigations have striking similarities to our own, indicating something odd is definitely going on. Even Living TV's *Most Haunted* visited the hotel in Series 4 and up to that point in time it was quoted as being one of their best investigations to date, coming so close to filming some good paranormal activity. I will now leave you with one of my most spine chilling moments that I have personally witnessed to date while investigating this 400-year-old building. I was investigating the area known as the back kitchens when I suddenly became aware of an overwhelming presence. I did not like what I felt so I made a retreat to a section of the kitchens where the lights were still on. As I climbed the four or five steps up into the lit up area I clearly heard footsteps coming up the stairs behind me.

I was being followed by something and I felt it did not want me there. My survival instinct took over and I ran like the wind. I was terrified and my heart rate shot up through the roof. I have never felt fear like it and I know for a fact there was an unseen presence there with me. The sound of the footsteps reinforced my suspicion and for once, on all the investigations I have attended and carried out, I lost it. This, along with all the evidence our team has collated does lead me to believe that the Schooner Hotel may very well indeed live up to its reputation for being the most haunted, or at least one of the most haunted hotels in Britain.

CHAPTER ELEVEN

CASE STUDY

WARKWORTH CASTLE, NORTHUMBERLAND

Warkworth Castle is situated on the east coast of Northumberland and has one of the best-preserved keeps in the entire country. It is built on a peninsula and is on top of an enormous hill, which is surrounded by the River Coquet which would have made the castle a very well defended fortress as the only way raiders could attack would have been from the south. The castle could not have been built on a better spot.

It was originally built as a wooden fortress in the mid-twelfth century and was built as a motte and bailey construction by Henry, the earl of Northumberland (son of David I of Scotland). At this point in time Warkworth was still part of Scotland but it was soon to be back in the hands of the English. Henry II reclaimed the land and castle and subsequently gave it to the Fitzrichard family who lived there until the fourteenth century. It was during the thirteenth century that the castle was rebuilt with stone and was turned into the magnificent castle we see today. The next owner of the castle was the [then] lord of Alnwick, Henry De Percy in which he carried out more substantial work on the castle turning it into one of the best fortresses in the land. However no fortress (no matter how well they are built) was untouchable and during the rebellion of 1403 the castle and the walls were severely damaged.

The castle then became property of the crown, who, in turn rebuilt it and handed it back to the Percys of Northumberland who lost ownership again, only to regain it in 1470. In 1572 the castle was laid siege to again and was subsequently left in a state of disrepair. The activity of the parliamentary forces in the mid 1600s during a stay at the castle further damaged the building. Other houses and buildings were made nearby with the use of the castles stones in the seventeenth century.

Warkworth Castle remained a ruin for a few hundred years until the third Duke of Northumberland decided to do some restoration and preservation work. Parts of the castle were excavated and other sections were rebuilt. The castle is now looked after and cared for by English Heritage and is an outstanding reminder of the turbulent days to which this part of the country was subjected to for hundreds of years. Of course a castle such as this, which is steeped with so much history, bloody murders, sieges, prisoners, pain, anguish and torment should be awash with ghosts. And you would indeed be correct, as there are many reports of phantoms and shades of the past that have been seen in and around this area.

I have talked to many people who believe they have encountered some of these figures from bygone days. One informant told me that one sunny evening as she was walking along past the castle she became aware of the sound of horse hooves, the clash of steel on steel and the roar of what she described to me as a thousand men. It sounded like a re-enactment of an old battle and indeed this is what she thought it was. However when she walked around the castle walls to the entrance of the castle the sounds abruptly ceased. It was then she realised the castle was closed and no one was around. "Unmistakably the sounds of ghosts" she told me. "What else could it be?"

Another quite famous ghost encounter in relation to Warkworth castle concerns a group of school children and their teacher visiting the castle on a beautiful autumn afternoon. Whilst partaking in a group study session they were all excited to see a man dressed as an old soldier complete with weapons and full battle attire. He walked into the keep and was subsequently followed by the teacher, as she wanted to congratulate this man for going out of his way to get dressed up for the children. Hot on his heels she saw him bear left and begin to ascend a stone flight of stairs. She caught up with the soldier just in time to see him turn another corner and much to her complete surprise, when she turned the corner she found herself in a corridor with no way out and no one in sight. There was no way out except for the way she had just walked in! Where did this man go? Who was he? And what had she just witnessed? When she asked the castle staff about a man dressed up they knew nothing of him and this, combined with the fact he just vanished into thin air, led her to believe she had seen a ghost. Had it not been for the rest of her class also seeing this soldier before venturing into the keep she would have thought she imagined the whole thing. An absolutely incredible account of a ghost at Warkworth Castle.

To investigate this castle it was decided that we should venture up during the day as to investigate overnight was out of the question. Access is not allowed during the night-time hours but as most ghost sightings and reportings had happened during the day, we figured it would make more sense to investigate then.

The castle was open to the public on the day we carried out our tests and we were fortunate enough to visit on a grey and rainy day. The rain and bad weather kept many potential visitors away, so we could carry out most of our tests knowing we were going to be uninterrupted. On our way in we had a chat with the English Heritage officer and explained we were going to be staying at the castle a little longer than the average visitor. We planned on staying all day and our main focus for the investigation was of course the keep. Out of politeness and respect for the staff and would-be visitors we asked if our objectives for the day were acceptable and we were told it would be fine. However there was just one condition, and that was to inform the warden of any ghostly happenings we encountered at the end of the day when the castle closed. We duly agreed.

As a member of English Heritage I was allowed access for free, however, my co-investigator for the day and very good friend Darren Olley had to pay the £2.50 fee to gain access to the castle. Not bad these days for 7 hours of investigating! After attending some amazing all night vigils it was now time to see what sort of results we would yield during the daytime. At 10 a.m. we arrived at the castle and made our way straight to the keep where we had a walk around all locations within these ancient walls and decided what areas would be suitable for our vigils. Due to the fact there were no loose floorboards as the floors were stone, and there were no doors that could be closed by draughts and winds, the baseline tests did not register an EMF readings in any of the rooms or locations. We ran tests in the entrance hall, the guardroom, the wine cellar, the pages room, the beer cellar, the goods hall, the tank room and larder, the great hall, the chapel, the buttery and pantry, the chamber and the kitchens. We completed the baseline tests by 10.50 a.m., and then had another walk around all over again, only this time we took some photos. I photographed an orb or two during these stages, but we came to the conclusion that these were in actual fact, as always, dust particles.

We decided to begin our investigation at the entrance and hallway, making it location one. We took up our positions and sat and waited. The entrance and hall to this magnificent keep was very dark and gloomy and one would expect to see or hear echoes or shades of the past. However on this occasion we sat there to no avail and not one paranormal occurrence took place. So we moved onto the next location, which was the guardroom. Almost straight away I photographed a nice moving light anomaly, not the usual kind of light form and at the same time a drop in temperature was noted. We then moved off into the room and passageway where the soldier mentioned earlier was said to disappear into thin air. We sat there for a while and although Darren Olley and myself do not claim to be gifted psychics or mediums, we both agreed that this area had a certain oppressive feel to it. We chose not to stay there in that atmosphere for much longer so we headed back into the guardroom and took more photos and observed for a while.

We then tried a few experiments in order to eliminate possible explanations for alleged phenomena. We simply threw up some dust from the floor and walls, and subsequently we got some good orbs as a result (nothing new there then). All was quiet so we decided to stop for a break. We sat on the stairs of the keep that face south overlooking the rest of this ruined castle. In the distance we heard the sound of two male voices. We could not make out what was being said and as we looked around we could see no one. We looked at each other bemused as to where these voices were coming from. Then from behind one of the ruined buildings emerged two middle-aged men deep in conversation. The castle staff had let in some more visitors. We knew this would happen and how disappointed we were to realise that the voices we heard were not ghostly. We laughed about it and then proceeded with our investigations. We ventured into the goods hall and tank rooms and began to take photographs.

Darren Olley then thought he saw a flashing light in the doorway to both of these rooms and told me straight away. When I took a photo, there was an interesting light anomaly on it and it was in the same area. Was it the same anomalous light? Then, as we were looking at the picture on the LCD screen on my camera we both clearly heard what we thought was a loud scraping noise coming from the opposite end of the chamber we were in. Upon investigation we could come up with nothing and no explanation was put forward by either investigator. So we decided to sit and observe a little longer but nothing happened. The noise we heard is still a mystery to us today. By now the castle had admitted more visitors and approximately six or seven people were now on site. We had to be extra vigilant in order not to misinterpret any potential phenomena that we might experience.

The buttery, pantry and the beer cellar were our next port of call. All was quiet in the buttery and pantry but the latter had something in store for us. When we were down in the beer cellar we were taking photos and commenting on how great it would be to ascertain a good photograph of a ghost. All of a sudden, when I took my next frame, lo and behold, there was some anomalous mist in the picture. Another odd thing about this picture was the whole frame had a blue tint to it, but all my other photos were perfectly normal.

Now it could have been breath, but Darren Olley and myself don't think it is as we tried in vain to reproduce another misty blue picture to no avail. The photograph was controlled, with the photographer (myself) actually taking time out to make sure breath would not be drawn during the exposure of the photograph. It was taken next to the beer cellar door entrance looking down the actual chamber and we were right in the centre of the castle. It is also worth noting that the temperature in this room was considerably warmer than in the other locations. After eliminating all potential possibilities for this strange blue photograph we were left with what we can only describe as a strange photo. We are not saying it is a ghost but we don't know what it is! We do know however, it is very strange.

We left the keep altogether and decided to do a vigil in the underground crypt that lies in front of the keep. The church that once stood within the castle grounds would have been situated directly on top of this crypt so we decided to leave a trigger object of a crucifix hidden away in one of the dark corners. Alas it did not move but one strange thing did indeed happen. Darren Olley's camera went off on its own. He was not holding it anywhere near the shutter release and when he was looking at the camera, the mechanism started, then the flash went off. I just happened to be looking in his direction and he immediately turned to me with a confused look on his face. He then came over and I could clearly see his hand holding the camera and it did not move at all! The shutter release was on the opposite end of the camera. He now owns a picture of the crypt floor.

It was now approaching the end of the day and the castle was about to close. In regards to what had happened, well ... what can I say? I didn't in all honesty expect to get anything remotely paranormal in the least. How wrong can you be? There was the scraping noise we both heard in the tank room, the camera going off on its own and of course the mysterious mist I photographed in the beer cellar. Unfortunately we caught no glimpse of the ghostly soldier nor did we hear the deafening roar of the battle from bygone days that had once been reported there, but we did indeed get something. Whether it was paranormal we cannot say for sure but it was very strange to say the least. The English Heritage guide thought our findings were odd too. He thanked us for letting him know what had happened and after letting us out the castle, locked up for another day.

CHAPTER TWELVE

CASE STUDY

JEDBURGH CASTLE GAOL, ROXBURGHSHIRE, SCOTLAND

Jedburgh Castle Gaol and Museum is now one of the finest examples of nineteenth century John Howard reform prisons in the whole of the UK. Prior to Howard's changes the prison was filthy, overcrowded and disease was rife amongst the prisoners who were once jam packed into the many small holding cells that this prison contains. Common criminals, murderers, debtors, children and even prisoners who were not yet convicted were all held together here in awful, squalid conditions.

The gaol takes its name from the magnificent medieval fortress (Jedburgh Castle) that once stood on this spot where the gaol now stands. This castle was one of the most important strongholds on the Scottish borders but in 1409 it was destroyed. In 1819 the town gallows occupied this site and in September 1820 work began on the new prison which was built in line with John Howard's fresh and new ideas with regards to cleaner and more refined secure units.

A gaoler's house was built in the centre of the complex and contained a two-roomed flat for the gaoler and a one-roomed flat for his assistant. On top of the gaoler's house there is a rounded turret containing the prison bell in which the bell rope hung all the way down through a small aperture on each floor. This was used as a fire alarm but was primarily used for an alarm should prisoners attempt to abscond from the prison. The gaoler's house is now a magnificent museum detailing the history of this site (and others in relation close by) with artefacts and prison memorabilia. It is well worth a visit.

Standing directly behind the gaoler's house to the south is the block for serious male offenders. This block housed nine sleeping cells and two condemned cells. The west block contained eight holding cells and was built to house female prisoners on one side and petty male criminals on the other. It was partitioned to keep the groups of men and women separated from one another. The east block

(Bridewell House of Correction) housed sixteen cells in all. Eight were used for sleeping cells and the other eight were used for work. The cells in this block were for solitary confinement and the prisoners held there only met up during periods of compulsory exercise in the yards.

Over the next few decades new laws were implemented and bigger and better equipped prisons were built which meant that gaols such as these would soon be a thing of the past and they would inevitability close and this is what happened in 1886 with Jedburgh Gaol. The inmates at this time were transferred to Edinburgh and Jedburgh Gaol was used as police cells until the new ones were built. The gaol was eventually sold to the borough of Jedburgh in 1890 for a sum of £800. Over the next few years the gaol was used for an abundance of things including a private home (Gaoler's House), the prison blocks were rented out for storage space, and local businesses could also hire them to run their businesses from. In 1964 Jedburgh realised this former prison's potential and it was restored to its former glory and opened as a museum.

There are many ghost stories linked with Jedburgh Castle Gaol and with a history as macabre, sombre, and as violent as this gaol, it is not surprising that ghosts and phantoms of former inmates have been seen and heard here. Cell doors have been heard to slam closed and every now and again it is believed you can hear the moans and cries of the prisoners that were once locked up here, some of them condemned to death. Cold spots have been detected in certain areas of the gaol along with the feelings of being watched while walking through the old cellblock passageways. Both staff and visitors alike have reported these ghostly encounters, some of which makes the blood run cold.

It is not surprising that when The North East Ghost Research Team was invited to co-investigate the hauntings we duly obliged.

The investigation was ran by a good friend of mine who is a founding member of the Haunted North East Paranormal Group. We arrived at the prison on a dark and cold October night and our first impressions of the building itself were of total awe. We met the other team inside and then we took a tour of the gaols and locations we were to be investigating. It is interesting to note that during the tour of the building when we were inside the west cellblock one of our team psychics, Suzanne McKay stated that she felt drawn to one side of the block stating it had a feminine atmosphere to it.

She told us that it might have been sectioned for female prisoners. She also sensed a spirit lady in her late 40s but her name was unknown to her. This west block did indeed house the female prisoners and as mentioned earlier on, was partitioned to keep the women on one side and the men on the other, a good start.

Baseline experiments had been carried out and a CCTV system had been set up in the Bridewell House of Correction prior to our arrival and all that remained was to split into groups and begin the investigations. It was decided by myself and the HNE founder that all seven members present from our team would be working together in one unit, and the HNE team in the other. We were now ready to begin the investigation. The write up you are about to read is based on The North East Ghost Research Team's perspectives of the night's events as unfortunately for the HNE group the investigation proved rather quiet indeed. I guess we were lucky! Having said that it helps our investigations when we have two very good psychics to work with.

10 p.m. saw the start of the investigations and we were posted to the west block, where Suzanne had picked up on the female presence earlier on. We put our heads together and formulated a game plan, as this wing was huge. We discussed splitting into smaller groups to cover more of the block and then, as we were talking, the lights went out and we were thrown into sheer darkness. The vigil had begun. I took some initial baseline readings with the EMF meter but lots of hidden wires and light switches made this task rather difficult to acquire a reading. The room temperature in the main corridor was 14 degrees and the doors leading outside were firmly closed. It was noted that a few of the cell windows rattled in the wind and dust particles filled the air so caution was taken (as always) not to accidentally misinterpret any alleged phenomena.

Motion sensors were locked off, and video cameras and EVP machines were left recording while we sat in the cells and observed. We observed for a while ... then we observed some more. Nothing! After 20 minutes or so I decided to take cell number 2 and sit in it on my own but nothing happened. At this point we then split into our smaller groups and myself, Mark Winter and Suzanne McKay headed downstairs to the debtor's room while Darren Olley, Julie Olley, Claire Smith and Glenn Hall investigated the upper cellblocks.

At 10.15 p.m. we tried some EVP experiments and called out to the atmosphere in the hope that we could ascertain some information from beyond. On listening back to the recordings we found we had no results whatsoever. So we moved on to another experiment. I had noticed a large set of stocks along the back wall so I decided to try a psychometry test. Psychometry is being able to sense and ascertain information from inanimate objects simply by touching them and although psychics seem to get better results I believe we are all capable of doing it. I asked Suzanne McKay if she would go first.

The first impression she got after she had touched the stocks for a while was that of a man named Elliot. She had the impression of chains hanging around her neck as though being forced into a prayer. She also said that these stocks were not part of the museum and were brought here from elsewhere. From where she could not say.

Claire Smith and Mark Winter both came up with the impression that the stocks were moving. They too sensed a chained up feeling. One has to say that chains are a little obvious, as you would expect those in the stocks to be chained up too. One odd thing did occur during this experiment. When we were noting down the results during the psychometry, we all heard a long drawn out guttural breath coming from the lower stairwell. I immediately ran up the stairs and asked the other group (who were at the other side of the cell block) if they heard the noise. They told me they had not.

We then switched locations and I asked Glenn Hall to carry out the psychometry test. His results were quite interesting indeed as he too picked up on the idea they may be from elsewhere. He also sensed two men and a woman and got the word 'fraud'. Upon researching these details I unfortunately came to a blank but that's not to say they may be wrong. It was an interesting idea and it proved to be worth trying. Meanwhile back in the upper west prison block Suzanne informed us that she felt there were three gravestones nearby which were significant to the gaol. She got the names Armstrong and Patterson. She was then drawn to cell 3 and when she looked in she felt as though she was being pushed back as if she was not wanted. An oppressive atmosphere then filled the room and feelings of sickness and illness were felt by everyone present. Before we had a chance to do anything else the atmosphere lifted and everything was fine once more; it was so weird. The rest of this vigil proved rather quiet but what an interesting start.

During a 15 minute break it was decided that myself and some of our team were going to have a walk around the whole grounds to get a general feel of the place and perhaps take some photographs. As I walked outside the cold wind blew hard in my face and although it was dry, rain was beginning to fall but only slightly. We made our way around the back to the serious offenders' block, which stood adjacent to one of the exercise yards. We turned and looked back towards the gaol and the view we were rewarded with was every ghosthunter's dream.

The cell blocks and gaoler's house with the turrets perched high on each corner were towering up into the dark night sky with only the full moon illuminating the scene. The wind was still blowing and every so often the clouds obscured the moon throwing us into total darkness. It was one of the many magnificent moments I have had during my ghost hunting and for me; it was the epitome of what we do. It was so aesthetically pleasing to the eye. All that was needed now was an accompanying apparition making its way across the grounds slowly disappearing into the night. But alas this did not happen.

We made our way back to our base room and proceeded with the investigations. We returned back to the west block and with permission from the HNE founder we were allowed access into the old gaoler's house (the museum). It had been decided prior to the night vigils by HNE, that this location was not available for investigation but we came to the agreement that we should (and quite rightly) be allowed in to investigate. The first to venture in was Suzanne McKay, followed by myself. All the lights were on and turning them off was out of the question for some reason but that did not bother us in the least. Since the museum was full of detailed information and gaol history I decided to blindfold Suzanne so she could not see any of the exhibits and their information. I asked her what she could pick up, if anything.

"It's an eerie and not nice feeling" she said.

"In what respect?" I replied.

"I am not sure, I do get the name James or John though, an authorative figure that sits at his desk searching through a log book," she explained. "He plays with his pocket watch. Also," she said, "This museum used to be private quarters and the names, Hudson, Hutson or Hutton keep going around in my head. I can't work out which one it is".

Very interesting indeed considering that this area was indeed the gaoler's private house and in the Bridewell House of correction there is an exhibit of a mannequin sitting at a desk looking through a logbook. His name is John Hutton. It is also ironic that James Hutton (the father of geology) is one of Jedburgh's famous and celebrated sons. It must be stressed that the information in these blocks were carefully covered up and concealed prior to the investigation so no clues would be given away. Of course the thought occurs that Suzanne may have researched the building before our investigations and most sceptics would say this was so. However if you have ever met and worked with Suzanne to the degree that I have you would know that this is not the case. Although her reading is subjective rather than objective it was nevertheless very odd indeed as it was quite accurate.

We then headed downstairs to the lower section of the museum and took a walk around. We strolled past an old wooden chair in an alcove next to another mannequin and thought nothing of it at the time until one of our team investigators, Darren Olley, heard the sound of creaking and movement coming from behind us. We were not sure as to what this noise was so we sat on the wooden chair to see if it made a noise similar to the one Darren had just heard. It did. Could there have been an invisible presence with us in the gaoler's house, who at that time fancied a seat? Or could the chair itself be haunted? It was an out of the ordinary occurrence definitely worth noting.

We then ventured back into block three and at this point I asked Glenn Hall and Claire Smith to investigate the gaoler's house/museum. In particular I asked Glenn if he would attempt to read the building to see what he would come up with. His first impressions of the museum rooms were of hustle and bustle and he felt it was once very busy in here. He sensed a woman that visited once in a while in a horse-drawn carriage and when this lady came, it was always a big occasion.

He sensed that a man named George was linked emotionally somehow to this lady but exactly how he could not say. He was then drawn downstairs and went straight to the old wooden chair and stated that he felt there was something about it. He then told me that he had the impression that people, on occasion, heard the chair creak when no one is around it as though someone was sitting down in it! This ties in perfectly with what Darren Olley had heard earlier on. Coincidence? I think not.

After 15 minutes or so they ventured back to the cell block we were in and told us his impressions. To say that we were amazed was an understatement and it seemed that this old magnificent building was beginning to tell us its story. While all this was going on Julie Olley and Mark Winter were positioned downstairs in the debtor's room and base room area. They too had an interesting experience while investigating these rooms. It appears that when they were sitting quietly in the debtor's room they heard a loud scraping noise coming from the base room area and went on for about a minute or so. Upon inspection they found the room to be empty and upon asking the others if anyone had been in, they replied that they had not. Mark was visibly shaken as we could tell when he relayed the account to us. It was now past midnight and the end of this vigil.

After a short break we resumed the investigations. It was our turn to investigate Bridewell House of Correction. We ventured in and split up into smaller groups. Suzanne McKay and myself sat in cell 3 and waited. Suzanne then picked up a feeling of oppression and got the words 'pilgrimage', 'destruction' and 'silence' but what they correspond to she could not say. In my later research I came up with nothing either. Everyone else in this block at this time did not report anything odd in the least until 1.21 a.m. when Darren Olley and Julie Olley reported an odd scraping noise followed by a breath. They were at a loss to explain what they had just heard.

We all regrouped and sat in the one section of the prison and called out to the atmosphere and we were rewarded with the sounds of strange knocking in response to our questions. A light flashed across the room just as we were leaving the cell, which seemed strange at the time but after a few enquiries we found out that someone was outside taking photographs of the exterior of the building at that precise time. It was now 3 a.m. and the end of the investigation and all in all it was not a bad night's work. Some odd phenomena had been reported earlier on with audible noises being heard and recorded and it was very interesting what our psychics had picked up on. It seemed to quieten down later in the investigation but that is the way things go. To be able to spend a night in such a place as Jedburgh Castle Gaol was indeed a great honour and a privilege and my thanks go to all those involved especially Steve Caldwell from HNE. I hope one day we may return.

CHAPTER THIRTEEN

GHOSTS OF NORTH WALES

On a trip to North Wales a year or two ago I took the opportunity to visit a number of eerie locations and landmarks that are rich in history and well heeled with ghost legends. During my time in North Wales I stayed in a beautiful bed and breakfast only a stone's throw from the river and my room commanded spectacular views of the captivating ruins of Conwy Castle. My stay here was for only one weekend so I decided to visit a small selection of what I thought were the most splendidly haunted locales.

My first port of call was of course the magnificent Conwy Castle. Conwy Castle is now just a ruined shell and a shadow of its former glory. Still, this gritty dark stoned medieval bastion dominates the area in which it stands and when one first catches a glimpse of this ancient fortress towering over the Conwy estuary, your breath is taken away. With the picturesque backdrop of the Snowdonia mountain range, Conwy Castle and its surroundings are well worth visiting for this reason alone. Built for King Edward I between 1283 and 1289 by Master James of St George, this castle is one of the finest examples of medieval military architecture there is in the UK today. Its two barbicans and its eight enormous towers rising up into the heavens still stand proud today and are a testament to the late medieval workmanship.

But it is not just the castle that is historic in Conwy, but the old fortified town walls too. The township of Conwy was once a walled town like Newcastle upon Tyne and these actual walls survive today almost in their entirety. The town walls, with three double towered gateways, and twenty-one (of the original twenty-two) wall towers that are still standing at their original height, make Conwy one of the finest examples of surviving fortified medieval towns in the world. During my visit I took the opportunity to walk around the entire length of the walls. It was a magnificent experience and at the highest section of the town walls, spectacular views overlooking the town of Conwy, the estuary and its castle on the horizon are there to be enjoyed by everyone.

I must return to my visit to the castle. It was about 2 p.m. when I arrived on a glorious hot summer's day. I made my way up the steep embankment path that leads to the ticket office and entered the castle through the small gateway that is situated through the turnstiles. As I walked into the inner section of the castle walls, the magnificent towers and courtyards within dominated my views and it wasn't until I climbed the vast amount of stone stairs that leads to the top of these towers, that I could see the outstanding views of the surrounding areas and, of course, the castle that lay beneath my feet. If you concentrated and listened hard enough, you could almost hear the sounds of the day-to-day goings on of yesteryear! Echoes from the past reverberate from around almost every corner and shades of the past are not that far away.

Conwy Castle is of course haunted by spectres and apparitions of long gone days and many ghost stories and accounts are often being reported from people all claiming to have had paranormal experiences there. One such account tells of how one individual was walking home one evening after she had visited the castle. She was the last visitor out that day and as she was strolling over the bridge that spans the river, she felt as though she was being watched. She looked around, thought nothing of it and continued with her journey. Then the feelings of being watched became stronger so she turned around again only this time she looked up to the castle walls. There to her utter astonishment she saw what she described as a figure of a man in some sort of armour and helmet standing still and looking directly at her! Fear overcame her and she ran home, terrified. Of course there may have been a perfectly rational explanation for what she had seen, until we find out that upon her return to the castle the following day to ask about this figure, she was told by the warden that after she had left, the castle was locked up for the night and no one could have possibly been perched high up on the castle walls, certainly not dressed in armour and helmet! Could it have been a ghost of a soldier, or guard on duty from long ago?

On chatting with the guides and officials of the castle I learned that there was indeed a resident ghost or two in the castle and one of them, I was told, was the ghost of the missing doctor. It is said one day a woman and her child fell down the long flight of stone stairs from the top of one of the towers after looking out for her husband. They were taken into a room and a doctor was assigned to care for them. For fear of the husband's anger upon his return from war, a servant locked the doctor in the room with the dying family and upon the husband's eventual return, he was informed of the news. When he opened the locked door he found his wife and child to be dead. There was no sign of the doctor. The husband by all accounts went insane with grief and died not long after and it is his ghost that is said to be seen near the area, and in this particular room, searching for the missing doctor.

Now this story is identical to an account from a house not far away called Plas Mawr and I wonder if perhaps this particular account has been mixed up with that one. I asked the guide if he could have been mistaken or perhaps misinformed and his reply was maybe he could have been but he wasn't sure. Further research did tell me that it was indeed Plas Mawr house in Conwy that housed this ghost, indicating just how easy it is to perpetuate the myths of ghosts in alleged haunted properties, even if one is not aware that one is doing so.

My next visit was to the beautiful Aberconwy House, which is situated on Castle Street in Conwy and is the oldest recorded house anywhere in Wales. It is said that parts of the house date back to the 1300s and the upper section of the house was finished around the fifteenth century. It is a wonderful old building, standing out on the corner of the main street and it does indeed have an air of mystery to it. I was eager to have a look inside and being a member of the National Trust I figured I could have a look in and spend some time getting to know its ghosts. I ventured in and was greeted by a National Trust official. I produced my membership card and asked almost straight away, "Have you got any ghosts here?"

He replied in the affirmative. "We do indeed," he said, "More than one by all accounts."

He then proceeded to tell me about the first owner of the house and how some people believe that his wife is one of the ghosts that resides in an upper room of the house and has been seen standing next to the fire. I was told that sometimes the sense of presence is so strong in there, that some of the National Trust volunteers refuse to go in. I was also told that when people were in that room alone, invisible hands have inexplicably touched them and a strange odour of flowers has been smelt which, I was told, was quite unnerving.

This was all very well but I wanted to speak to someone who had experienced ghostly phenomena first hand so I asked if any of the guides present on the day had experienced anything that they would consider being paranormal. An elderly chap said that he had seen the ghost of a man walking down one of the Victorian corridors. He told me that although he only seen him from behind he could tell that he was wearing Victorian attire. Research has shown that a man fitting his description once lived here at Aberconwy House and it is this chap that is believed to be the spectral visitor. By all accounts this fellow has been seen on a number of occasions and I was told he is quite harmless.

I took great pleasure in viewing the old magnificent rooms and corridors in this small, but captivating time capsule and was honoured to share my visit with the guide as he ventured around with me giving me a personal guided tour so to speak. It was a quiet day for visitors for some reason and I was the only one in at that time.

It did not take long to see the entire house so my visit was quite short albeit very rewarding, as we were lucky enough to encounter some ghostly – or strange activity during my visit. I was chatting with the guide in a room next to the Victorian corridor when we became aware of the sound of footsteps clearly making their way down the corridor outside. Thinking nothing of it we carried on talking half expecting someone to come in to the room in which we were standing. No one did.

We looked at each other quite bemused and ventured out to take a look to see if we could find anyone and there was no one to be seen at all on that level of the house. We were dumbfounded and the guide was overjoyed to say the least as it seemed one of the ghosts of Aberconwy House had decided to put in an appearance for us that day. I was so taken aback by this episode I asked him immediately if I could feature this paranormal occurrence in one of my future publications!

The next day came and after a stupendous breakfast, I was ready for my day ahead. I was off to visit one of the most remarkable castles that North Wales has to offer, Penrhyn Castle. If you have ever been to visit Penrhyn Castle you will understand when I say that this castle has to be, without question, one of the most magnificent palaces I have ever seen in my life. It stands nicely on a hill between Snowdonia and the Menai Straits and is one mile east of Bangor and again, is now in the hands of the National Trust.

Penrhyn Castle and estate was built in the early nineteenth century for the Pennant family on the profits made by Jamaican sugar and Welsh slate and within these magnificent walls lies an earlier castle and a medieval hall. There is also a library, a drawing room, and an abundance of other stylish rooms that are adorned with wonderful furniture, stained glass, and intricate handmade statues. The castle also has a wonderful one ton slate bed, which was made for Queen Victoria as well as a grand staircase, which took almost ten years to build. A collection of old paintings crowd the interior walls and these are a part of the castles treasures. At the back there is an industrial railway museum for the train enthusiast along with wonderful countryside walks, walled gardens and acres of beautiful landscape for all to enjoy.

When I ventured inside the castle I got the unmistakable feeling that I was being watched. It's not often I can sense things like this but every now and again it does happen. When I asked about any resident ghosts or paranormal activity the guide told me that although he was a little sceptical, he had heard one or two reports of ghostly phenomena which included the usual array of reported activity including cold spots and unexplained temperature drops, feelings of uneasiness, footsteps being heard in empty rooms, as well as the feeling of being watched. I got the impression that ghosts at Penrhyn are not discussed that much either because they believe they do not have any, or they prefer to let them be and not disturb them, which is commendable and understandable.

Past occupants include a chief steward of a welsh Prince, an archbishop of York, and a pirate who lived there over 400 years ago! So maybe the ghosts of these former residents still reside here at Penrhyn.

My trip to Wales was coming to an end and what a trip it had been. I had visited some of the most beautiful areas in North Wales and sought out some fantastic ghost legends and tales. I even experienced the odd strange happening myself. Needless to say I will indeed venture back across to Wales, and maybe next time venture a little further south. There is so much more to explore and many places I did not get a chance to visit and one day I hope this will be rectified.

CHAPTER FOURTEEN

CASE STUDY

KILLHOPE LEAD MINE, NEAR CUMBRIA

Killhope lead mine is located in the heart of the beautiful North Pennines between Alston and Stanhope in Upper Weardale near Cumbria and is surrounded by acres of lush countryside, woodland walks and aesthetic beauty. The mine was opened in 1853 and for 57 years the mine was a thriving industry which was run by locals and supplied lead all over the north of England and beyond. In 1910 the mine was closed only to be re-opened for a few years sometime between 1939 and 1945. The mine's giant waterwheel, which towers skywards, was built in the late 1870s and was one of many waterwheels which mines such as Killhope would use. It is now the only surviving waterwheel of its kind.

In 1980 the restoration work began at Killhope and today it is the one of the finest examples of lead mines that can be visited. It is a museum and popular visitor centre in which you can go and see how this Victorian mine was once worked. The mine itself tunnels deep under, and into, the solid rock and earth of the North Pennines and a cavernous and hollow labyrinth of tunnels and passageways is there to be explored by those brave enough to venture down into the dark and dank catacombs of yesteryear. On the ground level there are a number of edifices and buildings known as the miners' quarters, which are now museums and visitors today can see how these miners would have lived. Not much has changed and when one walks into the rooms it is like going back in time.

No one is sure if the area or the mines are haunted but there have been some strange occurrences reported here leading me to think they may well be. A local radio DJ and ghost hunter has visited Killhope on a number of occasions and has broadcast live investigations from the site and although I have never heard these broadcasts, I am told they were quite good with alleged phenomena occurring throughout the night. Staff here have also reported objects being displaced and moved in the Miners' quarters throughout the night. When opening up in the morning it was found that the old-fashioned draughts board and draughts pieces were moved from where they were originally left. Chairs and old furniture were also found to be 'out of place'. No one had been in to move them!

So who haunts the area then? Over the years there have been two recorded deaths here at Killhope. In 1864 it is reported that a mineworker, Graham Peart fell to his death here while working high up on a ledge. By all accounts he was distracted by something, lost his footing and fell, which ultimately sealed his fate. Another recorded death here is that of a certain Thomas Harrison who was blown to bits in 1878 while working with some gunpowder. Could these people still be at Killhope, getting on with their everyday duties unaware that they are dead? Or is it someone else, someone else who perhaps loved the place so much they simply did not want to leave?

Another legend and a potential candidate for a ghost is that of an unknown woman who wandered off into the deep woodland in search of her husband. She was never seen again and it is said that on dark foggy nights you can hear her calling out for the husband she never managed to find during her search when alive. Perhaps she still walks the woods in vain, looking for her long lost love.

As a [then] member of the North East Ghost Hunters I was lucky enough to be invited up to Killhope to investigate the miner's quarters and the haunted woods that surround Killhope (access down the mine was not allowed for us that night). Our journey began at 8.30 p.m. where I was met and picked up at Newcastle Central station by a few members of the group. The drive up there was quite long and we arrived at Killhope mine at 10.10 p.m., after driving through long twisting country roads, amidst thick fog rolling in from far away on the east coast. The atmosphere was good and our excitement was starting to build up, yet I felt apprehensive about the whole idea of spending the night in literally, one of the darkest places in the whole of the North. When we arrived the rest of the team met us and we were shown to our base room, which was one of the vigil locations. This particular location was the room in which the draught set and other effects had been mysteriously moved.

On entering the Miners' quarters we were then greeted by another well-known north-eastern paranormal investigator, and a number of his team. It was at this point an investigator tried to take a photo of the draughts board, and for some strange and unknown reason, his camera kept on spitting out the batteries! This happened a few times and it baffled everyone. On one attempt the batteries almost came all the way out of the camera. Then to add to the mystery, when he took out the batteries, the lights on the camera were still coming on! Possible camera malfunction or ghost intervention? The thought crossed my mind that a little residual energy left in the camera from the batteries could have accounted for the lights coming on after the batteries came out, but why the batteries fired out of the camera in the first place remains a mystery.

At 10.15 p.m. a digital thermometer was set up next to the draughts board, which was close to the fire. If any fluctuations occurred it would prove odd to say the least. The internal room temperature read 13.8 degrees. By 10.25 p.m. everyone had attempted to take photos of the draughts board and had experienced minor difficulties with their cameras. It is also interesting to note that a few people reported feelings of dizziness and sickness when they first entered the miners' quarters. At 10.30 p.m. we had decided to venture around the Killhope Mine site. But before we headed out we left an infrared night vision video camera recording, trained on the draughts set in the hope we might catch some paranormal activity. It got to 10.40 p.m. and we noticed the temperature had dropped to 12.3 degrees. We concluded it was probably a natural temperature drop.

We headed out and around the mine site and ventured to where the big iron waterwheel is and some of the outbuildings. On our way out a really odd thing occurred. Myself and another investigator both thought we heard the voices of two men talking or muttering coming from near our base room area from within the darkness. Could it have been the echoes of our own party? We will never know for certain but I recorded the incident none the less. After an uneventful hour of checking out the area we returned to the base room for a break. It was at this point, myself, and two of the investigators all heard what can only be described as a loud howl or scream, coming from the mine wheel area or from within the woods (we could not determine which). Could it have been a fox – or the phantom lady of the forest? The thought crossed my mind. Whatever it was, it sounded harrowing.

At 11.45 p.m. we decided it was time to have a walk through Killhope woods up to the seventeenth century thatch that is hidden deep in Killhope forest. On our way up through the trees, an investigator told me that he was picking up footsteps following us as we were ascending up the path. He picked these footfalls up on his low frequency sound audio enhancer. We looked around but could see no one. When we arrived at the seventeenth century thatch we went inside and it really was like something out of the Blair Witch Project. It was cold, dark, wet and very scary to say the least. A few of us, including myself, managed to get a couple of good mist photos and one picture had some moisture orbs on it. In all probability this was down to the moisture that was in the air. During our stint in the wooden edifice nothing paranormal happened.

At 12.10 a.m. we left the thatch building and set up a dictation machine recording in the hope of catching something strange on the tape. We also drew around a cross and left it on a windowsill as a trigger object. We walked about 20 feet away from the thatch and stood in the dark and waited to hear something … anything. It was not long before we all heard another very loud screech, scream or wail. We can't decide exactly what it was. Some thought it sounded like a fox scream, while others said it could have been the sound of steel moving and scraping, like the mine wheel turning, or perhaps an echo of it moving from bygone days but we all couldn't help thinking perhaps it was a ghostly wail echoing through the dark forest. Whatever it was, it sent shivers down the spine.

The time was now 12.20 a.m. During our descent back down to the miners' quarters I was walking at the back with an investigator for company, when I became aware of something behind me. It sounded like a footfall or two, followed by a breath or a grunt! I turned around and all I could see was the blackness of the forest. I was sure I heard something but to this day I don't know what it was. Whatever it was, it seemed to be really close to me and I was rather glad when we reached our base room.

At 12.30 a.m. we arrived back at the miners' quarters and had a short break before attempting the first séance of the investigation. The séance turned out to be quite good with lots of minor happenings (pardon the pun). It started off as normal with an investigator calling out and as usual nothing was happening. We gave it a bit more time and then reports started to come in that few people were feeling cold breezes, and presences were felt behind certain members of the circle. As always, the proceedings were monitored and when temperature drops were felt, they were backed scientifically by the investigator measuring the temperature with the temperature gun and other devices in his vast array of ghost hunting equipment. I soon took over the lead in the séance and was asking for phenomena when all of a sudden the name "Harrison" came to me.

About 30 seconds later an investigator asked the event organiser what the name was of the chap who was killed. At this point I shouted out the name I had just been given. To my surprise (and everyone else's too) when I said the name the atmosphere in the room changed considerably and everyone felt it. It was also reported that after I had called out the name, the room temperature dropped by a staggering 6 degrees in 2 seconds flat. The event organiser then confirmed a miner of that name had died at Killhope Mine and was alleged to be one of the possible spirits. I did not know this fact until after the séance.

At 1.30 a.m., after a break, an investigator had the idea to steal one of the miners' forks when we left the hut for our next walk to the seventeenth century thatch. The idea was to entice any ghost or spirit in there, into an outward manifestation. The forks and other eating utensils would have been very precious indeed to these miners, and arguments would have broken out about them. Telling the spirit he was taking it away from them would hopefully produce some phenomena. We all thought this was a good idea. We then made our way up the thatch and picked up the dictation machine and trigger object we left earlier. This had not moved. A second séance was attempted in this location but nothing happened.

After a while we came back down to the miners' hut to check on the place. Upon our arrival back, it was noted by one of the investigators that the forks on the table had been crossed over into an X shape. No one had touched them and they were left parallel before we went out. Isn't it odd how one investigator said he was taking a fork to aggravate the spirit and lo and behold, we get some good phenomena relating to the old cutlery! It was decided we should try another séance to attempt to make contact with whoever or whatever, was residing in there. We formed the circle and held hands. This time it was another investigator who started off the proceedings by asking if any spirits present would make themselves known. After a while he asked me how long my dictation machine recorded for and I told him about 45 minutes. He then asked the spirits in the room to try to communicate through the device on the floor (meaning my dictation machine) and then asked some random questions leaving a space in-between for any potential answers. The questions were varied: Are you a man? Are you a woman? Did you once live here? Did you die here? Do you mind us being here? etc.

Unfortunately when I listened back to the cassette there were no ghostly voices answering those questions. However what we did get was one or two crystal clear taps or knocks in response to some of the questions we posed. They were heard by everyone at the time and were picked up on the tape too, not bad results. Other phenomena included the sense of presence by one investigator behind her during the séance, which I think another investigator felt it too. However, time was now getting on and it was time to end the investigation.

All in all it was an eventful evening in which some good phenomena occurred. The howls or screams we heard emanating from within the forest, (on two occasions), along with the 'Harrison' séance, which resulted in the change of atmosphere, and the 6 degree temperature drop. The knocks and taps I picked up on my dictation machine were interesting too, as were the knocks we heard on command to certain questions we posed during the séance. The movement of the cutlery, which was left parallel on the miners' dinner table, next to the draughts board when we were all out and about, was a very good result too and we mustn't forget the mysterious footfalls we heard while venturing through the black, uninviting haunted forest. Earlier in the chapter I said that it is not known if Killhope was haunted. Now I have been and investigated the area first hand, I can say now that I really think it could well be, although more research is needed before any final conclusions are made.

CHAPTER FIFTEEN

CASE STUDY

THURCROFT MINERS' INST, ROTHERHAM, SOUTH YORKSHIRE

During my travels around the UK I get to meet the most wonderful people from all walks of life; people who have experienced ghosts first hand. Some people, as you can imagine are afraid of what is happening so we try to offer our assistance in the best way we can. Others take it in their stride and are more than happy to share their homes or properties with their guests from the other side. The good people in relation to this case were not frightened of what was happening to them, but called G.H.O.S.T. in to investigate the hauntings nonetheless to try and find some answers. A correspondence that was sent to our team, which we received after an appearance in a nationwide publication, reads as follows. I thought it would be best to publish the correspondence exactly how we received it although one or two minor details have been excluded for obvious reasons:

Subject: unexplained activity

My name is Cheryl Booth and I am writing to you after seeing you in a paranormal magazine. I am secretary for the Thurcroft Welfare Community Hall. Thurcroft has been a mining village from the late 1800's until 1997 when the Thurcroft Colliery closed. The hall was built in 1925 to provide a place for miners and their families to socialise. The hall was once used to hold tea dances and various film nights, using the projection room, which is situated at the back of the hall on the second floor, and did so for many years. The reason for contacting you is because there have been a number of unexplained and paranormal events reported to me by guests and staff, and there have also been a few odd experiences that I have personally witnessed.

Here are a couple of examples:

1) Last week I was alone in my office sorting through some paperwork when I heard one of the doors outside my office open. I immediately went to look and there was nobody there. Due to the size of the building, you can hear people moving about and walking through the building as it amplifies the sound, but I never heard anything other than the door opening. Shortly after I was picking some paperwork up off the floor and out of the corner of my eye, I saw somebody standing in the middle of the foyer. I immediately turned my head to look (thinking it was somebody who required some information or assistance) and the figure vanished.

2) Late last year we held a social night for user groups of the building. We had some music on low and halfway through the night we heard a number of 'footsteps' directly above us. First we thought it was the music so we turned it off but the noise continued. Thinking then that somebody was on the roof or had managed to get into the projection room, a number of us went to investigate (in separate locations) but there wasn't a soul in sight. About 10 people all heard these footsteps that night.

And finally

3) A member from one of the user groups was using the toilet facilities when they heard talking coming from one of the cubicles. They immediately opened the toilet door and the voices stopped! No other toilets were in use and all the doors were open.

Many more occurrences have taken place but there isn't enough room on here for them. I am not sure if this kind of building is something that you have investigated before, but if you want to have a look for yourself and hold an investigation, you are more than welcome, if only to help us understand what these incidents could be.
I have enclosed a rough drawing of the layout of the building so you can get an idea. Any information or advice you could provide us with would be much appreciated.

Should you need to contact me, you can do.
Many Thanks

Cheryl Booth
Secretary
Thurcroft Welfare Community Hall
Rotherham
South Yorkshire

As it said on the correspondence there have been more incidences reported but have not been included in the initial letter. When we arrived to conduct the investigation I promptly interviewed everyone present that night who had experienced a ghostly, or an unexplained encounter. I wanted a bigger picture of what has been going on in order to run and conduct a thorough investigation. An SNU committee member, June Thompson went on to say: "Sitting in the bar room for our Sunday evening spiritualist service, the kitchen door was wedged open. As the service went on my eyes were drawn to the fire door in the kitchen which can be seen through the bar room door. I saw a shape, which resembled a human form stood there in the corner. This happened on three occasions. On another Sunday evening we held our service in the side room. It was during the summer months so the only door into the room had been left open by using a chair, before the service began. During the service the chair was moved and the door slammed closed. When the door closed the chair amazingly wedged itself behind it making it hard for us to exit the room. When we did eventually get out the room, we searched the building for a joker but found no one. The premises were empty apart from those in our meeting room, and all the exterior doors were locked!"

Elaine Hollis, another SNU committee member who was present told me her accounts of what she had experienced.

"Although I can verify what June has said, as I was there too, I have also found this place to be very odd indeed. There is a certain feel to it and more often than not it feels as though you are being watched. On one occasion I walked through the main hall and into the kitchen to tend to some duties and when I returned into the hall I found three of the seats had been moved into the middle of the hall (which were all around the edge of the hall when I went in the kitchen) and were facing towards each other like in a circle. Very nerve racking indeed."

She went on to say: "It is rumoured that a death occurred in this building somewhere around the stage area in the main hall. Who it was though we are not certain. Also the old library room out back, which is now used as an office is often quite cold for no reason whatsoever, even in the summer. The smell of tobacco smoke often fills the room even though this is a no smoking building, we have never found an explanation for it".

My last interview before the investigation began was with Chris Wood. Chris is the bar manager/odd job man for the welfare building and is often in the building on his own through the night carrying out jobs. He told me "Working through the night on your own here is really not that bad. I know ghosts exist here and I feel we have a mutual respect for each other. I often hear doors opening and closing on their own and footsteps are quite often heard reverberating around the premises during the night. At first I thought we may have intruders in the building, or perhaps someone had been locked in but on checking for people and for a potential break in, I found nothing out of order and the building empty. After a while it just becomes second nature to ignore it. It is something you get used to".

My interviews were complete and now I had a better idea of what had been happening over the years at the premises. I was informed that lots of other folk had also had their stories to tell and I would love to chat to them all to hear their stories and encounters in the lovely old building. One day I will.

It was now time to carry out our preliminary baseline readings and prepare the building for the investigation to come. This baseline reading was rather odd as one or two anomalies were indeed picked up during the tests. Backstage, (a place where everyone agreed had a certain feel to it) a cold draught was felt by all and upon trying to locate its source we came up with nothing. Then, it simply vanished! We left a flour tray experiment in this area. The old library was of interest too as when we had ventured in there earlier to take our readings, we recorded the temperature at a steady 19 degrees. We needed to return a few minutes later and when we did, we found the room to be a lot colder than previously recorded. The temperature had dropped to 13 degrees. A 6 degree drop in only a minute or two! Trigger objects were left in this room too.

The rest of the baseline tests ran smoothly and nothing else was reported. We now had a basic reading of the premises for our records. During the baselines we also placed a trigger object in the projection suite on the second floor along with some motion sensors in the thin corridor that leads to the old office. Other motion sensors were placed near the newer main entrance where an apparition of someone had been seen in the past. We split into groups and began the investigation. It was decided, as there were four team members and four guests on the investigation, we should split into two groups of four, each containing two team members and two guests.

In group one there was myself, Lee, Chris Wood, and Cheryl Booth and our first port of call was the area backstage. The temperature measured 17 degrees and no EMF anomalies were recorded. This area was absolutely pitch black and it took some time for our eyes to adjust. Lee, when filming with his night vision video camera caught an amazing show of the strangest light anomalies I have seen to date. The odd thing about them is when I ventured over to have a look through the viewfinder I asked them to stop and they did! When I asked for a sign for any potential spirits to show themselves in some way, the light anomalies began once more!

Cheryl then felt a cold breeze and she told us she is had begun to feel rather apprehensive. Chris then claimed to see an orange light anomaly with his naked eye and said it was coming up the corridor and floating around at the top of the room. He became agitated and then emotional. Chris, who is a big strapping fellow, then began to cry uncontrollably! It is something I have never seen before on an investigation. (Well, not with a 16 stone, big burly lad like him).

There are only three explanations as to what was going on; (a) he was getting carried away with the whole thing and imagined it all as no one else could see this orange light that he claimed he could see, (b) he was making the whole thing up for whatever reason, or (c) he was a lot more psychic and in tune with spirits more than he gave himself credit for. I will go with the latter simply because when he told us where to point the video camera, lo and behold, we caught what looks like an orange light anomaly moving across the ceiling!

Although we could not see it with our naked eyes as Chris had, it verified to me something very odd was going on. Chris went on to say that his emotions were all over the place and that he felt a heavy pressure on his shoulders and back. Was he sensing some sad and tormented soul that for whatever reason still lingers in this area backstage? After all, we all felt this area had an eerie feel to it earlier on. It was an interesting first vigil.

Group two consisted of Drew, Fiona, Elaine and June and they were investigating the bar room. A relatively quiet vigil was held in here with only one or two possible psychic or ghostly occurrences. The first was when June and Elaine felt as though they were being moved, then felt a breeze across the room. No trace for the draught was found and June and Elaine suspected that this may have been the presence of a former friend who has passed into the next world. The other was a strobe of light which was seen in the room followed by an unexplained banging noise. The whole group witnessed this and no explanation was found.

On to location two and our group were due to investigate the projection suite on the second floor, a cold, dark and dusty environment, which was open to the elements due a broken window or two. We ventured up the flight of stairs, which, if had been any steeper would have been vertical, and entered the projection suite. If anything untoward happened in here getting out quickly would be rather hard indeed so great care had to be taken to say the least. The trigger object we had placed here earlier on had not yet been moved and despite some calling out, nothing much happened at all. However I had a bit of a fright when something prodded me in the lower back region while I was sitting on a chair. What it was for sure I cannot say.

Group two meanwhile were investigating the kitchen area where a human figure had been seen on a number of occasions. An interesting vigil was documented in here with the sound of some unexplained knockings being heard by everyone. They started off quite faint and built up into a quite loud noise. The knocks also came on demand when the investigators and guests asked for them. However they were not recorded on tape. After a break, our group investigated the bar area and group two investigated behind the stage. Not long after venturing into this location I heard the sound of what can only be described as a chair being scraped and dragged across the main hall floor, which was only in the next room. On venturing in to see if anything was out of place we found nothing.

This was quite interesting, as chairs have been known to move in this area and, although nothing seemed to be out of place, I did hear the sound of a chair being moved. I took my seat in the bar and sat in the darkness for a while. I called out to the atmosphere and took some digital stills but all was quiet. As I was sitting in the darkness the other three members of my group claimed to hear a grunt or a moan coming from directly behind me, however, I heard absolutely nothing. The rest of the vigil was rather quiet.

The other group, while backstage, sat in silence for about 45 minutes waiting for something to happen. Just as they were about to leave the area the lavatory (which is located in this area) flushed on its own! This is something else which happens here quite a lot but we were not informed of this. Upon walking into the Gents it was reported that you could hear the cistern refilling. The flush mechanism is the usual silver handle type, which needs to be pushed down hard in order to activate the flush. No one was in the lavatory at the time so it seemed this happening could well have had a paranormal origin.

To end the night and the investigations it was decided that a séance should be held backstage in order to try and experience more paranormal activity. It seemed that our first reactions to this area proved right and it was the most active area during the investigations. We took our chairs through, formed a circle and began the séance but not before setting up a host of video cameras on tripods to monitor the proceedings. The séance was led by Fiona and it lasted about 30 minutes. During the proceedings one or two light anomalies were caught on tape and the usual array of feelings were reported. Feelings of being touched, draughts and coldness were felt but nothing that we could class as good, objective evidence. However a sitter did report that she felt odd and said her arm went ice cold. My temperature gun registered a reading of 15 degrees on the cold arm and 27 degrees on the other! This was extremely peculiar to say the least. Perhaps there was indeed a presence there with us. It did seem likely.

It was now 5.30 a.m. and we packed up our equipment, loaded up the car, and got ready to come home. When chatting in the office Drew asked me if I thought the venue was haunted. Although I was compelled to say yes (as I thought it may well be) I said that conclusions could not be made based upon one night's investigation. The testimony of all those who I had talked to seem credible enough and a lot of the data we accumulated on the investigation does suggest the building is haunted, but more work needs to be carried out. At this point we were invited to return to carry out more research and on one cold night in February the following year we did. The same staff and community workers who had joined us the first time also partook in the night's investigation. We also had guest medium Ralph Keeton and Nikki Austwicke joining us on the investigation. (Ralph and Nikki will be introduced properly to the reader later in the book as this section of the chapter is detailing the account of what happened *after* Ralph and Nikki had been acquainted with the team). After the centre had closed for the night and all the centre users had left to go home, we locked all the doors and proceeded to carry out the baseline tests. While the baseline tests were being carried out I re-interviewed Cheryl Booth and June Thompson and asked them what had been occurring since our last visit. They told me:

> Well, basically it's more of the same really, chairs are still moving around on their own, and doors are opening and closing when nobody is around. Some of the cleaning ladies often tell us they see shadows flitting about and hear unexplained whistling coming from somewhere – but where? They cannot say. I also saw a full on apparition of a man who I thought was my father (still alive) and when I went to speak to him in the room I saw him walk into, there was nobody there at all and there were no doors or other exits for a normal person to leave by!

By now the baseline tests had been carried out and no anomalous readings were ascertained and we were now ready to begin the second investigation. We spilt up into three groups and headed off into the locations to see if we could document any more paranormal activity. As it happened, the night turned out to be rather good. During the course of the investigation various strange occurrences were reported by the team members and guests, including breaths and disembodied sighs, light anomalies, the sound of chairs being moved in the main hall when I was in the hall at the time – and even more odd – *no* chairs were found out of place! Lights were also being turned off while we were in the actual locations. Our guest medium also picked up on, and told the staff there, that there were indeed a number of ghosts that resided here.

One name in particular came up and that was a certain W. Gregory. This person was picked up backstage where Chris had his emotional experience on the first investigation. The office not far from this area does indeed have a plaque on the wall with a list of people relating to the centre who had died in the Great War between 1914–1918 and a certain William Gregory is named on the plaque. I can guarantee that Ralph did not venture into this room prior to him picking up this name so he could not have, and did not cheat.

Another interesting occurrence happened during my first vigil when Cheryl was looking through the doors in the main hall into the room that runs by next to it. She told me she thought she saw someone walk past the windows inside the other room. Now the interesting thing about this is that one of our team investigators, Drew Bartley, saw the exact same thing while we were on a break later on. He was quite dumbfounded by the whole experience and we could not duplicate what he saw by normal means. We thought it may have been a reflection in the window by someone in the hall with us but tests proved this was not the case. Combined with Cheryl's sighting earlier on this incident proved very significant indeed.

I guess it must have been Drew's night as he also saw a figure or a person quickly stick their head around a door and then withdraw it back. It was not one of the team nor was it any of the staff or guests that were there that night. We also know there was no one in this actual room at this time. Drew described him as short, balding, and quite chubby faced, just as Ralph had described one of the spirits earlier on! Again, Drew had no knowledge of this description by Ralph and was quite flabbergasted to say the least. Drew is rather sceptical and always puts other explanations forward to try and explain what has occurred but this time he was at a loss to explain it, and it was to get better – or worse, depending on your views!

On one of the last vigils of the evening Drew, Nikki, and Chris were backstage investigating when all of a sudden the three, for no reason, became scared. The room's atmosphere changed from being warm and normal, to an unnerving and intimidating feeling. Suddenly a thump was heard coming from the empty corridor and when all three turned around to see what it was, Drew was physically assaulted! As they were looking down the corridor into the darkness wondering what the thump was, from out nowhere came a tremendous blow to the top of Drew's head. The impact was so hard that his knees buckled and the sound of the 'slap' it made on the top of his head can clearly be heard on videotape, which he had recording at the time. The three screamed as they tried to escape. A normal, quiet vigil had turned into utter pandemonium. Later, I was told, accompanying the assault was the sound of an angry and evil howl that enveloped his head at the time of the attack by this invisible entity. This howl can also be heard on the videotape!

Drew described this encounter as the most terrifying he had ever witnessed and said that, at the time of the attack, he thought he was not going to come out of this one alive! Nikki and Chris also agreed beyond all doubt, that something otherworldly and petrifying had happened which indeed scared them somewhat. This can also be heard on the videotape. It is shocking footage to say the least and watching it makes the blood run cold. One wonders now if Drew is still sceptical! After the incident when I was chatting to him, I could clearly see he was shaken, upset, and very frightened indeed. This is not the Drew I know, and I have never seen him like this in my five years of working with him. But in true ghost investigator style – he marched straight back into the unknown to try and find out why this entity had chosen him for attack. Ralph told us that Drew was just there at the wrong time (or right time!) and it could have happened to anyone there that night. It was this spirit's way of saying "get out, we have had enough!"

We took heed, packed up our equipment and headed off home. The second investigation proved to be one of the best for the team so far and especially for Drew. Guest medium Ralph Keeton answered one or two questions that had arisen from the last investigation like who the ghost was backstage, and how many ghosts resided in the building altogether but, as with most investigations, more questions had arisen from this examination. One question we can answer from the first investigation is 'is this place haunted?' I can now say without a shadow of a doubt that yes, the place is haunted.

CHAPTER SIXTEEN

THE GHOSTS OF SWAFFHAM, NORFOLK

The elegant and charming Swaffham in the county of Norfolk is a quaint, but lively and bustling market town. It is situated on the edge of the Brecks nature reserve approximately 30 miles west of Norwich and boasts some of the most beautiful countryside in Norfolk. Swaffham, famous for its wonderful market place has an abundance of beautiful Georgian buildings and is rich in history as well as having great aesthetic beauty.

On a weekend visit to Swaffham, I stayed over at the old Red Lion pub, and the George Hotel, which are located in the centre of this ancient town. My purpose for the visit? I was attending a wedding, and although this was my primary basis for visiting, I made it my business to do a bit of ghost hunting and seek out some of the local ghost stories and encounters that may have happened here. It was inevitable that I would be successful and it was not long before I had my first lead. During a look around on market day I found a bookstall. While searching through the vast array of old and new books, hoping to find a work on Harry Price, I came across *Norfolk Stories of the Supernatural* of which I purchased.

"Got any more ghost books?" I asked.

"Indeed we have" came the reply. "Got one called *This House is Haunted*".

"Really? I will take that one too," I said. I snapped this book up which was written by Guy Lyon Playfair and was all about the famous Enfield Poltergeist case in 1977. It was a first edition from 1980 so I bought it. Little did I know at that time I would eventually meet the author of this amazing book at his home in London on a number of occasions, and become involved with him and his work with poltergeists in a way I never could have dreamed. As it transpired, I too investigated a vicious poltergeist case that is comparable to Enfield, and Guy Lyon Playfair wrote the foreword for the book that was written about it.

"Not from round here are you?" the bookseller observed.

"No, from Newcastle, down for a wedding, and a spot of ghost research, too."

"Researching ghosts, eh? Plenty of ghosts down in these parts," she said. "Try the Red Lion across the road, they are supposed to have one, and maybe take a look in the church yard too. Plenty of ghost stories attached to this grave yard."

"Swaffham church yard? Just over yonder?" I said. "That's where the wedding is, and I am staying at the Red Lion tonight."

"Well, you are in luck then" she said, "and if you have time, try to get to Raynham Hall, it's only a few miles away".

I bade her goodbye and followed up some of the leads that she had given me. I returned to my room, which was at the rear of the pub, got cleaned up and settled down for some lunch and a pint. The first person I spoke to told me she hadn't heard any stories of any ghosts that walk the Red Lion pub, but she was new to the pub although she had lived in Swaffham most of her life. A gentleman, also behind the bar, overheard our conversation and promptly told me that many a night he had been in the bar alone but felt he was not alone. He did specify that nothing definite had ever been seen (to his knowledge) but unexplained noises had been heard as well as one or two other people sensing someone of an otherworldly nature not too far away. Although these accounts are quite interesting, research has shown little to back up any accounts of any potential ghosts. This is not to say the Red Lion is not haunted, it may well be.

I moved on and questioned one or two of the locals with regards to the alleged ghost or ghosts that are supposed to reside at Swaffham churchyard. I had found out from one elderly local, that the churchyard at Swaffham is reputed to be haunted by the ghost of a monk. He told me that he is often seen gliding along the paths and in-between the gravestones before suddenly disappearing. Others have said that when they are in the churchyard they have felt someone tap them on the shoulder. When they look around to see who is there, they are shocked to find they are on their own. Swaffham church has another wonderful legend attached to its history and is known as the *Pedlar of Swaffham* and I will elaborate on this tale now.

The story goes that a local pedlar called John Chapman had a strange dream one night. In his dream he was told to go to London Bridge where he would hear some great news in regards to his life. He thought nothing of it until the next night when once again, he had the same dream. This time he decided he would act upon it. The following day, excited by this prospect he packed up some belongings, got his pet dog, and set off for the city of London. When he arrived at London Bridge he stood there and waited for his great news. He waited and waited but nothing happened. A curious Londoner eventually asked him why he should be standing on the bridge for hour after hour and was subsequently told about the pedlars' dream. The Londoner laughed in his face and said, "If I believed in my dreams I would be in a place called Swaffham, wherever that is, digging up gold from under an apple tree of a man called Chapman".

Disheartened by the whole episode he sadly made his way back home. Then it dawned on him. John Chapman had an apple tree in his garden and he wondered what would happen if he dug it up. He dug up the apple tree and found a small pot of gold coins. He kept the coins, cleaned up the pot and after finding a strange inscription on it that he could not understand, put it on his stall to sell. One day not long after, a passing monk was looking at the pot and asked the pedlar if he knew what the inscription read. The pedlar said "no" so the monk translated it for him.

Under me doth lie, another richer far than I

After the monk had left his stall, he hurried home and dug further down into the earth where his apple tree once stood and this time found a much larger pot, again full of gold. It was not long after this happened that the locals announced that they were going to rebuild the church in Swaffham. With the pedlar's newfound wealth, he donated the money to rebuild the north aisle and the tower.

An absolutely wonderful story with a happy ending for a change and interestingly enough, research has shown that in an ancient inventory logbook in regards to the rebuilding of the church, states that a local man called John Chapman did indeed pay for the work to be carried out. One also wonders if the ghost of the monk that haunts Swaffham churchyard is the same monk who translated the inscription on the pedlar's pot. An interesting thought occurred that this monk was meant to translate the inscription on the pot, ultimately leading to the church being rebuilt. Perhaps if the gold were not found, the rebuilding may never have happened due to lack of funds. An uncanny coincidence? Or spiritual intervention? Now, he may haunt Swaffham churchyard simply to look after and protect the church after it had been rebuilt. A fascinating idea, which could well hold some validity.

I now turn my attention to the George Hotel where we stayed for our second night. We booked in and almost straight away I asked about any resident ghosts. To my delight I was informed that the George Hotel was one of the oldest buildings in town and it seemed that a ghost known as the Green Lady resided within. This spirit woman wearing a green dress has been seen walking through the corridors in the oldest wing of the building and has also been seen in the lounge area. Every now and again, I was told, she has been seen in some of the bedrooms too. Unfortunately when I asked if she had been seen in the room we had booked I was told she had not been. Much to Jayne's (my partner) delight who is terrified of the thought of ghosts!

Other phenomena has been reported here with staff and guests being touched and slightly pushed when no one is near them. Staff in the hotel have experienced their shirts being pulled, and unexplained voices have been heard when no one else is around leaving them quite frightened to say the least. One kitchen worker ran out of the hotel in sheer terror after sensing someone who was not there. It was fascinating to talk to some of these witnesses who have experienced the phenomena firsthand and I was looking forward to spending the night here. Regretfully for myself, but thankfully for Jayne we experienced nothing paranormal during our stay there.

By all accounts nobody knows who this ghost lady is or why she haunts the hotel but an investigation there may throw up some answers. From what I was informed, the ghost seems to be friendly enough and judging by the stories that I heard during my visit I can only surmise that she is perhaps a former employee or a guest of the hotel who once stayed here. Perhaps she loved the place so much she did not want to leave. We hear this time and time again and it does indeed make some sense. Showing herself in spirit form, touching people and pulling their clothes may simply be her way to let you know that she is still around and is very happy to be so – as clichéd as this sounds.

Many of the ghost stories and accounts I learned about during my time in Norfolk were absolutely fascinating to hear and this visit gave me a chance to delve into some of the wonderful history and ghost legends that are attached to this particular village. Ghost hunting (for me) is not just about one off all night investigations, but paying visits to places like this, tracking down the alleged hauntings and listening to first hand accounts from the witnesses themselves and trying to piece together what has happened in order to try and make some sense of it. Working like this is just as satisfying as spending all night and awake in a reputedly haunted location. I left Norfolk with an abundance of true life encounters and one day soon, I hope to return and revisit in search of ghosts.

CHAPTER SEVENTEEN

CASE STUDY

WOODCHESTER MANSION, NYMPSFIELD, GLOUCESTERSHIRE

In early 2006 myself and two members of The North East Ghost Research Team travelled down to the beautiful Cotswolds in Gloucestershire merely to observe an investigation that was being run by Swindon based research team Paranormal Site Investigators (PSI). Founded by Dave Wood BSc and Nicky Sewell BSc Paranormal Site Investigators are, in my opinion one of the most thorough and professional investigative teams I have ever had the privilege to meet and work with in all my years of study in this particular field. Their scientific approach to their research combined with their methodology and practices are second to none and this leads me to think that they could well be one of the best psychical research teams in the UK. Is it any wonder that ghost hunting legend Peter Underwood FRSA supports their cause and patrons their team? It was indeed an honour to be asked by PSI to attend an investigation with them and on one cold January night that is exactly what we did. The venue, the magnificent Woodchester Mansion in Cotswolds.

Woodchester Mansion is set in a 400 acre landscape park and is a striking, but unfinished gothic mansion, which was built in the mid-1800s. It is believed that during the construction of this magnificent dwelling the construction workers downed tools and left for an unknown reason. Some believe that funds simply ran out and to finish the building was simply not an option. However, other rumours persist that something unknown, and disturbing happened during the construction causing the workers to flee in terror, never to return. Although confirmed reports of ghost activity only date back to the 1990s, rumours of earlier sightings do indeed persist. On 7 January 2006, eleven PSI investigators and observers from The North East Ghost Research Team conducted an overnight investigation at Woodchester Mansion.

We arrived at the venue about three hours early as we thought it would be better to find our way there first (as we were to travel about 300 miles and we were not sure how long the actual journey would take). Once we had found Woodchester Park, which is 4 miles southwest of Stroud off the B4066, we decided, as we had plenty of time, to visit Wotton-Under-Edge and seek out the very famous and extremely haunted Ancient Ram Inn. It was not long before we stumbled across the signposts for Wotton-Under-Edge and as we made our decent down the long and winding country road towards the village, I could feel a surge of exhilaration, knowing we were nearly there.

The Ancient Ram Inn is owned by John Humphries and is reputed to be one of the most haunted houses in the UK. The inn, which was believed to have been built around the mid-1100s as a drinking tavern, is now the epitome of all haunted houses with old creaky doors and floorboards, old mildewed tangs and musty odours, ancient warped walls, sinking ceilings, underground tunnels and stories of deaths and murders. Its resident ghosts include a cavalier; a woman called Elizabeth who was buried within the grounds of this house whose grave can still be seen today, a spirit man called Thomas, and a hooded figure believed to be that of a monk.

Upon our arrival we parked up in the courtyard of the Ancient Ram and knocked on the door to the inn, in the hope someone was at home. Much to my delight John Humphries opened the door and welcomed us in with open arms. In the space of one hour I was given a brief tour of the building and was given accounts of his ghosts (some of which are outlined above). I would have loved to have stayed and chatted longer with John but time was getting the better of us and we had to return to Woodchester Mansion for our rendezvous with PSI. I said thank you to John for his kindness and hospitality, made my way back to the car and we headed off into the night.

We arrived at Woodchester Mansion and Dave Wood and Nicky Sewell met us. We were asked to arrive an hour or two early before the rest of the PSI team as we were to be given some basic training, which the PSI team always give to their guests on investigations. We talked about ghost hunting methods, tests and experiments, media coverage, the PSI code of ethics, equal opportunities, race, religions and diversity, as well as a whole host of other topics, which I must admit I learned a lot from. The training was very thorough and was well worth participating in. PSI must be commended for applying such practices.

At night when the sky is clear and the moon is shining down on the magnificent, yet derelict and deserted house that is Woodchester Mansion, you can not help but think that this unfinished masterpiece is awash with shades of the past and every corner you turn around you would expect to run into a phantom of bygone days. The atmosphere blows you away and I suppose this is why so many people report ghostly happenings. Atmosphere takes a hold and the imagination runs wild and at the end of every dark corridor, there seems to be a ghost in waiting! Not the case with PSI. The following is a brief summary of the night in question and as you will see, everything is looked at and no stone is left unturned:

A wide range of environmental monitoring equipment was employed, and over 500 photographs and over 10 hours of audio and video footage were captured for analysis. PSI's investigations of such 'public cases' can be described as 'research investigations'. That is, such investigations are not phenomena-orientated; investigations and methods are strictly regulated and highly standardised in order to inform a wider body of research over time rather than 'solve any mysteries'. During the investigation, fourteen participants reported eighty-seven subjective experiences over three hundred and three minutes of field time.

After analysis, 57% of such experiences were categorised as 'subjective experiences'. All experiences that were not verified were ruled out as evidence, due to the possibility of cause by hallucination. Typically such evidence would be contrasted with medium and interview evidence; however such data was not available. One case stood out as significant when contrasted with historical evidence, but coincidence or misassociation could explain the experience. 35% of experiences were categorised as 'subjective-verified', however potential natural explanations were advanced for these experiences. 8% of the experiences fell into the category of 'whole-real experience'. Compelling natural explanations were advanced for each case.

Environmental conditions were consistently monitored throughout the investigation, but were recognised as being necessarily flawed. Five significant fluctuations occurred, three of these remained unusual but appeared to not be connected with any paranormal phenomena. Five hundred and eighty-nine photographs were taken and over ten hours of video footage analysed. Two hundred and eighty-nine photographs reveal unusual phenomena, most of which could be easily explained. Natural explanations were advanced for each of the photographs, including those that defied easy explanation. Eight units of video evidence were identified; most of which were explained by natural means.

Several structured field experiments took place during the investigation, few of which revealed significant activity. Ongoing research into correlation of paranormal belief, with phenomena reporting and research into the role of context in reporting phenomena were analysed. In each case results were mixed and did not add weight to existing theories, however possible flaws in methodology were discussed.

PSI investigation conclusions tend to err on the side of caution in their assessment of evidence. No evidence is regarded as proof of paranormal activity where a natural explanation can be identified. This highlights the deficit of robust experimental conditions that could be utilised in paranormal fieldwork. However, trends that emerge over the course of several investigations can inform PSI's extra-investigation research. Various units of evidence, in particular the atypical proportion of auditory perceptions, remained sufficiently

interesting that PSI is now in the process of conducting a longitudinal study of
Woodchester Mansion. It is hoped that this might shed further light on findings
and inform the general field of investigating the paranormal.
Dave Wood BSc. Co-Founder PSI.

Since this investigation the PSI team and I have become good friends and regularly
correspond with the occasional get together once in a while to conduct and partic-
ipate in psychical research. The North East Ghost Research Team hopes to learn
a lot more from PSI and we look forward to working with them in the future.
Incidentally, in the summer of 2006, Dave Wood and Nicky Sewell journeyed up
to the north-east of England to observe in a case I was investigating in which their
witness testimonies and statements can be read in a book I have co-written about
the case. *The South Shields Poltergeist*, (with a foreword by Guy Lyon Playfair,
as stated in the last chapter) documents the seven months my colleague and I,
Mike Hallowell, spent while investigating what is now believed to be the best
documented and most shocking poltergeist case since 'The world famous Enfield
Poltergeist Case' in which the late Maurice Grosse, and Guy Lyon Playfair were
the principal investigators.

CHAPTER EIGHTEEN

CASE STUDY

A MANOR HOUSE
MOST MYSTERIOUS

This chapter concerns a number of investigations in a very old haunted house located somewhere within England. The current owners of this particular manor house make it clear that media and publicity regarding the house is a no go. So, to respect their wishes, I will try to keep it anonymous to the best of my ability – and therefore not name the venue.

However, it is rather ironic to think that this house remains an anonymous location for my book, as it is one of the most famous haunted houses on the planet and many believe it is the most haunted house in Britain. It has undergone many investigations by many world famous ghost hunters – including Peter Underwood FRSA and his Ghost Club – it has been subject to an abundance of live radio broadcasts, the house has featured on countless television programmes worldwide, and has featured in hundreds of books and magazines dealing with the paranormal over the years.

Location names within this beautiful old house have been changed, but the facts, our findings on these investigations, and the ghostly happenings that occurred during our time there have not.

A BRIEF HISTORY

This old haunted house was allegedly built about 800 years ago but the present owners of the house don't believe this is so. The present owner has done a lot of historical research and can't find anything earlier than 700 years ago. The house once had a timber drawbridge; a thatched roof and a moat that to this day can still be seen. In days gone by, castles and forts had moats and drawbridges as part of their defences, but this house was different, it was a sign of stature.

When the house was first built it was actually called something else after the family who once lived there. They were very much devout Catholics – as was most of the populace of this particular vicinity.

One member of the family married, and eventually this new family became the next generation of the house and a certain famous man was eventually born here. He was sent away to be educated and it was there he became a cleric. He returned to England and after his death in the late 1600s it is said that (for some reason) nuns took his head back to where he was educated only for it to be brought back to this house after the revolution, where legend has it, it is buried in the grounds or behind one of the actual walls of the house.

It was during the reformation that priest holes were made at this particular house. There are two, one in the downstairs area which we will call the prayer room and one in a bedroom upstairs. The door-knocker on the original oak door is known as the 'Trinity and Sanctuary Knocker' and represents the Father, the Son and the Holy Ghost and if any monks were in the area at the time and needed a safe house this place would have taken him in and given him food and shelter. The priest holes providing the perfect hiding place should anyone come looking for them.

It is also said that during the English Civil War it is believed that Oliver Cromwell visited the house. We are not quite sure if this is accurate, however we do know Oliver Cromwell's soldiers and troops *did* stay at the house.

In regards to the ghosts that are said to haunt this beautiful old house and gardens, there are rumoured to be a good few. The sheer number of authentic and credible accounts that have happened over the years here does indeed reinforce the suspicion that this house could be one of the most spiritually active in the country. There are a number of ghosts inside the house (some rooms with more than one) and a number of ghosts in and around the gardens and that's all I will say.

Over the past few years I have had the privilege to be allowed access and run investigations here and collectively, I have spent almost a week at this property investigating its history and ghosts from top to bottom and having some terrifying, but in the same respect, rewarding experiences along the way.

Our first visit was a few years ago now, and I can remember the house coming into view for the first time as we drove up the derelict wooded lane that runs past this ancient dwelling. It was an awe-inspiring view, which sent shivers down the spine. We pulled in to the car park, got out the car and stood for a few minutes to take in the scene. It was a beautiful summer's day but you couldn't help feeling that there was a cold and eerie welcome awaiting us through the trees and inside the house. I walked through the car park and through the trees until I reached the huge old oak door. I knocked loudly upon the door but did not get an answer. No one was in, but it did seem, that from every window, a pair of eyes was peering down towards me on the path where I stood. I made a hasty retreat back to the car and informed the team.

We sat for a while in the cars chatting happily about the investigation to come and wondering what this old house had in store for us. Its reputation for ghosts rushed around in my head, making me feel more unnerved as time went on. Although we were excited at this prospect the nerves and anxiousness were beginning to set in. In the distance we all heard the sound of a car engine which, after a minute or so became clearer and louder. Someone was driving up the old private lane towards us. It was not long before a car pulled in behind us in the car park and a lovely lady got out the car and introduced herself to us as a very good friend of the property owners. She told us that she would be looking after us that night and she was there to let us in.

We emptied the cars and carried a vast array of cases and ghost hunting equipment into the house and made ourselves comfortable. Drinks and sandwiches were made available to us (which was very kind indeed) and as were tucking in around the table we were asked if we wanted a tour of the house. We duly agreed. The tour of the house took about an hour and proved very interesting indeed. During the tour Suzanne McKay and Glenn Hall both felt as though their hips were being squeezed while in a downstairs area of the house. A cold breeze was felt, and Claire Smith heard a voice calling her name. It was not any of us. Mumbling was also heard at the top of the stairs leading to the bedroom passageway.

Prior to our investigation starting, we set up some trigger objects. In one of the downstairs rooms we put down some rosary beads and drew around a crucifix. In the other downstairs location we drew around two round brasses, and in one of the bedrooms upstairs we drew around some toy cars in the hope the phantom children, who also haunt the room, would play with them. While we were getting ready to begin, Suzanne McKay and Claire Smith were in the entrance hall to the house with the big main door closed and locked. They both heard the sound of footsteps approaching the house from outside on the stone walkway, and when they reached the door they stopped. On opening the door to investigate they found no one was there. Very interesting indeed.

We decided to stay together as a unit while conducting our investigation, so we could place locked off cameras and dictation machines in other locations. During the first 10 minutes in our first location I could smell what can only be described as a foul stench but could not trace its source. A brilliant white singular light anomaly was photographed while in there and during a 5 minute stint in silence a muttering was heard by Claire and Suzanne but no one else heard this murmuring. Then Glenn reported his back went ice cold at the same time as my new torch batteries drained of energy. I called out quietly for phenomena to no avail. When we stopped for a break, Glenn and myself heard two distinct loud bangs coming from the ceiling above. There was no one upstairs at the time. After this first location we headed off to location two.

While we investigated this room we placed the video camera looking down the passage to the bedrooms and the dictation machine at the top of the stairwell. Suzanne felt something playing with her hair after I had asked for a sign. She sensed the words "I love your curly hair".

Claire, while sitting down on a chair felt something pulling and tugging her trouser leg which she said lasted for a good few minutes. We all said hello to what we believed were the active spirits of the children who are said to play in the room and put a teddy bear on the floor in the hope the spirits might move it. However, they did not. Suzanne said she got the impression that any spirits in there would let us know they were there when *they* were ready and not a second before. We ceased asking for phenomena and sat in silence but nothing happened. After this vigil we came downstairs for a break after sitting in the quiet and relatively inactive room.

Before resuming the investigations, myself and another investigator went upstairs to retrieve our dictation machines and cameras. While we were up there we both heard a blood-chilling long drawn out guttural sigh or breath coming from along the corridor. We looked at each other in total disbelief. We know no one was upstairs with us and in all honesty it scared us half to death. It was a hideous noise to hear and it is unfortunate that it happened while we were changing our tapes over, as it was not recorded. When we asked everyone else downstairs if they had made a noise like this, or indeed *heard* a noise like this, they told us they did not. It was quite harrowing to say the least.

Our next port of call was the larger of the locations downstairs. We sat chatting with the lights on for 15 minutes or so and then we turned the lights out. Soon, Claire felt her hair being gently tugged upon and Suzanne took a photo with what appears to be a face in the window. A detailed look at the photograph after the investigation proved the face to be patterns in the reflection of the window, a term in parapsychology called pareidolia which is where patterns are found in random things which are otherwise not there. Faces in clouds and in curtains are a good example and mistakes are often made in paranormal investigations due to this natural phenomenon. Two investigators then heard what sounded like metal scraping or sharpening near the fire in the hall, which was quite odd to say the least.

Upon re-checking the flour tray, which we had placed earlier on we found nothing had moved but we did discover two light fingertip dints in the flour along with a mark that looked like something had been dragged along in the flour. We were certain that the flour was flat and these indentations were not there before. No one had been remotely near the flour tray during this experiment. At this point in the investigation we all took a walk around the outside of the house and around the grounds where ghostly figures and dark shadows have been seen on numerous occasions. It was dark and atmospheric but we saw and experienced nothing paranormal. The next room up for investigation was the upper bedroom at the front of the house. This is where myself and another investigator both heard the loud and evil sounding breath earlier on in the investigation.

In this location Suzanne and Claire both felt pains in the chest whilst at the same time the EMF meter clicked at one milligaus (MG). I heard a popping type of noise when I was standing at the window. Where had it come from? I do not know. Suzanne sensed something was lurking at the door and it would not come inside the room. She then captured an amazing light anomaly on video camera floating around the room and funnily enough, its point of origin was at the door! The rest of this vigil was quiet.

The investigation was coming to an end but there was just one more incident I will tell you about. After we had packed up and we were ready to leave I walked through the house making sure we had not forgotten any equipment. On walking through the smaller of the downstairs locations I heard the sound of what can only be described as a baby crying. It lasted for just a second or so but it was long enough for me to identify what it was. It was not so much frightening but sad. We said our goodbyes and left.

After we returned home and slept we had to review our dictation and video footage for results. A number of recordings were made while we were at the location and they are outlined below:

1. The distinct sound of a dog's bark was recorded while we were in our first location and it came from *inside* the room where the dictation machine was placed. We recorded it twice in the space of 2 minutes and it can clearly be heard. When we asked if there were any dogs that could have made the noise from outside and at that time, we were told it was very unlikely. The only dogs around lived opposite and the owners were away with them. We were also told that dogs had been seen and heard on other investigations.

2. Another recording was of two distinct moaning sounds which lasted for about 2 seconds each. It sounded like a moan or grunt of a man and was also recorded coming from inside the room where the dictation machine was.

3. The sound of the door latch being moved was recorded during one of our vigils. It made quite a loud noise indicating the latch was moved with some force. There was no one in the room when it was recorded.

4. The sound of a whispering was picked up and it seemed to say, "Get out, get out my house". It was said twice within a space of a few seconds.

5. Some rather odd sounds were picked up while I was recording the tour of the building. One sounds like a breath and there are two more, but they have to be listened to, as I can't describe them in any way.

It was not long before The North East Ghost Research Team returned to investigate this wonderful locale and we have carried out a few investigations there. One investigation I wish to summarise to finish off this chapter was a joint investigation with the Ghost and Hauntings and Overnight Surveillance Team of which I was a founding member. The night of this occasion was rather interesting and three very strange incidences occurred which I would like to tell you about now. The first strange happening occurred while we were conducting a séance in the larger of the two downstairs locations. Drew Bartley and myself were filming the séance and Fiona Vipond was leading.

About 15 minutes in, she asked if the spirits in the room could make a sound for us and we were rewarded with a noise that reverberated around the house. It sounded like a handful of coins was thrown onto the metal fireplace and was very loud indeed. No investigator was, or could have been responsible for this. Upon looking around the fireplace for coins or anything else after the séance proved fruitless and nothing was found at all. It was very bad luck for us as just at this crucial time, both Drew and myself turned our video cameras to standby in order to relocate our position in the room. It occurred when our cameras were off. However I had forgotten about my dictation machine which I had left recording on the table. There was only about 30 seconds left on the tape when this incident occurred and when I played it back I was overjoyed to hear that we had indeed caught this phenomena on cassette.

The other two incidences are EVPs. The first one was recorded by Glenn Hall on his video camera during the same séance. After the noise of what we think could have been coins being thrown, Fiona asked if whatever spirit was there, could do the same again. On the tape you can clearly hear a voice, (which is not any of the investigators) saying, "YES". It is a long drawn out word and sounds almost like a guttural breath! Drew Bartley recorded the other EVP, again during this séance. When listening back to the recording two voices were heard which were not identified as any of ours. The first one spoke in a growl and it simply said "DARE COME THE DEAD!" A second voice immediately followed and was a voice of a woman. She said "BRING ME THE BIBLE".

These recordings along with some other EVP recordings we made at another investigation in Co Durham (see my first book, *Ghost Hunter, True Life Encounters from the North East* for a full detailed account) are some of the best results we have ever had in all our years of investigating. All that remains to be said is that this building may well indeed be truly haunted and it has been an absolute honour to be allowed in to carry out these investigations. We will undoubtedly return to continue our investigations in the near future. I just wish that I could tell you, the reader, the name of this wonderful place.

CHAPTER NINETEEN

CASE STUDY

THE JOLLY SAILOR PUB
NEAR SUNDERLAND

The Jolly Sailor public house is located on East Street, which is the main road between South Shields and the city of Sunderland. It is a former coaching inn from the eighteenth century dating it back to the 1700s. A very good friend of mine, Mike Hallowell, wrote a book called *Ales and Spirits, the Haunted Pubs and Inns of South Tyneside* and in it he talks about the Jolly Sailor. In it he says "When you walk in via the side entrance, you immediately become isolated from the traffic and other unwelcome signs of life in the twenty first century, and are plunged into a quaint old world of yesterday. When you enter the Jolly Sailor, the past greets you like a warm breeze".

I couldn't agree more because when The Ghost and Hauntings and Overnight Surveillance Team walked in via the same side entrance that Mike talks about, it was literally like a step back in time. On the right-hand side as you walk in, are the stairs leading up to the next level, and on the right-hand side half way down the corridor is the snug bar complete with oak beams across the ceiling with all sorts of memorabilia from the past hanging from them. Old-fashioned photographs and paintings festoon the walls, the red and orange lights dimly illuminate the room and the roaring open fire creates a fabulous echo of times gone by.

We sat down and made ourselves comfortable and it was not long before the present manageress and a few employees came in to see us. Drew Bartley and Fiona Vipond are regulars in this wonderful drinking establishment and it was Drew and Fiona who secured the investigation here for the team. The manageress and employees were to join us for the investigation but first I wanted to hear all about their ghostly encounters while working at the pub. I first spoke to Beverley Jackson who informed me that on one occasion while at the pub alone, she was in the kitchen getting on with her duties, when all of a sudden; she heard the fridge door open. When she glanced up she saw the door open and a man's hand holding the door from behind it. What was odd about this was that she couldn't see any legs where they should be under the door in front of the fridge. As she watched, the fridge door closed and a man was not to be seen anywhere.

She then informed me of another encounter in the pub that she experienced on the next floor up. "It appears that there is a playful ghost who likes to toy around with people's possessions," she told me. Getting ready to leave the pub she was putting on her coat and had a large bunch of keys in her hand. She put down the keys for one moment to put on her coat and when she went to pick her keys back up they were gone. She searched the room high and low as she did with the rest of the building. She then asked a friend who was downstairs at the time to help her locate her keys and they both searched high and low to no avail. They were just about to give up on their search when they glanced down and noticed that the keys were in the exact same place she had originally left them before putting on her coat. She is adamant that they were not there previously during the search and she is convinced that it was the actions of a mischievous ghost.

The Jolly Sailor pub is also famous for having an apparition known as 'The Green Lady' and she has been seen on occasion wondering around the upper levels of the inn wearing a long green flowing dress. She is believed to be a woman who once lived at the inn and was rumoured to have been courting a coach driver from Newcastle upon Tyne. She had big plans for her future with her lover until one day he abandoned her for another woman. This of course devastated her and legend has it, because of her sheer pain and anguish, she locked herself in her room and starved herself to death.

At this point the manageress told me of an experience she had one night while working in the main bar. She was standing behind the bar chatting to three of her regulars at last orders. The rest of the bar had been vacated and as these three regulars were friends of hers, she locked the doors and let them stay a little longer to finish their drinks. Before coming back to the bar she made sure no one else was left. She rejoined her friends and continued with her conversation.

The three friends drank their ale and she was just about to let them out, when all of a sudden she saw a figure walk past the door and along the corridor. "It happened so quick" she said. She thought she must have had another customer whom she had forgotten about or missed when emptying the pub at last orders. That is until she walked into the corridor to greet this person only to find no one was there. She looked in the lavatories, in the snug, and all around the pub but could find no one, no one except her three friends who were in the bar all the time. "Must just be another of the Jolly Sailor's ghosts," she said.

After listening to their encounters and after reading Mike Hallowell's chapter in his book on the pub, I was convinced the pub was haunted and was looking forward to see what G.H.O.S.T would uncover. Our team psychic was not on hand on this investigation so it was going to be purely a scientific investigation.

Had she have been there all my knowledge of the establishment and everyone's ghost accounts would have been kept from her to see what she picked up on the reading. I guess her reading will have to wait for another time and it will indeed be interesting to see what she comes up with.

After the pub had closed its doors we were ready to begin. Our first job was to conduct a thorough baseline test in all locations and rooms. This took quite a while, as there were at least 16 rooms to test for basic room temperatures, EMFs and the usual array of pre-investigation analysis. Draughts were located and squeaky floorboards were tracked down so we knew exactly what was what. If anything occurred, we had our baseline readings to compare them with in order to determine if it was paranormal or not. Trigger objects were placed in various locations around the pub, upstairs and down. These included a crucifix in the function rooms, motion sensors were placed either side of the corridor where the ghost was seen walking. A flour tray with some objects was placed in the snug area, and a doll was left in the private flat on the very top level of the pub. We were ready to split into small groups and begin the investigation.

I was working with Lee Stephenson and our first location was the bar and pool room on the ground floor. We ventured in at 2 a.m. and it was not long before we caught a nice moving light anomaly on night vision video camera. I took some digital stills in the hope we'd catch something paranormal but there was nothing. Five minutes later I called out to the atmosphere to see if any spirits present would give us a sign and almost straight away we both heard the sound of a footstep or two coming from along the corridor near the main bar. Upon inspection we found no one was there; no one of this world anyway! An ice-cold breeze suddenly rushed through the room and was felt at head height. Both Lee and myself could not work out where this breeze had come from. On the baseline tests in this area the windows were checked for draughts and nothing was found so this breeze remains a mystery. Was it spirits of the other world trying to make themselves known? Suddenly a loud crash was heard as if a tin tray had been dropped in the snug (which was empty at this point). Again on checking it out we found nothing out of place and everything was in order.

Drew Bartley, Fiona Vipond and the barman, Ben, were, at this time, investigating the function room on the next level up at the end of the building. When they swept the area with the EMF meter it seemed to go off for no apparent reason. It was then reported by Ben that he felt a breeze on his left-hand side and at this point a light anomaly was caught on video camera to the left of Ben. At 2.25 a.m. a séance was carried out and filmed. Nothing seems to have happened during the séance, or so they thought, until they checked the trigger object of the crucifix that had been placed on the table prior to the investigation. The investigators had checked this object before they started the séance and when they looked at it afterwards, to their astonishment, it had been completely moved. Ben, although a believer in the paranormal was absolutely blown away and could not believe what he had witnessed. I don't think he was expecting a result like the one he got.

Dale Bartley, his wife Kath and guest investigator Terry were assigned to the mid section of the building to investigate three of the end rooms. Nothing paranormal was reported during this vigil. The manageress and her friend Beverley Jackson were investigating the courtyard and they too experienced nothing.

Our second location (for Lee and myself) was the upstairs function room where not less then 20 minutes before the trigger object was moved. When we ventured in I noticed that the serving hatch doors between this room and the other bar were fully open. Earlier I had noticed they were closed so I radioed down to Drew's group and asked how they left the doors, if indeed they were touched at all.

"We left those doors closed," Drew said.

"Closed?" I repeated. "Are you sure?"

"Of course I am," he replied.

"Well the bleedin' things are wide open now!"

At this point I decided to play with the doors to see if the hinges were broken or to see if the doors would somehow open on their own. I could find nothing wrong with these doors and when closed, they stayed closed. After 30 minutes of sitting in silence and observing, waiting and monitoring this room we headed back to base for a break. Nothing at all had happened.

Drew, Fiona and Ben were now investigating the downstairs bar. A small EMF reading was made in the corridor but one very interesting thing was noted. The entire group heard a creaking noise and what they described as footfalls emanating from within the corridor just near the main bar, exactly where Lee and myself heard them during our first vigil. It appeared that we had a phantom that liked to walk this area of the pub but who it was we didn't yet know. Perhaps a reading from the North East Ghost Research Team and G.H.O.S.T psychic, Suzanne McKay is required. This may shed some light on the matter.

The two other groups, once more failed to experience anything untoward during this vigil. Not that it bothered the manageress and Beverley, as they have experienced plenty in the past. However for Dale, Kath and Terry it was proving to be a quiet night. We ventured upstairs as one big group to hold a large séance in the function room. We prepared for the séance by placing the seats in a circle and set up the video cameras to record the séance. The séance lasted for about 20 minutes and the phenomena experienced by the sitters was very subjective.

Different techniques were tried to entice spirits in and to attempt communication but nothing much happened at all in the way of good phenomena. During the séance (for some unknown reason) I was given the name 'Elizabeth' and I thought this might relate to the alleged Green Lady who is said to haunt the inn. A single flash of light was then seen by myself but I figured it might have come from Kath, who at this point was taking notes and had a torch. However she did say at that time the torch was turned off! After the séance we headed back downstairs for another break.

Onwards with the investigation and at this point (as Lee had gone home) I joined Dale and Kath. Terry had agreed to stake out the cellars on his own, so we investigated the snug area. Although the snug room is reputed to house the presence of a woman (not the Green Lady) nothing at all happened during our vigil in there. Terry also reported absolutely nothing during his vigil in the cellar. Drew, Fiona and Ben however caught some odd light anomalies while out in the courtyard while using the video camera. The manageress and Beverley, although they felt they were not alone and being watched while staking out the flat on the upper levels, said very little had happened. The last vigils were now underway as the cleaners were due to arrive. It was 5.10 a.m. so I decided to spend the last vigil alone in the cellar.

I was feeling brave and although I was beginning to tire, I knew the ice-cold atmosphere and freezing cold air would wake me up. It certainly did! The noise of the generators pumping away in the pitch-blackness was deafening and my only source of light was coming from the LCD screen on the video camera. I called out to see if could get any results and I was rewarded with a nice show of light anomalies. But that was it. After 10 minutes the batteries ran out, throwing me into total darkness so at this point I climbed up the ladders and made my exit. The rest of the vigils were quiet.

While preparing for a second séance in the snug area we all heard noises and movement coming from along the corridor. We were all accounted for in the snug and then we realised – the cleaners had arrived! Nothing paranormal there! But it did mark the end of our investigation. We packed up our equipment, said thank you for the hospitality we had received and left the premises.

14. The magnificent Woodchester Mansion in the Cotswolds. Picture courtesy of the Woodchester Mansion trust.

15. The Treasurer's House in York. Perhaps the scene of the most famous ghost sighting in history.

16. The gravestone of infamous highwayman, Dick Turpin.

Left: 17. The oldest pub in York, The Black Swan, haunted by a woman in the bar and a ghostly pair of legs.

Above: 18. The old gateway to Greyfriars Cemetery.

19. A gravestone commemorating the Skye terrier that was known as Greyfriars Bobby. The ghost of Bobby is said to be seen scampering around Greyfriars Cemetery on occasions.

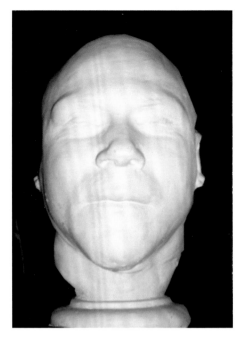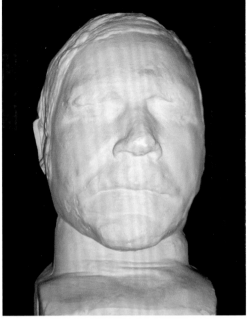

Above left: 20. The death mask of infamous Body snatcher and murderer William Burke before his hanging – from the author's collection.

Above right: 21. The death mask of infamous Body snatcher and murderer William Burke after his hanging – from the author's collection.

Left: 22. The City Hotel, Durham City Centre was the scene of a remarkable reading from psychic Ralph Keeton. Picture © G.H.O.S.T.

Above: 23. The impressive ruin of Tattershall Castle in Lincolnshire.

24. The Grange at Hurworth-on-Tees. Cindy and Colin Nunn from API have continually investigated this building for the last six years.

25. Washington Old Hall in Tyne and Wear, where a strange and eerie mist was seen to move through a wall by two investigators.

1. Borley Church, Essex.

2. The author in Borley Churchyard next to Henry (Harry) Foyster Bull's grave. A former Rector of Borley and son to Henry Dawson Ellis Bull who built the Rectory in 1863.

3. The author standing on Hall Lane, Borley, Essex. The Rectory stood to my left behind the wall. No trace remains.

4. The new prison block and courtroom at Inveraray Jail haunted by the ghosts of former inmates.

Left: 5. The ghost train at Blackpool pleasure beach, haunted by a man nicknamed 'Cloggy' whose footsteps can be heard clumping around the tracks.

Above: 6. The Ship Inn Pub, Exeter. At one time, Sir Francis Drake's favourite drinking establishment. Could his ghost still linger on here?

Below: 7. The author sits on the stairs in the courtyard leading to the Great Hall. Chillingham Castle, Northumberland.

8. The author outside The Plough Inn at Wigglesworth, North West Yorkshire.

9. The enchanting Culzean Castle near Maybole, Ayrshire. Haunted by an unidentified apparition on the oval staircase, a woman with a long flowing dress, and a phantom piper.

10. The ruins of Greenan Castle on the Ayrshire coast, built by the Clan Kennedy around 1600.

Left: 11. The Schooner Hotel in Alnmouth is said to be one of the most haunted hotels in the United Kingdom.

Above: 12. Warkworth Castle in Northumberland where phantom soldiers have been seen and the sounds of battling warriors have been heard.

13. The Ancient Ram Inn, Wotton-Under-Edge, Gloucestershire. Picture © Chris Howley.

CHAPTER TWENTY

YORK:
THE MOST HAUNTED CITY
IN THE UK?

The city of York dates back almost 2,000 years when it was first occupied by the Celts. Then when the Romans were at the height of their supremacy they moved into the area and founded *Eboracum*, the Roman name for York. The Romans moved north in AD 71 from Lincolnshire to invade what was then *Brigantes* as they acknowledged the area as a superior locale for a military stronghold and a Roman base. The Roman governor of Britain, Quintus Petilius Cerealis brought his troops here and it was not long before new roads and a civilian township was built up, making Eboracum the leading city in the Roman Empire. The Roman Legions occupied Eboracum until around the fifth century and their headquarters were based where York Minster now stands. Underneath the minster there are the remains of the Roman headquarters and settlement, which are open to visitors and well worth a visit if you are into Roman history.

After the Romans departed from Eboracum the Anglo-Saxons began to invade and eventually Eboracum became *Eoferwic* and was ruled by King Edwin of Northumbria. After that came the Vikings who renamed the growing city *Jorvik* in 866. The Normans came next to York, which saw the onset of William the Conqueror (the duke of Normandy) in 1069, which of course was only three years after his notable victory in the Battle of Hastings in October 1066 when he defeated King Harold who had originally invaded England from Norway. Hell bent on destruction and obliteration he caused mass damage. In time, the city began to rebuild itself and in no time the minster was rebuilt, churches and abbeys were erected, hospitals and monasteries were made, and it became a fine trading municipality, which made a lot of money and prospered through its trade and imports.

Through the years and as time progressed, each period has left its mark on the city of York. If one has a keen eye for detail and knowledge of history, it is not hard to find the remnants of the Middle Ages, Tudor, Elizabethan, Stuart, Georgian, Victorian and the Edwardian times. It is all there, some easy to find and some hidden away in what is now a modern city. Although the old buildings, edifices and ancient structures reflect the city's past there are also the echoes of the past in the form of the people that once lived, worked, fought and died here. These are the ghosts of York and there are so many documented cases of apparitions, spectres, and shades of the past being seen all over this ancient town, that it has been labelled as the most haunted city in the UK. Many other cities also lay claim to this title as being 'the most haunted' but I genuinely believe York is the true holder of this prestigious label. Having said that, if York is not the most haunted city in the UK it has to be the most *famously* haunted city in the UK for it is in York where the Treasurer's House stands, where the most famous apparitional sighting in history was recorded.

It was back in 1953 when apprentice plumber Harry Martindale was working down in the cellar of Treasurer's House. He was an 18 year old lad at the time and he was working alone drilling some holes in the ceiling for some new central heating. He suddenly became aware of the sound of a note being played by an instrument that seemed to be coming from way off in the distance but he thought nothing of it. As he continued to work he heard the sound of the instrument blowing again and this time it seemed louder, or was it closer? Suddenly, out of the wall, which he was leaning against with the ladder, came a Roman soldier. The soldier's helmet was at Harry's waist height as he was on the ladder and he immediately jumped down from the ladder and hid in a corner of the cellar where he watched another twenty or so Roman soldiers, along with a horse, walk through the cellar wall.

Curled up in the corner, absolutely terrified, he watched this amazing spectacle until the last soldier emerged and disappeared through the opposite wall. The sound of the instrument grew quieter as the phantom army of Roman legionnaires moved further away. He then ran out of the cellar in terror and sat at the top of the stairs to try and come to terms with what he had just witnessed. The curator of Treasurer's House saw him and simply said, "By the look on your face, you have seen the Roman soldiers."

This account turned out to be one of the most authenticated ghost sightings ever and remains so today. Certain things Harry noticed about these Romans were unknown at this point in time. It was only when more research had been done and new things were found out about the Roman legions did people begin to take Harry's sighting more seriously. One such discovery was the old Roman road called *Via Decumana* that ran under Treasurer's House right through the cellar where Harry had seen the Roman ghosts. Harry reported that he could only see the Romans from the knees up and it was later discovered that *Via Decumana*, the

Roman road, ran 18 inches under the cellar floor! The Romans were walking on the original level of the road!

I visited the Treasurer's House a few years ago and up until that time no one was allowed down in the haunted cellar. It was closed to the public. However on the day of my visit I was informed that the cellar was opening for public tours and the first ever tour down there was the very afternoon I had paid my visit. I was overjoyed and immediately paid my fees for my tour. Not only was I going to see the famous cellar, I was one of the first members of the public to be allowed down there since Harry's sighting in 1953. This was indeed an honour and a privilege and I was very fortunate to have visited on that particular day. I spent some time looking around Treasurer's House and took some time out in the beautiful garden until it was time for our tour. I was pleasantly surprised to find out that there were only four of us booked in for the first visit.

Our guide met us and we made our way downstairs and through the door that leads to a long passageway with a sloping path. The ceiling became lower and the passage became narrower as we ventured further down towards the cellar entrance so I was relieved that it was necessary to wear hard hats for the tour. We reached the entrance and I was the first to step in, and I walked onto a wooden platform that protected the old Roman road underneath from wear and tear during the tours, and left the very wall where the ghost soldiers had walked through all those years ago clearly visible to see. We were down in the cellar for about half an hour as the guide related the famous ghost story to us. It is something I will never forget.

During my stay in York I also visited the condemned cell where legendary highwayman Richard Dick Turpin spent his last night before he was executed near York Racecourse on April 7th 1739. The condemned cell is housed at the York Castle Dungeons, which are now part of the York Castle Museum, which has 400 years of history on display. The dungeons are a menacing place and you can't help thinking that they may indeed still house some of the prisoners of the past in the form of spectral beings. The ghost of Dick Turpin himself is said to haunt his condemned cell, which I also spent some considerable time visiting. The York Castle Museum is actually housed in the city's old prison buildings and the museum gives a fascinating look at prison life of 200 years ago.

It also includes a genuine cobbled Victorian street. Chatting with the some of the staff I was informed of a ghost or two that reside at the museum. There is, I was told, a spectral woman in black who has been seen sitting next to one of the old fireplaces and she has been seen by a number of different witnesses on a number of different occasions. The sound of a lady engaged in beautiful song has also been heard when staff are on the premises but no trace can be found of anyone when they have looked for its source. Then of course there are the old cell blocks which I touched upon earlier. Here, the sound of doors slamming closed are often heard, along with the tormented cries and the snivelling and whimpering of those condemned to death.

On the trail of Dick Turpin I also visited the site where he drew his last breath at Tyburn and subsequently I sought out his final resting place, which is located opposite St George's church in a small area of land barely recognisable as a grave-yard. Here he is buried in a rather large plot of land. Large because it is believed that he is buried with his trusty steed 'Black Bess'. The grounds in which he is bur-ied are right in the middle of a private housing estate and it was at the local pub, we decided to go for a drink and have our lunch. During our lunch I asked the local publican if there were any ghost stories attached to the area in which Dick Turpin was buried. "I am not quite sure" she said "but you can ask old George".

Old George was sitting in the corner supping a pint of bitter so I ventured across and introduced myself.

"Are you George?" I said.

"Aye lad," came the reply.

"What can you tell me about the ghosts, then?" I said.

"Ghosts!" he said, "Not sure if there are ghosts but strange things do occur in these parts," he told me.

He went on to tell me that he lived locally, just across from the grave of Dick Turpin and quite often he used to hear, many years ago, what he described to me as the sound of a galloping horse thundering past outside his house. Heard by the other residents – I was told – these sounds couldn't be traced to any source as when they look out the windows nothing could be seen although the sounds continued. He went on to say in a rather puzzled manner that although there was a concrete road outside his house the galloping sounded like it was on grass or a soft surface rather than the clip clopping of hooves you would hear if it were on the concrete.

"Very interesting, if true. You must have a great attention for detail as not many folk would notice such things," I said to him.

"Well, I was a policeman when I was younger" he said. "But I am still confused as there is no grass or fields anywhere near my house."

I explained that it might be possible that if the sounds that he heard were ghostly echoes from the past, and they may have been somehow imprinted onto the atmosphere, and what he (and his neighbours) were hearing were indeed psy-chic recordings of bygone days from when this area was in fact fields and old dirt tracks. The thought also occurred that if these accounts were true and the sounds of ghost horses were heard thundering by, perhaps it might be the ghost of Turpin himself on Black Bess. After all they are only buried a few yards away.

I was also eager to visit the ancient pubs and inns that York is famous for. My first port of call was the Black Swan which is located on Peasholme Green. It is York's oldest drinking establishment and is a beautiful medieval timber framed public house with a fantastic seventeenth century interior although some parts date back to the 1400s. It was originally a family home to the Bowes family in which William Bowes became Lord Mayor of York in 1417. On my visit I chatted with the owner and the first thing I asked was, "Could our team spend a night here investigating the ghosts?"

I was politely refused and told the ghosts are to be left alone and not disturbed. I respected the decision he gave me and asked if it was acceptable to have a look around after I had drunk a pint of his finest ale.

"No need to look around" he said, "One of our resident ghosts sits right here in the bar in that seat next to the fireplace. She sits looking into the fire and you can not see her face as it is covered with long black hair, and no one knows who she is".

I sat down with my pint next to where the ghost is seen and began to soak up this wonderful atmosphere. "We also have a ghost of a man in a suit and hat who wonders the rooms upstairs", he went on to say. "And a pair of ghost legs have been seen on the upper levels too".

"Not uncommon" I replied. "I have heard of other ghosts similar to this one where the upper torso has only been seen, or like your ghost here, just the legs. It is not as uncommon as one may think". I then took another mouthful of ale. "If I can't investigate overnight with the team, I may book in to one of the haunted rooms to see if I meet your resident ghosts," I told him.

"By all means" he said, before handing me a leaflet listing the room prices. I studied the price list for a while and then said, "Good value for money here!"

I saw off my pint, said thank you for the time he had given me and headed up the road to York's most haunted pub, the Golden Fleece.

The Golden Fleece is also reputed to be the most haunted pub in the UK and was established in 1503. After ordering another pint of fine ale I enquired about the resident spirits (and I didn't mean the Jack Daniels). I was told there are an abundance of ghosts said to roam here at the inn including a woman in a Victorian dress who is seen walking through a wall. The ghost of a mischievous young lad tugs and pulls the trouser legs of people in the pub and a ghost of a Canadian airman resides on the upper levels. Disembodied voices and laughter have been heard literally scaring the witnesses half to death and poltergeist-like activity has also been reported downstairs in the bar. After staying for while to soak up the atmosphere and after I had spoken to the staff we made our way back to our accommodation. I stayed in York for five days and in that time I visited an abundance of places, which are reputedly haunted. There are far too many to include here in this chapter so I will now briefly summarise and detail some of the haunted sites I visited.

At the York Arms pub, I was told the ghost of a lady appeared in the gent's toilets, and I was told that the ruins of St Mary's Abbey were haunted by a ghost monk which has been seen from time to time, however my short vigil there one evening proved rather fruitless. Clifford's Tower, by all accounts is haunted by ghostly blood that is said to pour down the interior walls. It is said that a mass suicide occurred there many years ago and many visitors who go there feel 'ill at ease'. On a visit to Trinity churchyard in Micklegate I found out that inside there is a spectre of lady who is looking for her child, and outside in the graveyard there is the ghost of a headless phantom who wanders around aimlessly. The magnificent King's Manor, I was informed, is said to be haunted by a number of ghosts; one being a woman dressed in Tudor clothing who is believed by the locals to be Anne Boleyn and another being a phantom monk. Then of course we have the ghost of the weeping girl at number 5 College Street. She is believed to be a victim of the plague. The Roman Bathhouse pub is said to be haunted by a Roman soldier who has been seen down underneath the pub in the old ruined Roman baths. It is said he vanishes into thin air not long after he is spotted. York Minster, Micklegate Bar, Bootham Bar, The Theatre Royal, Ye Olde Star Inn, The Cock and Bottle pub; the list just goes on and on.

Although I was there for nearly a week I did not visit half the haunted sites I would have liked to. Now you can understand why that this wonderful and historic city is reputed to be the most haunted city in the UK. During my visit I spoke to many wonderful people who told me some fascinating ghost stories that were attached to their premises and buildings. In all honesty I had heard some of the stories before through reading and learning over the years. However it was nice to hear these stories and ghost accounts coming from the horse's mouths so to speak and I so look forward to my return to York to seek out the ghosts of what I believe could be the most haunted city in the land.

CHAPTER TWENTY-ONE

CASE STUDY

THE MCORVILLE INN – ELWICK – HARTLEPOOL – NEAR MIDDLESBROUGH

The quaint little village of Elwick is situated in Hartlepool in Teesside and is roughly eight miles north of Middlesbrough. It is off the beaten track and as you stumble across it, you automatically think that you are in the heart of the beautiful English countryside. It is an enchanting little hamlet with only a few watering holes, a number of houses, a post office and a village green. The village is rich in history and there are many ghosts said to reside in some of the wonderful old houses and properties in this area.

I think Elwick's most famous legend concerns a local woman many years ago who was accused of being a witch. I spoke to the [now] resident of the witch's house Jayne Lavelle, and she told me that the witch lived at what was known as 'B Cottage, Elwick' and she was known as old mother midnight of Elwick, or widow Pavey. She was a herbalist and known locally as a medicine woman. One day she made up a batch of potion for a local ill person but unfortunately after the administration of this herbal remedy, her patient died. Because of this incident, the 'local witch' was subsequently tried, and burnt at the stake outside Hart Church and is believed to be buried on the spot where she was burnt alive in unconsecrated grounds.

Across the road from the two pubs which are situated in this village lies an old huge house. Here it is said that one night the owner of the house woke up to see a glimmering mist form floating over by his bed. When he called in his two sons to see this spectacle, they too caught a glimpse of it before it disappeared into nothing. What it was they have never found out. The local post office also has a reputation for having a ghost. Doors often open and close on their own, things are constantly moved around and shadows have been seen occasionally flitting about the place. It is my hope, one day that we can go in to investigate these strange occurrences and try to shed some light on to what is going on here. But it is one of the pubs situated here in this charming old village called The McOrville Inn that our team were called in to investigate.

The McOrville Inn was named between 1845–1894 after it had been previously known as The Fox and Hounds. It was named after a famous horse called McOrville who was the son of Orville, the winner of the 1802 St. Ledger. Every summer for twenty years this stud stallion would tour the area on a weekly basis for all to see. He died on 21 February 1842 at the age of 32 years and such was his reputation that the local coroner issued a death notice for him. It is believed by locals that the horse 'Old McOrville' is now buried in the village field with a large stone marking his grave. Village historians once visited the pub and they believe that some parts of the building date back to the 1600s based on the beams they discovered up in the loft area. If true this would make this inn very old indeed. I spoke to the pub owner and landlord Darren Holmes and he told me a little about the history and the ghosts there. He went on to say:

Here are some of the different things that have occurred here over the years. Before we actually bought the place there was another couple in here. They went on to tell me that the bedroom, which I now sleep in, was once occupied by them. They woke up one night to find the room was literally full of smoke or mist and could not see a thing. So they jumped out of bed thinking their property was on fire and when they ventured out into the hallway there was no other sign of smoke! They checked the whole place over looking for a potential fire and when they ventured back into their bedroom all the smoke, or mist, was gone. This happened on more than two occasions.

Another story concerned my brother who has a room at the back of the house, which was once a kitchen. On a number of occasions he has told me that he has woken up and seen a figure of a man standing in the room looking over his bed. Sometimes he said he would see this figure and feel it as it shook his bed which frightened him quite a lot. We know of one person who has actually died in the bar. The guy (who shall remain anonymous) was a well-known figure in these parts. His family had owned the pub for a long, long time and the story goes that during Sunday lunch here at the McOrville he dropped down dead with a heart attack and because the pub was so busy and most people were drunk, people did not actually know he was dead and just left him where he lay, stepping over his lifeless body to get past him. It was not until some time later they made their grim discovery.

Another past landlord told me of the ghostly happenings that occur down in the cellar under the pub. He went on to say that countless times he would go down to the cellar thinking that he needed to change a pump, as the beer flow would cease, only to find the pumps had been mysteriously turned off. This is the exact same experience that we have had here since moving into the pub seventeen months ago. I have also experienced weird light formations and an illumination over in that corner near the side door, and have sensed people in here with me when I know I am on my own.

Let us not forget the old stables that are housed out back too. They do indeed have a certain feel to them and we use one as a coalhouse. On occasion when I am out back getting coal I often have this overwhelming sense of presence and I feel that something or someone is coming towards me. Again I am not afraid but more interested in these phenomena. There is also a story concerning an actual handprint of a small child in one of the bricks in the walls to the old stables. The story goes that children were employed in those days to make bricks as well as work down the local mines.

One day when a young lad was making these bricks, a whole load of newly built bricks accidentally fell down upon him and crushed him to death. During his fight for life under these new, but not yet hardened bricks his handprint was impressed into one and it can still be seen to this day. It is believed that the ghost of this boy haunts the area of the stables near to where his handprint is still seen in the wall although they are not sure where exactly he died. The pub has an amazing atmosphere and the people are so lovely who frequent the pub, both past and present! And I am not frightened of the ghosts in this pub one bit.

So there is plenty to go on, with what Darren Holmes has told me and all things considered, it could be an interesting investigation. Attending the investigation was spiritualist medium Peter Crawford who organised the event, along with one or two other guest mediums. Britain's top exorcist Ralph Keeton and his girl-friend Nikki Austwicke were also there too. Ralph came along to meet the Ghost and Hauntings Overnight Surveillance Team to see how they worked on investigations, as a friend of Peter Crawford's had invited us along to co-investigate. Ralph, famous for his work as 'Britain's number one exorcist', also worked with the *Most Haunted* team for five series. He is also the founder of the International and National Psychic Team who have featured many times on Sky and National Television.

We arrived on the night in question at about 10 p.m. and went into the pub, which was still busy with all the Friday night drinkers who were out enjoying themselves on this cold, December night. We sat down and made ourselves comfortable in front of the roaring fire that stands in the main bar area. We began to chat amongst ourselves and it was not long before we were soon introduced to everyone else who was going to join the investigation. Everyone hit it off very well, and we all got on like a house on fire. Ralph, when he ventured in, came across to G.H.O.S.T. and began chatting to us straight away. As well as getting down to the nitty-gritty of ghost talking and business, he also regaled us some serious yet humorous stories from his *Most Haunted* days. He is a total joy to listen and to chat to, and he is a man with extreme knowledge in the paranormal field. It turns out he was looking for a ghost hunting team to work with in 2007 for some new television shows, projects and ghost investigations. I thought I might take the opportunity to chat to Ralph about his experiences with the *Most Haunted* team and find out exactly what he had been up to with them. This is what he told me:

I feel very privileged to know the *Most Haunted* crew and I have been at many of the TV shoots for the *Most Haunted* programme in the past. My first introduction to them was at The Jamaica Inn, in Cornwall. I attended and brought another now famous medium with me who I was representing at the time. Having met up and eventually gotten to know the full team is an experience I'll never forget, both Karl Beattie and Yvette Fielding made me very welcome into the group. The MH Team are a great bunch of people and easy to work with, allowing you space to do your own thing and you could clearly see they'd become a close family. It was really nice to meet up with Derek Acorah again as I'd met him before on other locations. Richard Felix, as usual is always full of life, boisterous as ever providing detail after detail as his passion for ghostly adventure has no bounds.

I then asked Ralph if there were any special moments he could tell us about. One in particular came to mind:

Richard Felix, Derek Acorah and myself went out in the pouring rain onto the moors of Bodmin, while filming at The Jamaica Inn in the hope of seeing or hearing the Bodmin Beast that is said to haunt the area. I felt awful sitting in Richard's new Range Rover with muddy feet, soaking wet through and not finding a thing after filming for over half an hour. Having said that we all nearly had heart attacks when the lights of Richard's Range Rover shone into the eyes of a staring sheep on the moors. We all laughed hysterically when we realised it was not the beast! But it just goes to show how the mind can work when in those frightening scenarios. Resulting from working with the MH team I have now worked with Sky, Discovery, Channel 4, the BBC, and have filmed for a Sony Pictures Christmas children's film *Monster House* producing a half hour documentary for Steven Spielberg. I also now run a team at exorcisms.co.uk where I work with investigation teams, radio presenters and alike continuing the search for 'ghostly' activity throughout the UK.

So our work was cut out for us tonight. Or was it? We figured if we proceeded with the investigation in our usual professional manner, we would have nothing to worry about. So that is what we did and at the end of the night we were told he would like to work with us again, on a more professional basis. Anyway, on with the investigation and by the time the bar had emptied and we sorted ourselves out it was about 12.30 a.m. and we were ready to begin.

Our first port of call was to investigate the cellar under the pub and everyone present on that night ventured down to conduct a séance in the hope we could make contact with any of the spirits of the McOrville Inn. The séance proved quite good with a lot of data picked up by some of the mediums. The first thing that was picked up was a spirit woman with grey hair, and a centre parting down the middle of her head. Peter Crawford picked up on this spirit and he told us that this woman was scurrying around as if she was looking for something. He went on to say that she was a nice old lady who was simply looking for something she had lost. When asked to give all a sign, knocks and bumps were heard in the cellar and people felt all sorts of mysterious pains, ailments and feelings of extreme coldness. At this point Drew Bartley, Fiona Vipond, and Lee Stephenson all caught light anomalies on their night vision video cameras.

Drew Bartley and myself were also there to monitor the proceedings with our EMF meters and digital thermometer guns and sure enough anomalous readings were ascertained. Ralph Keeton proceeded to call out in response to this spirit and every time he asked a question, we were all rewarded with bumps and bangs emanating from within the room somewhere although everyone present remained perfectly still. Then the impressions came through that this particular area might have been used to slaughter animals. I ventured upstairs to talk to Darren Holmes about this and he confirmed that in the past, animals were slaughtered around here as part of the industry, but where exactly he could not say. It would be interesting to find out if indeed it was on this spot.

Then a medium said that she got the impressions of stables and the death of horses too which is interesting as there are old stables out the back and if I can remind you, it says that the horse 'Old McOrville' is buried in the village green. When asked if she knew anything about the old stables out the back she told me she did not and was indeed quite surprised by the revelation. It must also be noted that it was *after* this séance when the pub owner Darren, announced that he was taking the group outside to see the old stable area! I had known simply because I interviewed the landlord prior to investigation. So it was an interesting start to the examination. One other thing worthy of note is that upon everyone's exit out of the cellar I proceeded to take a few photographs. The first two pictures came out normal but the third frame was obscured by what I can only describe as a thick, dense anomalous mist! I find it rather odd that this should happen just after the séance. Could something have been brought forward by the séance? It's a teasing thought, and if true, I may have caught it on camera.

We retire upstairs for a bit of a break and we were all treated to sandwiches and cakes courtesy of the landlord Darren Holmes. After a while we spilt into two groups to cover more of the building. One group covered the area next to the disused fireplace at one end of the huge 'L' shaped bar, and the other group ventured over to the area where the fire was, at the other end of the pub. The G.H.O.S.T investigation team along with Ralph, Nikki, and a few of the mediums decided to hold a table-tipping experiment while Peter Crawford and his group sat in silence and monitored their respective area.

Before we began the vigil in the bar, Drew and myself ventured downstairs into the cellar to set up some locked off equipment. A set of motion sensors were used along with a trigger object. We came back upstairs, joined our group and proceeded with the investigations. The circle was formed around the table and Ralph proceeded to ask the spirits some questions. In a sturdy and dominating voice he called out, "If there is any spirit here in the room with us tonight, please try and give us a sign". Nothing happened, so he called again. "If there is any spirit here in the room with us tonight, please try and give us a sign". Still nothing, so he tried a different approach. "If we can ask our energies and our guides to combine, to bring forward any energies within this room, any energies in this area. I am going to ask that you can step forward and that we can use the table to communicate, I am going to ask the group that is sitting at the table if they can combine their energies and focus on the table. Make sure your hands are touching, thumbs to thumbs, and little fingers to little fingers! I am now going to ask the energy to go through to the table and the first thing I am going to ask the energy to do is..." At this point Drew filmed a light anomaly moving across Ralph. He told Ralph and Ralph said; "Yes, it's just stepped forward."

"I am now going to ask you to creak the table, don't force the table but slightly creak the table so we know that you are here." A little time went by and we all heard the table creak.

"Right, I am going to ask the energy to step forward and make yourself known to us, please make yourself known." The sitters now reported that the table was beginning to move slightly.

"Please creak the table," Ralph said.

"If anyone is here with us, can you move the table for us?" At this point we all heard the wooden leg from the table scrape across the floor.

"Thank you! Can you do that again, please?" Sure enough the table began to move. "Ok, can you show us a 'yes'?" The table moved one way. "Can you show us a 'no' please?" The table moved another way. At this point I tried to get under the table in the hope that we could see the thing lift off the floor. Drew had the same idea and was attempting to take photographs. I was also closely monitoring the hands of all the sitters and took great care to study them all meticulously. It appeared that everybody's hands were resting so lightly upon the base of the table that cheating, at this stage in my enquiries, was ruled out.

By this time the table was rocking violently all over and was up on one leg. We came so close to having the table lift up off the floor but alas, this did not happen. What did occur were knocks and bumps and the occasional sound like a footfall that was heard in the bar. All of us monitoring the table-tipping heard this. It was as though someone was strolling around in the bar area trying to make themselves known to us. I even walked down the bar, had a look around and saw no one in this area. I then asked the other group at the other end of the bar if anyone had been down here and they replied no one had. So who, or what had we just heard, and who was communicating through the table?

Ralph, now curious as to what was being heard clumping around the bar area decided to venture over and have a look. When he got to the middle of the bar area he suddenly stopped and said, "I am feeling there is a presence right here."

"Is it male or female?" I then asked.

"I can't quite tell at the minute, I just know we have somebody here." This astounded me, simply because when I was interviewing the landlord earlier on, he told me of the person who had died right here at this spot. Could Ralph have been picking up on this person's spirit? It seemed to be the case. Again this is another true life encounter with spirits that personally for me, goes a long way to support the theories of ghosts and maybe an afterlife. It certainly supports the theories of spirit mediumship in some people! I knew for a fact that no one knew about this spot in the pub and Ralph had sensed it. Could this have been the same person we all heard moving around here not less than 2 minutes ago? It appears likely that it could have been. The table at this point had calmed down and whatever spirit had came through seemed to have dispersed. It was a fascinating experiment to watch and it is something I will not forget. Whether the table-tipping experiment can be deemed as good objective evidence is another story but nevertheless it proved very interesting indeed.

The other group were having a little success too within their group. I ventured around to see what was happening. I was told that the door to the top of the cellar stairs kept opening on its own even though the handle closed it tight. I sat myself down and called out to the atmosphere in the hope this would occur again. Never in a million years did I expect to see the handle move down, and the door slowly move open, but I did, twice in the space of 10 minutes. It was absolutely incredible and there was no way that a draught or rational explanation could explain that one. This has to be one of the best ghostly phenomena I have ever witnessed on investigations, and believe me; I have seen some incredible phenomena! I just wished that I had my spare videotape with me. When I retrieved it from my holdall, the door (surprise surprise) would not open for us anymore! I put my camera away and taped the proceedings with my dictation machine.

When I asked Peter Crawford about any other impressions or anything else that may have happened he told me about a wonderful friendly energy of a lovely lady. He felt her presence for about 5 minutes until it faded and told me her name was Sarah and she resembled the lady in the Mona Lisa picture. It was at this point when Ralph turned to me and asked me if I had anything to do with cartwheels!

"Cartwheels?" I said. "There is a cartwheel on the front of this pub," I told him.

"No, no, no, this has something to do with you," he exclaimed.

"No, I cannot think of anything." I said

"Oh well, never mind" he then said.

It seems he was reading me and it did not dawn on me until I was going through my notes after the investigation that I remembered that years and years ago my mother went through this phase of garden ornaments and one particular large garden ornament that everyone was buying were these huge wagon wheels or cartwheels to either lay on the lawn, or have mounted on the walls. My mother had a few in the garden. Could it have been these he was picking up on? Or the fact that I once broke my hand no sooner had I mastered the art of cartwheeling at my local Judo club? (Mediums do work in rather odd ways).

I then called out to the atmosphere to see if anything would happen and to my utter joy the door opened once more but only this time I managed to catch the sounds on audiocassette tape. (Granted, not as good as videotape, but a good result nonetheless). At the same time, with my naked eye, I saw two amazing light anomalies float across the top of the door! What an amazing investigation. It was time for one last break before our final vigil of the night.

We ventured outside into the old stable area. The wind was howling through the trees, and the rain was lashing down upon us. The stable doors were crashing in the wind and it was cold beyond all belief. Most normal folk would be tucked up in a nice and warm bed at this time of the morning, but not us! What made the situation so surreal was that we were standing there in almost sub-zero conditions, soaking wet, tired and cold, calling out to the atmosphere in an old stable with Ralph Keeton, Britain's number one exorcist and the man behind Hollywood's new movie, *Monster House*! It does not get better than that.

The vigil in the barns was uneventful and it was quite hard to determine what noises may have been paranormal due to the gale force winds reverberating around (and inside) the old stables. However, one stable proved rather odd. This is the stable where Ralph had wanted to stay for a while and when we got in, we were not disappointed. The wind was confined to being outside this particular area and after asking Alice (the lady who Ralph sensed) to show us some signs, the light flex hanging from the ceiling moved back and forth on command! It stopped when it was asked, and resumed when it was politely asked too. It was quite incredible to say the least. Some cynics will say it was the wind, but hey! You were not there! I am a sensible investigator with an inquisitive mind and a yearning for the truth. If it were the wind, I would have said so.

So the investigation had now came to an end and what a night. A fabulous haunted venue with many reputed ghosts and shades of the past. It was indeed an honour to be asked to go and co-investigate with Peter Crawford,

Ralph, Nikki, and all the other guest mediums.

CHAPTER TWENTY-TWO

THE SCOTTISH HIGHLANDS

The small village of Carrbridge is located approximately twelve miles south-east of Inverness and about five miles north-west of Aviemore in the highlands of Scotland, and I stayed at the Carrbridge Hotel when I came to visit in my search of ghosts. Carrbridge sits in a valley at the foot of the Monadhliath mountain range, and is just north of the Cairngorms. It is surrounded by acres of lush countryside, peaks and forests. It is a picturesque landscape every way you turn and there is no escaping the aesthetic beauty this tiny little hamlet offers. The village itself consists of a main road, a village shop and post office, a couple of pubs (which I must say served excellent beers, single malts, and magnificent pub food) a hotel or two, a playing field, adventure playground, school and village hall and that is it. This remote and isolated village is a wonderful retreat for those who just want to rest and enjoy the surrounding beauty or take time out and it was a perfect base for my visit.

As mentioned earlier I stayed at the Carrbridge Hotel, which sits at the north end of the village next to the river, which often floods when the water is in spate. Time after time this little village is subject to flooding in the spring when the snow on the mountain peaks begins to melt and literally tons of water rush down the mountainsides and into the river causing damage to the area. Usually the damage caused by these frequent floods is not that bad with the water levels reaching quite a height, but not a dangerous level. However there have been some disastrous floods, which have caused untold damage to the area. On the 8th July 1923 the village was flooded, with torrential rain and thunderstorms. Down the mountainsides gallons upon gallons of water came and this resulted in the collapse of six rail and road bridges and total devastation in the Carrbridge area creating thousands of pounds worth of damage and creating havoc and inconvenience for months after.

An earlier dreadful flood in 1829 also swept away bridges but amazingly what was left after these floods remains upriver west of the Carrbridge Hotel in the form of an old stone arch, spanning the river. It is now known as the Old Packhorse Bridge and it is here, allegedly, where a ghost man has been seen silently standing at the ruined bridge at dusk. Sitting having a drink in the hotel bar I got chatting to an old fellow who relayed this ghost account to me. I told him I thought the story was very interesting and asked him how he knew about the phantom vision at the bridge and if there was anything that backs this haunting up historically. He went on to say he knew it was real, as he himself had witnessed it on a number of occasions while out walking his dog. He went on to say that on one occasion, it disappeared before his very eyes as he was making his approach to the bridge from along the woodland path.

Intrigued as I was with this story I decided to venture out there the following evening at dusk in the hope that I may catch a fleeting glimpse of the apparition that this fellow claimed was real. I sat down at the end of the ruined bridge and waited. The gushing sound of the river flowing by made my time there much more tranquil, and I could have just drifted off into a nice altered state of awareness, a perfect alternate state for perhaps tuning in to the world of spirit! The sun was sinking, casting a bright red-orange glow across the sky while the birds were sitting perched on their branches filling the dusk air with their beautiful evening song. It was like something from a fairytale and I felt I was a million miles away from any civilisation. The phantom did not put in an appearance for me, but there were other nights I could return.

I returned to the hotel room, got changed, and headed down to the bar for an evening drink with my other half. The following day we were heading off on one of our excursions and we were going to Inverness. Jayne had shopping in mind but I wanted to visit the old castle that stands by the River Ness. We agreed to go our separate ways in the afternoon after we had dined and spent the whole morning together. We finished our drinks and retired to our bed. The morning came and it was not long before we arrived at our destination. After our morning together I set off for the castle and found out upon my arrival that it was now a sheriff's court.

The present Inverness Castle was built between 1833 and 1836 and stands overlooking the River Ness. It is a magnificent red sandstone construction and was built by the architect William Burn. I was informed that since 1057 there have been a whole host of forts and castles that have stood on this spot, which tells me that there must be ghosts, and sure enough, there is. I was informed by one of the castle staff, that in the section that is known as the castle garrison that is open for the tours to the public, strange occurrences have indeed taken place. Unseen hands have pushed people, while others feel ill at ease in certain areas. A sense of presence has been detected by visiting psychics but as yet no one has been able to put a name to this alleged presence. I was also informed about the local legend of King Duncan who, by all accounts has been seen walking along the banks of the River Ness just beneath the castle. Macbeth and Lady Macbeth in William Shakespeare's famous 'Scottish play' murdered King Duncan so perhaps the ghost of King Duncan really is just a legend after all.

Our next trip out, a few days later, took us to the beautiful shores of Loch Ness where the breathtaking ruins of Castle Urquhart stand. Records show the earliest castle there dates back to the 1200s and although fortifications have stood here for over 800 years, most visitors nowadays who visit Loch Ness are usually here to see one thing and one thing only. Whether the Loch Ness Monster exists or not still remains a mystery but still, in their droves the visitors come in search for her. I must admit during my time at Loch Ness and castle Urquhart deep down I was hoping for a sighting although my primary objective was the ghosts of Urquhart. These haunting ruins of one of the largest castles in Scotland stands on a rocky outcrop overlooking the famous Loch Ness and fell into decay in 1689. In 1692 it was blown up to prevent the Jacobites establishing any occupation here and has stood as romantic ruins ever since.

Not long ago I had a chance to go and investigate Castle Urquhart overnight. This investigation was going to be broadcast live on the radio but other ghost hunting commitments in York had been arranged first so unfortunately I had to decline the offer, which was a shame. Nevertheless a colleague of mine, and team associate Drew Bartley, from the Ghosts and Hauntings Overnight Surveillance Team managed to investigate the castle and this is what he told me upon his return:

It was a surreal experience creeping around the pitch black ruins in the dead of night listening to the waves from the loch smashing and crashing up the rocks that lay only yards away from where we stood. The ruins of the castle are said to be haunted by the ghost of a man who carries a long stick and this is exactly what one of the investigators claimed to have seen standing amidst the ruins. We did not know this at the time and this reported sighting correlates with other sightings. It seems this investigator may have just seen the ghost of Castle Urquhart. Another investigator, while down in the old cellars reported that the door latch to the cellar was repeatedly moved up and down as if someone was trying to get in from the other side. Inspection proved no one else was there however the wind factor leads me to believe that this was the cause of the phenomena. The other investigator disagreed. It was an interesting investigation and well worth partaking in.

After our visit to nearby Drumnodrochit and Fort Augustus, (where a local told me about a magnificent abbey that has been converted into luxury self-catering apartments that is reputedly haunted by the ghost of a Benedictine monk), we made our way back to the hotel. Time was getting on and although I so wanted to visit the abbey in search of this monk, time had beaten us. Perhaps one day I may book in to one of their splendid apartments and spend some time up at the Abbey.

We arrived back at our hotel in time for a traditional Scottish evening meal, which consisted of tatties, neeps and haggis (potatoes, turnip and haggis). Incidentally, our hotel in Carrbridge was located about ten miles north of the famous Ben Macdui. This magnificent peak, which is part of the cairngorm mountain range, is world renowned to the ghost enthusiast for the spectre of a large grey man is said to haunt it. Known as The Grey Man of Ben Macdui, this terrifying phantom has, on many occasions, frightened the life out of literally dozens of climbers over the years and his appearance often results in climbers fleeing the mountainside in absolute horror. Too many reports have come in over the years to dismiss this mystery as imagination or flight of fancy.

The Grey Man has also been heard as well as seen. His footfalls have been heard thundering down the mountain paths in the dense fog by climbers only to be surprised by a giant figure that manifests itself in front of them before they take to their heels. More often than not the pounding footsteps follow the climbers as they are running away and it is only when they reach the bottom of the mountainside that they realise the footsteps behind them have ceased. One account says that in 1943 a climber on Ben Macdui, was confronted by the Grey Man and out of sheer terror he fired his revolver at the human figure which remained unharmed! Once again the climber fled in terror. Many well-attested and documented reports of this spectre have come in over the years and although I have travelled the country far and wide in search of ghosts, this is one phantom I would *not* like to come face to face with. There is definitely something macabre and sinister about this mountainside haunting and I, for one, will choose to avoid Ben Macdui.

I will end this chapter with an odd story regarding the hotel room that we stayed in during our time in the Scottish Highlands. I had asked the staff at our hotel if indeed there were any alleged ghosts there and was told although there might be, they were not too sure. I can verify, as too can Jayne, that there is something rather odd indeed going on in the hotel, well, in our room anyway. I will not say what room we stayed in although we would not forget in a hurry, but needless to say I believe it to be spiritually active. Subtle things were happening during our stay there such as the light in the toilet and shower room was found on in the morning. This happened on a number of occasions although we were certain we had turned it off the night before. Our bedroom door was found unlocked one morning after we had returned to our room the night before and locked it before retiring to bed! But the strangest thing was hearing the shuffle and padding of footfalls in our room during the dead of night. It was I who heard these and it is just as well because if Jayne had heard them, we would have been on the next train home. I said nothing and convinced Jayne that the doors, and the toilet light phenomena was down to ourselves being rather careless although I am certain we were not.

So there you have it. A memorable trip way up north in the Highlands of bonny Scotland. A holiday, and tracking down the shades of the other world all rolled into one. An added bonus with a haunted hotel room, or was it? Was I mistaken, dreaming or imagining the whole thing? I am confident that I was not but I will let you, the readers decide.

CHAPTER TWENTY-THREE

CASE STUDY

THE DURHAM CITY HOTEL
A READING FROM RALPH
KEETON

On a dark and cold January night we arrived at the 500-year-old former manor house that is now known as the City Hotel. It is situated in Durham city and is just around the corner from another famously haunted pub called Jimmy Allen's. I came here with the Ghost and Hauntings Overnight Surveillance Team, and our guests for tonight were Ralph Keeton and Nikki Austwicke. We had met Ralph and Nikki at another investigation at the McOrville Inn at Elwick and it was decided we should invite them to one of our investigations. Ralph Keeton is known internationally as 'The Exorcist' and is reputed to be Britain's number one. Ralph and Nikki agreed to attend this investigation with us and since then, they have subsequently become members of the team. It is one of Ralph's exorcisms that is behind the story of Steven Spielberg's and Robert Zemeckis's classic movie *Monster House*, and his website can be visited at www.exorcisms.co.uk.

Not much is known about the City Hotel regarding its history and whether or not it did indeed have ghosts. We arrived in Durham at about 10.30 p.m. and made our way to the hotel where the owner Paul met us. We made ourselves comfortable and waited for Ralph and Nikki to arrive, which they did at about 11 p.m.. We chatted for about an hour while waiting for the pub to empty and then we set about our usual pre-investigation tasks. The baselines were carried out first, followed by a reading from our guest medium Ralph Keeton.

For our investigation we were allowed into six of the hotel rooms, the 200 year old grand staircase (which is a grade listed staircase) and the main bar downstairs. Throughout the baseline tests we determined that all areas had no anomalous readings in regards to the EMF sweeps and the average temperature of the rooms were 18–19 degrees. A few windows were noted to have had a slight draught coming from outside and one or two rooms had some very squeaky floorboards so care was taken not to misinterpret any possible phenomena that really would have had a natural cause. However the bar showed a temperature reading of 24 degrees simply because not less than 20 minutes before it was full of revellers and I think body heat would have accounted for this.

We began the reading of the City Hotel at about 1.00 a.m. and it was filmed and recorded for documentation purposes. Our first area for investigation was the front of the bar and this is what Ralph told us:

> In this area I am standing in now there is a young girl. She is about 13–14 years old and she has very long hair, very very long hair indeed. She would have been reported, if anyone had seen her as what is called a white ghost! While chatting to you guys she literally floated in here and it is this area in which she wanders. Rather than make the area go cold, this girl does the opposite and makes people feel rather hot and sweaty – it's a bit like a hot spot rather than a cold spot. I think one or two may have seen her and she is going to come through tonight. She either lived here or has been associated to this building somehow as she knows it quite well and we may see a flash of white light in this area as this is how she will show herself to us.

We moved down the bar and stood in the area where the pool table was and continued with the reading. Ralph picked up on the fact that the building was in actual fact two buildings rather than one. Paul, the owner confirmed that this was true. He went on to ask if a chimney, or an open fire had been taken out of the area and that too was confirmed by the owner. Ralph continued, "This is going to sound pretty obvious but you are going to have movement around this bar area and wisps of smoke and mist have occurred here. You also have a door that needs to be slammed closed at times."

This too was confirmed as correct as the fire exit door sticks and has to be closed with force.

"Is there a recurring problem in the ladies' loos?" Ralph asks.

"No" came the reply. At this point they began to smile and laugh. "So why are you laughing?" I asked them.

"Because we have the problem in the gents' loos!" they said.

"You see, I am getting the ladies…with me it's the ladies' loos, I am going to go down there, I need to see what I feel when I go down there" Ralph said. We walked to the bottom of the corridor and immediately Ralph turned to the wall on the left-hand side and said, "I want to go that way."

"You can't, we don't know what is in there, but we do know it used to be part of this building," came the reply.

"Yes, I can feel it" Ralph said. "I feel like I want to walk that way. I also feel sick down here too because I have the feeling that anyone coming down this way may indeed feel sick and that is due to the presence that is down here. He is a prankster and likes to joke around by making people feel ill at ease and it is this guy that blocks up the loos, he is a total joker and we are going to have some fun down here later on."

"It's quite interesting that you said the word 'he'," Nikki said.

"Did I? That is interesting, I must be subconsciously picking up that this is a male then," he said.

We then ventured back into the main bar and Ralph picked up on a spirit presence that had just come to him. As it turned out this was a spirit that was to be all too significant to the pub, the owners, and bar staff and locals, so due to personal reasons, I will not elaborate on what was picked up and who came through to Ralph. What I will say is that this reading was almost perfect in every way and things were sensed and picked up on that no one could have known except the pub owners and the barman. The look on the barman's face after the reading said it all. He then picked up on the date 1840–1842 and told us that a hangman or executioner once stayed or lived on the premises. Then he began to talk about three creaky steps on an upper level and asked if there were any. He felt that someone walked on the stairs and when they tread on these three particular stairs, people become aware of the presence. He then asked to go upstairs to continue his reading.

We reached the 200 year old listed stairwell and almost straight away he decided everything was all wrong. "I am all disjointed, I don't feel right here," said Ralph. "The layout, the walls are all in the wrong place and I feel the grand staircase should go down where the floor is now situated and again I just want to go this way". He pointed to the wall.

Paul, the owner, again confirms this is correct and tells us that there were indeed more stairs that led down where we were standing. There was also another part to the building, which was not there now. This is where Ralph had wanted to go. "Beeston or Beaston," he then said, "Who is Beeston?" Then he told us that we would get some activity down the corridor, which led to rooms 4–6 so we all had a walk down there. He picked up a large slightly deaf woman who was very domineering and bossy to say the least. He also told us that the level of the floor was not at its original height and said it should be far higher up. Then he said there is a weird ghostly smell connected to this area and at that point I felt a cold draught or breeze blow right across my face. Drew Bartley felt another cold draught while sitting in room 4.

This is where the reading became rather odd for me in more ways than one. Ralph explained that this domineering woman had an affinity for me and was drawn forwards when she heard my voice. He said there was a Scottish connection with her and she attached herself to me when I came to this area. I then felt dizzy and disorientated and found it hard to focus but said nothing just yet. I thought it might have just been me feeling odd but I thought maybe this was the spirit woman making me feel this way as it has happened before on other investigations.

Ralph then said to my utter astonishment that people would feel disorientated and dizzy while up in the area!

"I've got swords," he said. "Two swords crossed over." I began to think for some strange reason that Ralph was beginning to read me because I own two swords. One wooden one called a Bocken, and a steel samurai sword from Japan. I told him about my swords.

"You have two swords? Do you have problems with your jaw or your tooth or some problem inside your mouth at the minute?"

"I do indeed" and I went on to tell him what I had been experiencing lately.

"Right, we are going somewhere with this. The woman we have with us here recognises these similarities between you and herself and that is why she likes you," Ralph said. "So this hand," he went on to say, "I am talking about this finger, which is your left hand and your middle finger is sore. A joint or knuckle that has been broke or dislocated and is now in pain". I told him that the very knuckle was broken during some martial arts training a few years ago. It all seemed surreal as what he was saying tied in with lots of different little aspects of my life. "So why has she latched onto Darren?" Drew said. After a few seconds of deep thought and concentration Ralph said, "It's his voice, she is recognising Darren's voice. The more you speak the more she will come forward as she finds you very interesting. If you do a vigil up here later on and you ask for phenomena you will get it, that I promise," he said. At this point I became very dizzy again and nearly lost my balance. I felt unwell with it and this time I told everyone.

"This is what I felt too", Ralph said. At this point in the proceedings I decided to leave the area because I could now barely string a sentence together through being disorientated and dizzy, combined with feeling quite apprehensive and unnerved. We left this area for the time being, and ended Ralph's reading. Little did I know that this was the start of something incredible.

After a short break we decided it was time to split into groups and investigate the building to see if we could document and experience any paranormal phenomena. Drew, Jason (a guest) and myself went back to the corridor to rooms 4–6 to see if indeed we would get any signs, while Lee, Fiona and Jonathon went to rooms 2 and 3 and Ralph, Nikki and Andy went along the corridor next to the loos. Since time was getting on we designated ourselves 30 minutes in each location before coming back down for a short break. We arrived back upstairs and more or less straight away I began to feel disorientated and dizzy again so I called out to this spirit lady in the hope she would give us a sign. After a while nothing was happening so I tried again. It was then that Drew swept me with his EMF meter and we ascertained a reading of 2 MG. We went into room 4 and sat down for a while. I called out again and asked for a sign and it was at this point at 2.49 a.m. that Drew and myself clearly heard someone whistling from down the corridor. Now we know for a fact that no one was down there at the time so who whistled we could not say.

The rest of this vigil was quite interesting as we all heard a loud bang or a series of bangs, which sounded like a rumbling noise at which we were at a loss to explain. Our guest, Jason, described it as furniture being dragged across the floor. It seems Ralph's prediction for phenomena in this area due to my being here was proved correct! We then ventured into room 6 along the corridor and held a séance during which one or two light anomalies were caught on night vision video camera. After the vigil had finished we returned down stairs for a short break. We returned up to this location, only this time we decided to bring Ralph to see if he could continue his reading of the area, and maybe me.

At 3.30 a.m. Ralph began to tell us that this spirit lady was only coming forward that night simply because I was present. He told us that this was her area and this is where she would stay. In other words she would not be coming home with me after the investigation (which in all honesty I was rather pleased to hear). At this point in the investigation I was leaning against the wall with my right arm while listening to Ralph when all of a sudden it was pushed from behind at the elbow making me stumble forward a little. "You were just pushed there," Ralph said.

"It sure felt like it," I said.

Then within the space of 5 minutes the same thing happened again only this time it felt a little harder. At this precise time a light anomaly was filmed behind me right at the crucial moment. I then felt weirdly exhilarated and delight came all over me, for what reason I could not say. We moved back into room 6 and the reading and the investigation continued.

Now, I am going to tell you what I got when I was talking to the others down-stairs, I am getting the impression that this building was used for pirates, now when I say pirates I don't mean the seafaring swashbuckling vagabonds that sail the high seas in search of treasures, no! I mean it was a place for storage of illegal things and I must stress its not recent. We are going back a good few years here! At this point I decided to call out to the atmosphere in the hope that this lady could give us another sign and then I started to see little light anomalies with my naked eye floating about the room. These anomalies were not the usual kind and when I say that, I mean they were not white, or bright ones but rather the opposite. These little orbs of energy I was seeing were black in colour. I thought it may have been my eyes playing tricks in the dark but Ralph assured me that there were such things as black orbs. Black orbs, he went on to say were a negative energy.

Ralph then said that the spirit lady who has the affinity with me was standing close by and seemed to be leaning over me as though she was pressing herself upon me. He then got the sensation of absolute pain and agony coming from her and said this pain went back to about 1827. She was then next to me and was touching my head. "Fish, fish…she hates fish," Ralph said as he began to hold his throat. "Why is she telling me to tell you that?" he then went on to say. At this point in the reading I went white as I was overcome with surprise and shock. That very day at work while eating my lunch, which consisted of a scabby portion of chips, a pile of mush those at the work canteen call peas and a battered fish, I had a large fishbone stuck and lodged in my throat and I literally thought I was going to choke to death on it. It was lodged in my throat for about 25 minutes until it became dislodged and swallowed with some dry bread I was told to eat by a woman at a neighbouring table. I subsequently left the rest of my lunch and decided I was going to give fish a wide birth from that point on! "Well she has literally told me to tell you this, she wanted you to know this". He then said to me the strangest thing. "Why have you cried? Have you been crying?"

Again you could have knocked me down with a feather. Just that morning before I went to work there was an incident at my home involving our daughter Abbey that resulted in myself and my partner Jayne shedding a few tears. I will not elaborate on what actually happened but I did indeed cry a little that morning. I had never cried or shed tears for a good few years (except the day she was born) and I did that day and for Ralph to pick up on that really did astound me. He said to me, "I am seeing through your crying eyes". I explained what had happened and he went on to say that this woman knew I had been crying when I came into her domain this evening and she wanted me to know that everything would be right in regards to what happened.

Now, writing these words a few weeks after the event I am glad to know that Ralph, and the lady in question were indeed right and my daughter is absolutely fine, as are myself and Jayne. In retrospect, thinking about everything that went on in that corridor makes me really think about the whole 'psychic' thing and convinces me even more than ever that there is indeed something in it. The vigil then came to an end and we all re-grouped in the bar downstairs for a break.

That night's investigation is one I will not forget in a hurry and my experiences with the reading I received from Ralph combined with my uneasy feelings earlier on really made me think hard about everything and it had a very profound effect on me, but the night was not over yet. We still had one more investigation location to stake out and that was the corridor that led to the toilets. After our final break we headed off to our last location. We headed down the corridor to the toilet area and made ourselves comfortable and started to call out to the atmosphere in the hope that we would get some good paranormal activity. It was so dark down there you could not see your hand in front of your face and as I began to attempt spirit communication we all became aware of what sounded like a man's guttural breath or someone clearing their throat. It was certainly not one of the investigators and it came from directly behind where I was standing, which was with my back facing into the gents' loos as I was peering round the corner along the corridor.

After a discussion of what, or who it could have been, we called out again to this spirit man. It is interesting to note that when Ralph was reading the area earlier on he claimed the spirit down there was indeed a man. It looked as though he was right again. The time went by and nothing else seemed to be happening until we all heard the shuffling of footsteps coming from the opposite end of the corridor. Upon inspection of the area we found nothing untoward and no one was around to account for the shuffling we heard. It seemed the vigil was producing some good results. The trigger object we had placed down the corridor failed to move and the EMF and temperature surveys provided no anomalous readings.

The end of the vigil and investigation quickly came so we tied up our loose ends, finished off the experiments, gathered up the equipment and headed off home for some well-deserved rest.

In summary the investigation as a whole was rather good for me personally as I was subjected to what I believe was some very strange phenomena. Along with the reading from Ralph, it certainly made this an investigation to remember. The rest of the group's investigations unfortunately provided me with very little in the way of information as a quiet night was had. There was the occasional knock and bump and feelings of coldness, but nothing that could have been deemed as credible and objective paranormal phenomena. I guess working with a medium most of the night does break the monotony of what may otherwise be a dull and long evening with only few possible phenomena encountered. Having said that working without a medium can be just as rewarding if one is patient and tenacious. That night's investigation was very satisfying indeed and I look forward to a second investigation there in one of the oldest and most historic hotels in Durham city centre.

CHAPTER TWENTY-FOUR

SCOTLAND'S HAUNTED CAPITAL THE GHOSTS OF EDINBURGH

Edinburgh is Scotland's capital city and is laden with history. It is a place I have visited dozens of times and is a city I have an affinity with. During my days as a young lad my parents would take my brother and I on holiday to a caravan park just over the borders and we stayed at a wonderful little place called Coldingham not far from St Abb's Head. From here we ventured to places of interest such as Eyemouth, (which is just back over the borders in England), St Abb's Head, and of course Edinburgh. In those days holidays were fun and the treasured memories I have from these family trips away are ones I will never forget.

I think my interest in the paranormal and all things 'ghostly' may well indeed have partially stemmed from these holidays as we often used to go out for 'spooky midnight walks' with my parents down the village and through the churchyard at the dead of night peering around every gravestone and corner with the full moon shining down upon us, hoping to see a ghost. My father would tell stories about the headless horseman that gallops down the old country lane at midnight while we were standing in the pitch black of night with only my small torch as a means of illumination and I can remember being scared out my wits waiting nervously for the phantom horseman.

During these holidays we would visit Edinburgh at least twice and go shopping, sightseeing, and do the usual things a family would do while on holiday. Trips to Edinburgh later on in my life came and went, but I had never attempted to track down any ghosts nor did I even visit any alleged haunted sites with the intention of investigating the ghosts or hearing of the ghostly tales that may accompany these locales, until now. A week in Scotland's capital in a beautiful family-run bed and breakfast located only 5 minutes from Princes Street was ideal for what was required.

Edinburgh is rich in history and ghost legend, as are most of the cities and towns I have visited in my search for ghosts and like the rest of them, Edinburgh has had its fair share of disasters, doom, gloom and tragedies which I believe, leaves its mark for the future generations. Sieges and bloody warfare, witchcraft, diseases, murders, and plagues have all hit Edinburgh and have left their mark in one way or another. Perhaps the most infamous and heinous crimes Edinburgh recorded were that of William Burke and William Hare otherwise known as Burke and Hare, the Edinburgh body snatchers. It was common practice back in those days to buy the bodies of the dead; to dissect and study them for medical science and big money was paid for the bodies used.

Burke and Hare, who originally came from Ireland to Edinburgh in the early 1800s, had the gruesome idea of digging up the recently departed in order to sell them for the easy money. The doctor they sold the bodies to, Dr Knox, was of course in on the act and the twosome became a deadly threesome. When the grave robbing became known to the authorities, guards and lookouts were assigned to all the cemeteries in an effort to quell this odious crime. But this did not stop Burke and Hare, they wanted to keep their steady income coming in so they decided that rather than dig the bodies fresh out the ground, they would supply their doctor with fresh corpses in which they had murdered themselves. And so began an appalling and gruesome chain of murders in the Edinburgh region and in total, over sixteen innocent people fell victim to the evil of Burke and Hare. Eventually they were caught and on 28 January 1828 William Burke was publicly hanged in front of 25,000 people. William Hare was offered a pardon if he confessed to the murders that he took part in, and it was this confession that led to Burke's hanging. Hare was set free and it is believed he was last spotted in Carlisle in 1868. Dr Knox was never charged for his part in the whole sordid affair and after mass riots outside his house, he left Edinburgh and died sad and alone in London in 1862. It is interesting to note that prior to William Burke's hanging, a cast of his face was made with plaster. It was called a death mask and it was common practice back in those days. A cast was also made of Burke's face *after* his execution and both photographs of those death masks can be seen in this book.

One of the places I wanted to visit during my time in Edinburgh was the magnificent Edinburgh Castle. Built on an extinct volcano, it stands at the top of the Royal Mile and houses the oldest building in Edinburgh, Saint Margaret's chapel. I spent a couple of hours exploring the place and taking in the breathtaking views the castle has to offer. I enquired about any potential ghosts the castle may have and I was informed about the legend of the lost ghost piper whose bagpipe music can be heard emanating from the tunnels that are hidden deep in castle rock and under Princes Street. Edinburgh Castle, it seems, has the exact same legend and ghost tale attached to it as another famous castle I visited during the course of my research. Culzean castle on the Ayrshire coast (which is also featured in this book) also boasts of an underground tunnel which a piper attempted to walk through while playing his pipes as people listened on to see how far he would go and ultimately he was never seen again! As with the Edinburgh Castle legend, his ghostly pipe music is still heard quite often emanating from the tunnels deep underground. Further research has shown me that yet another castle called Gight Castle in Aberdeenshire also has the exact same ghost legend attached to it indicating that some castles in Scotland may like this story so much it has been adopted as their own leading me to believe there is nothing to them but a good old fashioned story! Having said that the story must originate from somewhere and may indeed have an element of truth behind it, but from which castle it originates is anybody's guess.

Needless to say I was rather disappointed to hear of the exact same legend in relation to three different Scottish castles. I dare say the same occurrence *could* have happened in all three of the castles' histories resulting in the loss of the piper and ultimately his return in the form of a phantom that plays the pipes, but it is highly unlikely. I just wonder how many more castles in Scotland there are that tell this ghost story of underground tunnels and a ghost piper?

After we visited the castle we left the Royal Mile and headed down the old stairwell that leads down towards the north side of the old town and we found a beautiful old cobbled street, which is known as the Grassmarket. It is tucked away behind the magnificent castle and it was here where they once carried out the public hangings. Alas this was not where the infamous body snatcher William Burke met his grizzly end, although Burke and Hare did work this area! No, that was on the head of a stretch of road now called George IV Bridge (formerly Liberton's Wynd), which can be reached by following the road along from the Grassmarket and heading up Candlemaker Row. At the east end of the Grassmarket where it connects with the lower end of Candlemaker Row, stands a round and raised stone composition with a St Andrew's cross in rose-coloured cobbles. Inscribed upon it are the words

'For the protestant faith, on this spot many martyrs and covenanters died'

It was in this precise spot where the Grassmarket gallows once stood. (X literally marking the spot). Here, over 100 people met their deaths on the gallows in front of a huge and angry justice-hungry crowd of people, all cheering and laughing as the guilty died with the hemp around their necks.

Just yards away from where the gallows stood is an old drinking establishment and it is called the Last Drop. A beautiful old building which of course I had to call into for a visit. I asked the barman if the name of the pub bares any relevance to the area in which it stood and I was informed that the pub *was* named the 'Last Drop' to commemorate the last hanging in the Grassmarket, a macabre reminder of those horrific times of a bygone era. It is also the only building in the Grassmarket that retains its original form and design from the outside. I asked if the building had any ghosts and was subsequently informed that on many occasions the ghost of a young Irish girl had been seen and heard playing and running about in the bar area. It is also believed that one or two of the former victims of the nearby gallows make their presences known to bar staff and visitors alike. Strange goings on occur from time to time and some say those that died are not too far away.

I left the Last Drop and continued with my journey through Edinburgh. I ventured up Candlemaker Row knowing that just around the corner is the site of what is probably known as Scotland's most recent, and terrifying case of psychic disturbance. It is here at Greyfriars cemetery and the Covenanters' prison where the infamous Mackenzie Poltergeist is said to scratch, attack, bruise and maul the unsuspecting visitors to the area. George Mackenzie is said to be the cause of all this terrible activity, hence the name. He was an employee of Charles II and was in charge of the prison in the seventeenth century. He persecuted the Scots Presbyterians known as the covenanters and often locked them away in the prison and sentenced them to death with relish and amusement on the nearby gallows at Grassmarket. He was an evil man and was known as a hanging Judge. His tomb is nearby the prison, but it is not here where he haunts. He chooses to wreak havoc in the old Covenanters' prison.

Why he has came back after all this time to haunt no one is sure, but one theory is that in 1998, a local chap desecrated and vandalised George Mackenzie's tomb and it was not long after when all the disturbances began. Of course when I paid my visit to the Covenanters' prison, the gates were locked and access was denied, unless I returned later as part of a paying group. Needless to say, I did not. I can't help thinking that at the beginning back in 1998 there may have been one or two genuine paranormal occurrences which were mistaken for poltergeist activity here at the prison resulting in mass hysteria and thus a huge psychological ball of activity began to roll, but I may be wrong! After all, poltergeists (in my opinion) are not spirits of the dead. This ghost story ultimately has led to the churchyard being one of the most frightening graveyards in the UK and has done wonders for the Edinburgh tourist trade as people come from far and wide to experience the wrath of George Mackenzie.

A wonderful ghost story attached to the graveyard that is a lot better known is that of Greyfriars Bobby. Bobby was a Skye Terrier and belonged to a local policeman called John Gray. When John Gray was taken ill one winter, Bobby stayed right beside his master until he passed away. Even after he died good old Bobby stayed with his master and even followed the funeral procession into Greyfriars churchyard. After the grave was filled in Bobby was able to sit on the bare earth that covered his master. Bobby was fed by the local graveyard attendant James Brown, who felt sorry for him, and was often taken to the castle by some of the many friends he had made during his vigil at his master's grave. During the summertime Bobby made himself useful by chasing all the cats away from the cemetery, which of course pleased James Brown.

By now he was becoming a well-known and faithful little dog and word spread fast of Bobby's loyalty and devotion. For fourteen long years Bobby took vigil at his master's graveside and when he eventually died, he was buried in a flowerpot at the front of Greyfriars churchyard. He lay there for one hundred years before a stone was erected to mark his grave. Some say that Bobby never existed at all but there are one or two exhibits and photographs available that prove Bobby was indeed real. Even today, it has been said from time to time you can still see the ghost of faithful Bobby running around Greyfriars churchyard chasing the cats away.

One of the official residences of the Queen, the Palace of Holyroodhouse stands at the east end of the Royal Mile at the foot of Arthur's Seat. My visit there coincided with a visit from Prince Andrew, the Duke of York, who had been staying there for a few days. As we arrived he was preparing to leave and we were fortunate enough to see him depart as we entered the palace. Holyroodhouse Palace is famous for having some odd phenomena occurring there but it was the bloodstained floor in the Mary Queen of Scots' bedroom that I had come to see. I ventured inside and duly looked around the magnificent palace before venturing up to the bedroom in the upper section of the palace.

Upon entering the room I was met by a guide who told me the story of how the bloodstains came to be. David Rizzio and the young queen had formed a close relationship when she had arrived in Scotland. Mary's husband, Lord Darnley, did not approve of this friendship and became increasingly jealous of the two so with the help of a few of his comrades he began to plot the demise of the young queen's companion. One night in 1566 Darnley and his companions burst into the queen's apartment and seized Rizzio. They stabbed him repeatedly and his blood spilt all over the floor. Repeated attempts were made by the murdering mob to clean up the blood but the blood kept returning. The guide then showed me the actual bloodstains on the wooden floor and as I examined them closely she went on to say that it did not matter how many times the red stains were washed away, they would always return. Even the when new floorboards were placed down in the room in an attempt to rid the floor of these red stains the blood returned to stain the new wood!

I then asked the guide if she, or any other of the guides had had any strange experiences while working there and she told me that although she had not, some of the other guides got certain feelings and impressions from this room. She also said these guides did not like being in there alone and would prefer it if they did not have to use the Mary Queen of Scots room. I then asked if Queen Mary herself had ever been seen in there and was told as far as she knew, she had not. After seeing the bloodstains and listening as to how they had come about, I said thank you, bid the guide farewell and I left the Palace of Holyroodhouse.

I stayed in Edinburgh for a few days in my search for ghosts and I did indeed have an agenda. Part of this agenda included a trip down into Mary King's Close – one of Edinburgh's deepest secrets. Again, this is another tourist attraction that trades upon its amazing history and its ghosts but I wanted to know for myself whether or not Mary King's Close was as haunted as people say it is. I turned up at 12.30 p.m. and booked my tour with the guide for 12.40 p.m. There were only two or three people in my tour group and after a brief introduction of what was what, we headed down into Mary King's Close.

"I am glad there are only three in this tour," the guide said. "It will make it easier to identify if we are joined by an uninvited fourth party".

"Are you for real? Or does that happen quite a lot?" I said to him.

"Oh yes indeed, we are often joined by guests from days gone by on these tours, it happens quite a lot. I have to headcount everybody as we move from room to room, house to house just in case we are joined by the spectres that roam the close".

"I am sorry to sound cynical but is this not just 'tour banter' to hype up the experience for the visitors?"

"Young man! I can assure you what I tell you is the truth. Ghosts are reported down here quite a lot of the time, don't you know Mary King's Close is one Edinburgh's most haunted areas?"

"I have heard something to that effect" I continued.

By now we had ventured into the first house on the close and the tour had began. I have to say that Mary King's Close really is a frightening and foreboding place. When I ventured into the first house I became all disorientated and quite dizzy although I said nothing to the guide or the other two guests on the tour. I looked at the floor to see if it was uneven as this could account for the disorientation but was surprised to see the floor was flat in this room. Feelings of dizziness and diso-rientation are often associated with haunted locations and the thought occurred that the spirit people of Mary King's Close could indeed have been affecting me.

On with the tour and it was not long before we entered Annie's room. Annie is the ghost of a five-year-old girl who was sensed and seen by a medium while being filmed for a television programme. She was seen sitting on the floor crying. When the medium asked her what was wrong the girl replied she was lonely and could not find her dolly. Being the warm-hearted lady she was, this medium went out and bought the ghost girl a new dolly and left it for her in the room. From that moment on visitors to Mary King's Close bring the young ghost girl a toy or a dolly to play with and Annie's room now is festooned with these toys. A touching and heart-warming story but whether or not it is true nobody knows. Perhaps she is just a made up tourist attraction.

However this visit, for me, proved rather interesting indeed as I experienced what I would deem to be paranormal experiences while being down in the close. In one room on the tour I had my face touched by invisible hands and in another section of the close we all heard the sound of a dog barking. No dogs were down there and as we were way below street level it was unlikely that it could have come from above. The guide told us that barking dogs were often heard down in Mary King's Close. It was rather odd to say the least.

After about one hour down in Mary King's Close we ventured back up to the top once again, being head counted for the last time by the guide. Mary King's Close is a wonderful and historic piece of Edinburgh's history and it would be an honour to be able to investigate the close in more depth. The possibility of an overnight investigation there is indeed on the cards and by the time you read this chapter; the investigation may well have been carried out.

And so my time in Edinburgh came to an end and I had enjoyed a fabulous week away. There are many other haunted sites to visit and there are many more magnificent ghost stories to tell from Scotland's capital and I dare say a whole book could be written on the ghosts of Edinburgh, but alas I must tie up this chapter here. I had visited the haunted venues and sought out the ghosts and legends of all the places that I had on my agenda and I guess I will save the rest for my inevitable return.

CHAPTER TWENTY-FIVE

THE GHOSTS OF DERBY

Derby, in the Midlands is yet another city that is claimed to be the most haunted city in the UK. Like Edinburgh, York, London, and other big cities that are rich in history and laden with shades and echoes of the past, Derby too has a macabre and gruesome record in which people from those bygone days are still said to wander aimlessly around in search of rest and release of torment.

In around 1349 the Black Death hit the old town of Derby killing many thousands of people. Some of those unfortunate victims, however, did not die of the plague but were pronounced dead from the symptoms of this 'Black Death' which included deep sleep and coma. Often mistaken for a dead body, these inert, but still alive individuals were brought out of their homes to be taken away and buried. You can't imagine the pain and torment some of these people must have felt as they woke up to find they had been buried alive! Some of the stronger survivors of this living nightmare, it is said, were known to have clawed their way out of their shallow graves or kick and scream until they were released from their coffins prior to burial. But think of those unfortunate people who did not have the strength to do this, those unfortunate souls would have died a horrible and painful death either suffocating or starving to death in their pitch-black tomb. If they were lucky, the plague would kill them first. It is no wonder that Derby has the highest rate of ghost sightings of plague victims. However, there are many ghosts reported in Derby who are happy ghosts and are quite prepared to stay where they currently reside.

Derbyshire, and the city of Derby are situated right in the centre of the UK, in The Midlands. From all over the UK and from all directions people would visit, pass through, ply their trade, look for work, etc. and Derby was seen as an enormous crossroads or intersection. It was like the grand central station for the inhabitants of Britain and for many years it was literally the dead centre, or hub, of the UK.

Because it was so busy, and so many people inhabited this area along with the constant flow of 'passers by' and 'visitors passing through', crime was almost certainly rife and this is evident due to the fact the Derby once housed no less than five prisons. Many executions took place in Derby including Britain's last hanging, drawing, and quartering, and Britain's last 'pressing to death'. Derby is also known for its hanging on the gallows, as is a lot of places, but Derby lays claim to be the first city to hang its criminals by way of the 'drop system'. Up until that point in time people were strung up by the neck, with their hands tied behind their backs and were made to stand on a horse cart. The horse carts were towed away from under their feet so they would be left hanging by the neck and subsequently they would slowly strangle to death. Sometimes it would take up to 15-20 minutes for a person to die. The drop system made hanging much easier as the necks would snap as a result of the drop. It was like a new, cleaner, quicker system that was soon employed all over the country.

The city of Derby has indeed seen it all, and its claims to be one of the most haunted areas in Britain could well be true. There are many locales, areas of the city, pubs, hotels, parkways and roads that are said to be haunted and one of the biggest, or at least the best known, ghost walks in the country takes place in haunted Derby. Run by local historian and ghost investigator Richard Felix this ghost walk has seen more than 50,000 people in the last 10 years or so traipse the city in search of ghosts. Richard, better known for his appearances on Living TVs *Most Haunted*, is a friend of Ralph Keeton (who also appears in this book) and is probably one of Britain's better known ghost researchers and historians. My colleague, Mike Hallowell, and I had the privilege of working with Richard Felix as he shared the stage at a charity investigation where the three investigators addressed over 250 people on the subject of ghosts. It was followed by an all night investigation at the haunted venue and to meet Richard on that night was something I will never forget. It is one of Richard Felix's haunted buildings that I would like to talk about now, Derby Gaol.

Derby Gaol is reputedly one of Britain's most haunted prisons and it was built between 1750–1756 after the original prison (which was situated elsewhere) was condemned after 200 years because of the filthy conditions in which the prisoners were kept. Hundreds of prisoners died due to disease and illness caused by raw human sewage, rats, and vermin which swept through the old cells. When the old prison was condemned, it was dismantled and parts of the old prison were used to build the new prison. This new prison was built to house about 30 prisoners. The crimes of those who were kept there ranged from petty theft to murder and over the next few hundred years literally thousands of inmates occupied the prison and the famous condemned cell that is situated in the gaol. Like most condemned cells, it was the cell where the prisoner would spend their last night on earth before being led to the gallows. You cannot begin to understand the pain, anguish, torment, and the fear these criminals must have felt while spending their last night alive in that cell.

It is said that these emotions, feelings, and energies were that strong they have somehow engrained themselves into the fabric of the walls of the condemned cell as though the bricks have acted like a psychic tape recording. Screams, wails, and cries are often heard emanating from within the old prison walls and it is said that some people can pick up the feelings of pain and suffering that once went on in here and feel it for themselves, even to this day. I have heard that people leave this area in a state of terror, or they are emotionally drained after being in this cell for a while. Some can't even bear to enter the cell as the ghostly residual energies are said to be that over-powering. It truly is a place of immense sadness and fear and it is no surprise that the condemned cell is the most haunted part of the prison.

The rest of the prison is not without its ghosts too. Doors have been heard to slam closed for no logical reason when no one is around to close them, phantom footfalls have been heard on many occasions walking up the corridors sending chills down the spines of those who hear them and the smell of smoke has often been reported too along with an abundance of apparitions that have been seen there over the years. The prison is a magnificent visitor centre and is a testament to how old prisons used to operate.

North East Ghost Research Team member Suzanne McKay spent the night there in Derby Goal a while ago in search of its resident phantoms. I asked her what sort of a night she had and she told me it was rather eventful to say the least. Among the phenomena recorded was the mysterious smell of tobacco, or smoke. Unexplained temperature drops were recorded, and a sound recording was made of a cell door slamming. Overall, she says, it was a good night. So if you are not too afraid of the resident ghosts that may just make themselves known to you, I would recommend you pay the place a visit if you are ever in the area.

I now take you to another of Derby's haunted locales, and that is Ye Olde Dolphin Inn. This magnificent old pub is said to be Derby's oldest public house and it dates back to the early 1500s (around the same time as York's oldest pubs). Looking at it from across the road you can see that it is indeed very old and the Tudor style exterior beams give the pub that extra air of mystery. In my opinion, it is stuffed with ghosts. I was only in Derby for the day as part of some time away in the Midlands, and it was here I had my pub lunch and pint of the landlord's finest. The atmosphere there was happy and joyous, just like a good traditional British pub should be, but something also felt distinctly macabre. Perhaps it was my imagination, or perhaps my preconceived ideas of what the pub was going to be like got the better of me, yet I still felt unnerved.

I had to ask the bar staff if there were any ghosts in the pub, as I wanted to satisfy my curiosity and obtain first hand accounts of any resident ghosts. I was informed that there were ghosts in the pub (which I knew really as that is why I was there) but there was no one on hand that could have given me a first hand account. Visitors to the pub had seen a ghost of a lady on numerous occasions and I was told about the mischievous cellar ghost who interferes with barrels and pipes. Since time was short and I was not in Derby for long, I ate up, swilled my ale and bid the staff farewell and ventured on to my final venue in my search for ghosts in Derby.

Derby Cathedral is situated in the centre of Derby and is the smallest cathedral in the country. It is the seat of the bishop of Derby and the area around it, and I am told, is very haunted indeed and a number of ghosts have been reported there. An old friend of mine had a brother who lived in Derby and it was he who informed me of the alleged ghosts around the old cathedral. He would come to Newcastle on occasion to visit his brother, and when I ventured to my friend's house to join them he would tell me the stories of the ghosts. He knew I had a fascination with the supernatural and took great pleasure in letting me know just how haunted his 'now home town' was. I will not talk about my actual visit to the cathedral, or the haunted grounds around it although it was fascinating for me. However as I found no one to speak to in regards to the alleged haunted area I will elaborate on what my friend's brother relayed to me.

He first told me that the most famous of the ghosts there is that of a phantom called The White Lady. She is reputed to be seen wondering around near the back of the cathedral and has been seen by many people. She simply vanishes into thin air leaving those who see her rather shaken up. Another ghost, he went on to say was that of a young woman who has been seen weeping as she makes her way through the cathedral grounds. Sometimes only the sound of her crying is heard and her image is not seen. Amongst other ghosts haunting the area, one particular story is quite heartbreaking, and that is the ghost of a former executioner who was once a criminal himself. He is said to haunt the area unhappily.

I was told that this story is probably one of the better-known ghost tales of Derby. When he was alive he was offered a pardon for his own death penalty by the authorities on the condition that he was to become the next executioner. However – the next people to incur the death penalty were two of his own family members, his brother and his father, and he agreed to carry out their executions in order to save himself. After he died it is said that his miserable, and perhaps guilt ridden ghost haunts the area and cannot rest until his father and brother forgive him. Although I spent some time around the grounds and inside the old All Saints Church as it was formerly known, looking around and taking photos, I did not see any of these alleged ghosts I had been told about before my visit.

Before I knew it my short time in Derby had come to an end and it was time for me to leave this wonderfully haunted city. I wanted to stay there overnight and explore a lot more of this wonderful metropolis but alas, it was not to be. However I am glad of the time I managed to spend there seeking out what ghosts I could. After all, had I not, this chapter would not have been written. My short visit there gave me the time to at least accumulate *some* ghostly tales and talk to a few people about the ghosts of the places I have mentioned herein and with the help of my friend's brother (who incidentally wished to remain anonymous) and my own team colleague and fellow investigator Suzanne McKay, I was able to put together this short, but nevertheless interesting chapter on some of the ghosts of Derby.

CHAPTER TWENTY-SIX

CASE STUDY

WASHINGTON OLD HALL
TYNE AND WEAR

Washington Old Hall is located in Washington village in Tyne and Wear. The hall dates back to Saxon times – as far back as AD 973 – and was once owned by the ancestors of George Washington of the American War of Independence fame, hence the name. Formerly owned by the bishop of Durham, the estate at Washington was exchanged by him during the twelfth century and came into the possession of the first William of Washington.

The hall was added to the original building some time later and by the end of the nineteenth century it was used as a place of dwelling for about thirty people, all living in terrible and cramped conditions. Nowadays it is open to the public and is owned by the National Trust. This building is said to have only one ghost and it is that of the Grey Lady. She is said to walk the upper floors of the building. The Grey Lady has been seen countless times walking along with her head bent over weeping. Why this is, no one knows. However, our investigation there proved very interesting indeed. I had always wanted to spend a night there in search of its resident ghost and one night back in 2004 this was made possible. As a member of the National Trust I had visited Washington Old Hall on a number of occasions and found the place to be of great interest.

On the night of the investigation everyone concerned met at the old hall at 9.45 p.m. and at 10 p.m. we went inside to get ourselves sorted out and ready for the night's investigation. Another group of investigators had also booked the hall for the evening (Fiona's team) so we decided to mix in and work together. They were a spiritualist group from Durham. Before any of the investigations and vigils began baseline tests were carried out in the building to determine all baseline readings and no anomalous readings were ascertained. Trigger objects in the form of crucifixes and large keys were also placed down and drawn around in certain locations within the building, in the hope that some interaction with the ghosts of the old hall could be made.

A large wooden cross was placed in the panelled room downstairs on a wooden chest to the right-hand side of the door, and two motion sensors were placed either side of the trigger object so if the cross moved then the motion sensors should be activated indicating paranormal activity. Well, that's the theory anyway! We also drew around four old coins and left them on the wooden chest too. A thermometer in the panelled room read 18.8 degrees. A humidifier and two thermometers were set up in the bedroom upstairs and they read 63% humidity and 19.5 degrees.

We were now ready to begin the night vigils. It was 10.40 p.m. and my group's first designated location was the panelled room on the ground floor. We headed off to our location, which also included the great hall and the kitchens. The other group stayed upstairs to investigate the bedroom and main hall area. Our group then split into two smaller groups so we could cover more of the ground floor area. I stayed in the panelled room with a few other investigators and everyone else made themselves comfortable in the great hall.

At 10.42 p.m. a séance was held in the panelled room while the investigators were in there to try and draw in any alleged spirits that may be present. Members of the other group of investigators and psychics took part in this experiment. I stayed out the circle and observed, took photos and generally monitored the proceedings. The group seemed to have a lot of success in picking up spirits and generally sensing things however I saw heard and felt nothing as I watched in anticipation from the sidelines. I also called out to any residing spirits for phenomena to no avail. Well, nothing that satisfied my curiosity anyway. That however was to change later on!

At 10.55 p.m. the two groups that were downstairs swapped locations and we then entered the great hall area of Washington Old Hall to continue with the examination. I personally saw and heard nothing paranormal although it was more of the same with the mediums in this location as it was in the last. It was all very interesting to watch the mediums at work but for me personally, I wanted to see or experience something for myself rather than watch these sensitive people see, feel and experience everything. They picked up on an abundance of spirits and trapped energies contained within the hall but I was not too sure about what they claimed to be sensing. The ghost of Washington Old Hall is supposedly said to walk the upper corridor of the building and that is said to be the only ghost. Were the psychics picking up on other spirits that others had failed to detect? After 20 minutes the vigil came to an end and we all had a break.

It is interesting to note at this point just before our break when others were in their respective locations, two of the other group's investigators experienced something odd in the ladies' toilets. They told me that they both felt rather uncomfortable simultaneously while in there and again at exactly the same time, they both agreed that a presence was felt. Whether they did or not I cannot say for sure but the investigators were both adamant that they had experienced something strange. I was also informed on our break that one of the visiting mediums had picked up on a female called Annabel in the exhibition room. I was then informed that the spirit of a man called Albert Radcliffe haunted the bedroom next to this and he was quite happy to remain there. However another spirit of a man called Jack was not happy about Albert being there and Jack would not give up the room for him. It seemed Albert wanted Jack's room.

Another ghost was allegedly picked up on and it was yet another lady. She refused to enter the bedroom because of Jack! This lady was apparently on another level, or residual layer, to the other two alleged spirits but nevertheless was fully aware of them. Personally this does not make sense to me unless people from all different time periods in our physical world can meet up on the other side (after death) on the same plane of existence. For example, could the spirit of King Henry VIII who was born in 1491 be fully aware of Elvis Presley who was born in 1935, in the spirit world, a difference of 444 years in total? It's a mind boggling and extreme thought, but who knows for sure? At present I would suggest to the reader that these impressions that were relayed to him about what was sensed on the first vigil should be taken lightly due to the fact I cannot find any verification to back them up.

At midnight and after another break it was time for location three and this time the investigators were upstairs in the hall, bedroom and toilet area. Apart from the mediums doing their usual stuff, I again experienced nothing. In the ladies' toilets, a psychic picked up a whore named Alice and she was allegedly hung from the rafters.

"The bitch deserved it," said the medium picking her up – obviously speaking the words of another spirit. Then without any warning, the medium began to cough and choke as he held his throat. He looked to be in quite some pain and it appeared that he was picking up on this poor woman's death by hanging. Groans and wheezing came from the "possessed" medium and in all honesty I did not know what to make of the situation, so I continued to observe and see what happened. After a while the medium came round and almost fell to the ground with what they call "spiritual drainage". He was tired and very weak from this ordeal.

Apart from the medium allegedly suffering this lady's fate by being slowly choked by an invisible rope, nothing much else happened. Nothing you could hang your hat on anyway. I then decided to venture out in the main hall area and sit in the dark, silent and foreboding atmosphere to see if anything paranormal would occur. Although I did hear one or two strange knocks and bumps emanating from within the room, I surmised it was the wooden floorboards settling down and thus came to my own decision that nothing paranormal was occurring at this time. I then went and sat in the bedroom on my own for 20 minutes while the teams swapped over their positions. Nothing paranormal occurred.

Another break then took place followed by more vigils. In my group we continued to investigate the upstairs area of the old hall, and the other group of investigators went back down stairs to the great hall, kitchens and panelled room.

Our group's investigations proved rather dull with nothing at all happening in the way of paranormal activity. However the other group's investigations told quite a different story indeed. I was informed of what went on after the first of a few séances were held in this location. This is what I was informed of by Drew Bartley, a very reliable witness that up to this point in his life was a total sceptic:

Can I just say that we had two séances and we got responses to every question with loud bangs in that corner of the room (referring to the corner where the spinning wheel is). The trigger objects moved twice and there was a shadow moving across the wall and it was seen by all of us. I got touched, and two other investigators also got touched, when we tried it again she [the spirit] came back again and we could all hear her moving around the room and we know everyone was accounted for and in their place. We could hear something in and around the room by footsteps upon the creaking floorboards. The vase in the middle of the table in which we had the circle actually moved and we all heard it slide across the table. I am a very sceptical investigator, but something was definitely happening in there.

I was also informed that Drew Bartley and another investigator, (between the two séances that were held in this duration of time), heard movement from within the empty Panelled Room whilst they were in the kitchen area of the hall. They had both heard knocks, bumps, the shuffling of feet, and a sigh or a breath emanating from within the empty room.

Of course they decided to look in to the room and see what was happening. When they ran in they both saw something move across the room as they entered it. They described this to me as a four to five foot tall shimmering grey mist. This materialisation then drifted across the room and disappeared through the oak panelled walls. Both investigators were clearly surprised by this 'grey mist sighting' and both came across as very excited. In all honesty they were ecstatic about the whole experience.

The investigators then decided a third séance should be held and this time I was in attendance. If anything else would happen, at least I could see if for myself and personally verify something odd was definitely going on. We began the séance and in the circle were the other witnesses to the good phenomena that had previously been reported. This attempt at spirit communication proved to be quite worthwhile but according to Drew, it was nowhere near as active as before. This third séance provided more activity with investigators being touched and tickled. All the members of the group heard knocks coming from within the room and I *thought* I saw a figure standing behind a circle member during the proceedings. When I mentioned this the medium leading the séance confirmed there was someone there in the corner of the room. Had I actually seen the ghost of Washington Old Hall? I was then informed this is area was where a lot of the anomalous noises came from earlier on in the previous séance, a very interesting result, wouldn't you agree?

So, what can we say? What a climax to a night that had started off rather slowly to say the least. For me on a personal level, it ended on a quite a high with fantastic results. Had we really made contact with the ghost of the old hall? And if so, was it the Grey Lady that is believed to walk the upper floors? Drew certainly seems to think so. If true, it would indicate to me that the Grey Lady must be able to move around the place as an *active* spirit and is not a place memory or residual ghost as most people think. If it was not the Grey Lady of the old hall, more than one ghost must indeed haunt this magnificent old building. Either way we have learned at least one thing about the ghost or ghosts of Washington Old Hall.

CHAPTER TWENTY-SEVEN

CASE STUDY

THE GRANGE – HURWORTH-ON-TEES

The Grange at Hurworth is situated in Hurworth-on-Tees on the County Durham and North Yorkshire borders and was once used as a beautiful Victorian mansion for the Backhouse family. The building work was finished in 1875 by the famous architect Alfred Waterhouse on the site of the former Hurworth cottage. It was built as a wedding present for the nephew of Alfred Backhouse, James Edward Backhouse when he married Elizabeth Barclay Fowler in 1873. They had fourteen children and when James died in October 1897, he left the house to his eldest son, Edward.

Around 1912 the occupation of the Backhouse family came to an end and as far as records can show between 1912 and the 1950s the house was occupied by two more families, the Rogerson family and the Spielman family. In 1955 the Grange was once again put on the market and was subsequently purchased by the Reverend William Donnegan and the Hospitaller Order of Saint John of God. The nearby Holy Family School of Saint John of God was relocated into the Grange and was used as a school for boys for those wishing to become Hospitaller Brothers.

In 1967 the brothers decided to sell the Grange and close down the school. It was then bought by Durham County Council in 1968 who in turn gave the property to Hurworth Church Parish Council, and on the 20 September 1969 opened this former beautiful stately home as a community centre, which is still being used today by the locals and the community of Hurworth-on-Tees.

Over the years the Grange has reputedly been subject to paranormal activity and phantoms and spectres are often seen wondering aimlessly along the corridors and then suddenly disappearing. Doors are said to open and close on their own, and often cold spots and unexplained temperature drops have been reported, giving the Grange a reputation with the locals as a very haunted building.

Invited along as a guest of the API team, myself and Glenn Hall of the North East Ghost Research Team joined other guest investigators and API founders Colin and Cindy Nunn for a night's investigation into these strange goings on. Upon arrival at the Grange at 7 p.m. on a nice summer's night I found myself being drawn to the stairwell (without any prior knowledge) and correctly identified the area where one of the Grange's many ghosts walk. A photograph had been taken on this staircase on a previous API investigation by Colin Nunn, of a ghostly pair of legs. On the next exposure taken they were gone. Somehow I knew this was the area where the ghost had been seen, and where the mysterious photograph had been taken.

I was then asked what my initial impressions of the building were, and immediately I said the place has feel of "the cloth" and mentioned it had a church connection to it. Again at this point I had no idea about the association with the Hospitaller Order of Saint John of God! A tour of the building prior to the investigation proved very interesting for me too as I also sensed an oppressive atmosphere in an area which has known reported paranormal activity. I felt unwell and dizzy and I had to leave the area. After the investigation I was informed that in that area, some despicable acts of cruelty and abuse were carried out. Due to the nature of this disgusting behaviour I will refrain from going into any detail. Never, had an investigation venue spoken to me in this way before so I can only surmise that the spiritual energies (either active or residual) contained and held within the walls of this beautiful Victorian building must indeed be very strong.

At 10 p.m. we split into our respective groups for the investigation and our group headed up to the top of the building and investigated the upper levels. As we were getting settled into the vigil we all heard three distinct loud bangs in quick succession and we were all at a loss as to what they were and where they came from. Various light anomalies were caught on video camera throughout and some serious temperature fluctuations were also recorded. Furthermore, there were the sudden gushes and draughts of ice-cold air which we all felt during the course of the investigation and upon inspecting all the doors and windows in the vicinity, we found them all to be closed. So what could have caused this phenomena that none of us could explain?

I spilt from the group to spend some time alone to get to know the place. The temperature was a steady 16.5 degrees in the corridor and an EMF sweep showed no particular anomalies at that stage. I did not stay apart from the rest of the group for long, as 5 minutes into my solo efforts I distinctly heard three sighs or breaths with a two second gap between them, and they came from right behind me in the corridor. The rest of the group were in a room along the corridor so that discounted them. I quickly rejoined the group and reported my findings. By now it was nearly time for our first break in the investigation and while we were getting our equipment together we all heard a thunderous succession of banging as though someone had fallen down a flight of stairs. In all honesty it scared us half to death but inspection found no cause. There was nothing out of place that could have made the noise. We were the only ones in that wing of the building so I conclude whatever it was could well have paranormal origin.

Location two found our team in the main entrance hall and stairwell to this wonderful Victorian abode. After only 5 to 10 minutes the video camera that was left running during the investigation turned itself off, something that really shouldn't have happened. This happened three more times during the course of the second vigil. Was there something in there with us that did not want us to be filming? This seemed to be the case after realising the camera worked just fine when we took it to another location, eliminating the notion that the camera was at fault.

I took vigil at the bottom of the stairwell in the entrance hall hoping the ghost of the lady frequently seen there would put in an appearance. She did not but I did photograph one or two light anomalies with my digital still. I then took a number of time-lapse shots with my Nikon SLR in the hope that I might catch a ghost or spectre on film.

During our next break Cindy Nunn and another investigator headed up to the second level to retrieve some equipment and they made a hasty return after both claiming to see a figure walk past a frosted glass door, which turned and looked at them. I know that no one else was up there as everyone was in the break room with myself. However, unfortunately no hard evidence such as a photograph was acquired, which just leaves the testimony of the two witnesses, and judging by the speed and the noise they made while thundering back down the stairwell and the honesty and integrity these people have, I think they did indeed see a ghost or a figure that could not be explained behind the glass door.

Now it was our turn to investigate the very area where the figure behind the glass door was seen. (Incidentally, this is the exact area that I had to leave earlier on before the investigation began due to the oppressive feel to it). We made ourselves comfortable and listened, watched and observed.

In the presence of the North East Ghost Research team psychic we conducted a séance in what is now called the test room. This proved rather interesting in the way of phenomena, as the two girls who sat in felt unwell and hot, while the psychic (Glenn Hall) felt nothing at all. I however must have been having another one of my moments so to speak as I came up with the names Edward James Thomas, and described him as a priest with grey wavy hair and a thick black moustache. There is indeed an Edward James relating to the history and of course there is a link to the church, so wouldn't it be amazing if there was a priest with grey hair and a black moustache? Other sounds were reported too during this séance including the sound of children's laughter and playing outside behind the Grange, which was heard by all present and on looking out the window no one could be seen. All the sitters heard various knocks and bumps.

Our last port of call was the cellars, reputedly haunted by a grey lady who is seen quite often by all accounts. However apart from light anomalies caught on video camera, and a single footstep heard by Glenn, it seemed she did not want to put in an appearance for us tonight. Then, we thought we were rewarded with a good result. A night vision video camera was recording while we were all in the cellar area and it picked up what sounded like an evil, demonic voice of a man saying "no". The EVP recording was only discovered after the investigation and it sends shivers down your spine. However, Cindy and Colin reviewed the footage after the investigation, and they realised it was the sound of Colin's voice saying 'Woah'. Woah, for those who don't know, is an expression of surprise similar to 'wow' and sounds like the word 'no'. It appears at the same time Colin caught a light anomaly, which surprised him while he was filming. His reaction was caught on another video camera and subsequently was regarded as paranormal activity.

One has to be so careful when examining buildings and investigating haunted properties for evidence of ghosts or paranormal phenomena. Misinterpretation of the data can so easily happen as you have just seen and one wonders how many investigation 'units' or 'ghost busting teams' out there misinterpret their data. This ultimately results in the teams advising the property owners that their premises are well and truly haunted when in actual fact they are not!

Anyway – the cellar most definitely warrants further investigation. All in all though, I feel a fine investigation was had by everyone present and we investigated the building from top to bottom with some very good evidence recorded and documented. My sincere thanks go to Colin and Cindy Nunn for giving us the opportunity to investigate this former Victorian stately home and I look forward to making a return in the hope one day, we do catch a ghost on film.

CHAPTER TWENTY-EIGHT

CASE STUDY

THE GRANGE – HURWORTH-ON-TEES REVISITED

After a gap of almost two years I approached Cindy and Colin Nunn from API (Anomalous Phenomena Investigations) and asked if the North East Ghost Research Team could return to Hurworth-on-Tees to re-investigate the Grange. After a few days Cindy contacted me and told me that the investigation could go ahead. Although Cindy and Colin would attend, the North East Ghost Research Team would be left to our own devices and we would run the investigation for ourselves.

You would have read in the previous chapter about our first investigation there – which was quite interesting – so there is no need for me to mention or discuss any of the history or alleged ghosts in this particular chapter as by now you should all be well versed with it. What I will specify is that in this chapter there is a reading from team psychic Glenn Hall who, as you would have read, attended the investigation almost two years ago with us. Care has been taken to evaluate what Glenn sensed, and picked up on, due to the fact he has indeed been there once before and could have remembered (consciously or sub-consciously) some of the details and facts that relate to the last investigation, and indeed, the Grange itself. Anything that came up again during the reading was automatically disregarded as evidence for obvious reasons.

On the night in question we arrived at the location at about 8.30 p.m. and immediately went about taking pictures of the building's exterior. It was a lovely summer's night and after a baking hot day it was nice to have the air cool down in the evening. Since our last visit, there had been a few changes too. I noticed that a huge copse of trees and bushes had been removed from next to the car park revealing more of the Grange and making an all round better photograph. We were also informed that the chapel area, along with the attic rooms were out of bounds as work was being carried out. This, although unfortunate, was not too bad as there were a few locations and rooms that were open to investigation that were not open for us on our previous visit. These rooms, of course, had been investigated and monitored by API – with some positive results, and as usual all these results were kept from us until *after* our latest investigation. However, API had not had these new rooms read by a practising psychic so it would be interesting to see what Glenn would pick up on and see if it correlated with the API results.

This is another positive angle to hit the investigation from as not only do we explore the building and its ghosts, but also I get a chance to investigate and scrutinise the team psychics and see just how good they claim to be. And in most cases they are very good indeed! It is always a good feeling to know that the information they have received (for want of a better word) was not known to them prior to the investigation, and in this case, with these particular rooms that we had not previously investigated there was no chance of cheating or prior research as details had not been made public. Only Cindy, Colin, and API knew and they weren't saying a word!

I have to admit that when I ventured into the building on this occasion, it did not speak to me like it did on my first instance here. If the reader can recall, on my initial visit I sensed and picked up on information that I knew nothing about. I sensed the lady on the stairwell, and at one point I had to leave the building as I was so affected by strange feelings that I had experienced in one of the locations where bad things had indeed occurred! This time around the building seemed calm, serene, happy even.

At 9.30 p.m. we decided we should have a walk around the building and familiarise ourselves with the layout. It had been almost two years since our last visit and three of the new look team had not been at all so I thought this was for the best. After the tour it was time to set up any experiments and conduct our baseline survey, which went rather well with the average temperatures reading between 15 and 19 degrees. Nothing paranormal there. The EMF tests also showed no anomalous readings and all squeaky floorboards, draughty corridors and windows, and other normal occurrences that are often mistaken for paranormal activity were noted down for the record.

During these baseline tests we placed down various trigger objects or interaction experiments in the hope we would get good results. A crucifix was placed down in what we called the 'green room', my beam barriers/motion sensors were placed on the main entrance stairwell where the White Lady has been seen to walk, a flour tray was placed down with objects in one of the rooms that we had not investigated before, namely the changing room, and a bell was drawn around and placed in another location which had also not been investigated – the Hadwin Lounge.

Cindy had decided she would join us on our night vigils, whilst Colin would monitor the CCTV system he had set up. He planned to sit in our base room when his cameras were trained on the main stairwell and view the images through the laptop computer. This area is where the ghost lady has been seen, and is also where Colin took an anomalous photograph of what looks like a pair of legs!

That said, it was now time to push on with the investigation and we began the evening's examination with a reading from Glenn Hall. We began in the Hadwin Lounge at 11 p.m. Straight away Glenn picked up on what he called a 'French connection' to the building – and got a female presence – and then told us that the games poker, billiards, and bridge came to mind as though this room was once a games room. Cindy, who also joined us on the reading, was not too sure about the games room but clarifies that there is indeed a French connection to the grange.

He then sensed that a wedding had taken place around the time the building was being built. It turns out that when James Edward Backhouse married Elizabeth Barclay Fowler back in 1873, the house was built for them as a wedding present. At 11.10 p.m. we moved on to the first floor landing just outside the chapel area. Glenn then asked who had seen the shadow or human shape that had moved past the frosted glass window that is in the door at the end of the corridor, as he felt this phenomenon had been witnessed. It was Cindy and another investigator who saw this figure on our first investigation, knowing for a fact that this area was locked off and no one was in there.

Glenn was on the first investigation and knew about this occurrence so, technically, this section of the reading should be discarded. I am not saying Glenn remembered this from our first visit and brought it back up in the hope we would have forgot about it although that is possible. I think he may have had it stored subconsciously in his mind, and seeing that same doorway and corridor triggered his mind to give that impression, so to him, it *felt like* a psychic impression.

"Ah!" I hear you cry. "So does this mean *all* psychic's impressions are really suppressed memories from previous visits to places and seeing certain areas and locations again essentially triggers what the psychic perceives as alleged impressions?"

Well, in my opinion and to answer that in one word, no! And why? Simply because some psychics have been known to pick up on incredible information at locations they have never visited nor have they read, learned or studied prior to their first visit, Glenn being one of the few I have met to do this. This theory, granted, could account for *some* impressions relayed by the medium, but not all of them. Glenn then told us that he had picked up on two people, a maid and a janitor. He got the names 'James' and 'Blackie' and told us that Blackie might be a nickname. Suddenly he got a feeling of claustrophobia and felt he was surrounded by hundreds of people. He then said the building at one time may have been used for refuge after a river bank had burst and had flooded the local area.

Cindy then astounded us all by confirming exactly what Glenn had picked up. In the mid-1800s a river did indeed break its banks and the Grange was used for

refuge. At 11.15 p.m. we ventured into the two rooms that we had not investigated on previous investigations there, and they were the changing rooms. Whilst
sitting in there we were all surprised – and rather happy – to hear a footfall or two
emanating from along the empty corridor. Furthermore, these footfalls, or shuf-
fles, were accompanied by what we all described as a breath or air as it is being
exhaled from the lungs – then, to our delight, the lights flickered in the room. It
seemed someone was making himself or herself known to us – and we all experienced it. To top it off, a black cat was sensed and once more Cindy confirms that a
ghostly black cat has been seen on occasions in the main body of the building.

At 11.25 p.m. we moved along the corridor and continued the reading in the
green room. This is the room where the séance was held on our first investigation
here and it turned out to be rather interesting, as you will have already seen by
reading the previous chapter. Two youngsters of the same age were picked up but
they were not twins. They were in their early teens and were, by all accounts, quite
religious. Glenn got the word Catholicism and got the impression of a school. The
French connection that was mentioned earlier on in the Hadwin Lounge came
back with a vengeance as he then asked who John was; Glenn was now anxious to
know exactly what the French link was – if any.

Cindy was compelled to explain that the building at one time was used and
owned by the 'Saint John of God', which originated in France, and was a catholic
seminary for boys. Pretty interesting stuff to say the least. We then moved through
the door (which was the door that figure had been seen through) and along the
long corridor to the top of the main stairwell. At this point our medium began
to feel dizzy and disorientated and took a few minutes to compose himself. He
then, as I completely expected, sensed a mature, but stubborn, 'stuck in her ways',
woman who has been seen on the stairwell. This comes as no surprise to me as the
medium is very good indeed.

At 11.55 p.m. we entered the main room on the ground level and Glenn sensed
the room had a military or soldier feel to it. We later found out from Cindy, that
in the early 1940s, British Army soldiers were based here during the Second World
War. That was all Glenn managed to pick up at that moment in time so we finished
off the reading in the cellars that lie underneath this magnificent old Victorian
mansion.

Glenn didn't pick up much in the way of information but did get one or two
impressions. He sensed a coal fire burning and activity around it – but couldn't tell
us where exactly it was. Cindy confirmed the use of a coal fire along with a storage
area for coal. He also picked up a brawl in the passageway area involving a man
in his forties and a teenage lad. No one knows who this could have been. Despite
these few impressions one or two anomalous happenings did occur down there
during the reading. During the proceedings a knock or thump was heard coming
from along the corridor, which no one could explain, and Claire Smith complained
that her face was burning up one side. After checking, it was discovered there was

an eight degree difference in temperature on one side of her face in comparison to the other. Paranormal or not, who can say? But it was an odd occurrence nonetheless.

After the reading had finished we returned to our base room for a short break before we split into our respective teams and began the investigation. Darren Olley, Glenn Hall and I began our investigation in the Hadwin Lounge, while Julie Olley, Claire Smith, Mark Winter and Cindy Nunn began in the changing rooms – it was 1 a.m. These two locations had not been investigated by our team before and we thought the vigils may prove interesting – our vigil yielded no results but the other group's findings were not that bad.

Cindy called out to the atmosphere and was rewarded with what sounded like shuffling or footfalls in the hallway – just like we had experienced earlier on in the reading. Again, all investigators present heard and verified them. When Cindy asked if whoever it was making the noises, would do it again only louder, they were all astounded to hear definite footfalls along the corridor. No one was there. It was then asked if the spirit present was a member of the Backhouse family and another noise was heard in the form of even more footfalls. This noise was heard by only two investigators, Mark and Cindy.

Then, at this point a light anomaly was seen via night vision camera but the experient, Mark, thought it could be dust. At 1.30 a.m. the team called out once more and reported that the area felt colder than it was originally. Had a sprit presence entered the room? Or had the temperature naturally fallen? I guess we will never know for sure.

It was at this point in the investigation when Colin and Cindy had to leave due to other commitments the following day. This meant we had the run of the Grange. While packing up their equipment from the base room the light suddenly went out and wouldn't come back on – well not for a while anyway, then it went out again. Normally you would think (as I did) that the bulb or the electrics were at fault but this was not the case. Apparently it had happened before on Cindy's other investigations and tests had proved the bulbs, and the electricity were not at fault. So another strange occurrence – I am not saying it was ghostly, but it was very odd nonetheless.

We continued the investigation with our group spending time in the changing rooms and the rest went to the Hadwin Lounge and the main stairwell. Oddly enough, it was all quiet in the Hadwin Lounge and the top of stairwell as it was for us, yet the activity in the changing rooms seemed to be rather consistent. Glenn Hall and I both heard the sound of a door creak and click closed while standing at the top of the stairs, just along from the changing room area. No one else was down stairs at this point as we took a good look, and the other team were along the corridor on the same level as us. So that one remains unexplained. A few more knocks, bumps and bangs (as if someone was through in the green room moving about), made this vigil worthwhile but we were no closer to determining who the alleged spirit could have been and why they were there, with us, in the first place.

Other vigils included long and quiet stints in the cellars, the main stairwell, the large room on the ground floor, and the base room but to no avail. Still that is the nature of ghost hunting. Sound recordings were unsuccessful too, as were the lock off video cameras and trigger objects. Still, the earlier investigations proved rather fruitful with some odd phenomena documented. It just remains to be said that overall the investigation was rather quiet but not entirely a 'write off' and our thanks go to Colin and Cindy from API for giving us the chance to re-investigate this magnificent old house.

CHAPTER TWENTY-NINE

MORE JAUNTS TO OTHER HAUNTS

During my travels throughout the United Kingdom I have been fortunate enough to be able to stay overnight and investigate some very haunted sites; some well known, some not so well known. I consider myself very lucky for I have travelled around Britain seeking out these ghost tales and visiting so many wonderful places and spoken to so many wonderful people, which I have included so far in this volume.

You have just read about the cities and locations I have travelled to in search of ghosts in the chapters presented herein but alas, there is more. I have covered a whole lot more of this wonderful isle on my quest and a lot of the places I have visited do not warrant a chapter for themselves. So I have decided to include some of these haunted places and locales in another chapter briefly detailing a number of the other venues I have visited during my years of ghost hunting and research.

BELFAST, NORTHERN IRELAND

On a trip to Northern Ireland a year or two back I was fortunate enough to visit one or two of the fantastic haunted areas located in Belfast city centre. Since we only had a short afternoon in Belfast I was only able to visit a couple of the allegedly haunted areas. We were due to catch a bus later in the afternoon, and head off through the beautiful County that is Antrim, and up the north-east coast of Northern Ireland to Londonderry. It was here at Londonderry where we stayed for a couple of nights. I was fighting in the world master's judo tournament that was being held here and this was my main reason for visiting. However I had other plans too, as I wanted to at least try to fit in a visit or two to some haunted locations while I was in Northern Ireland.

In Belfast, prior to heading off for our bus trip I managed to find a local haunted area, which is quite famous for its ghost. We were fortunate to be in the area of Vicarage Street and I had remembered from past research and other ghost books that a woman haunted this area and was said to have been seen on numerous occasions by lots of credible witnesses. This ghost woman is said to haunt the area and has been seen walking around the vicinity, some times during the day and other times at night, with a pack of cigarettes in one hand and a cup of tea, or coffee in the other. No one knows who she is or why she remains there.

Another fascinating story is of the ghost of the old linen mill. Helena Blunden allegedly haunts this location after falling down a flight of stairs resulting in her death in 1912. She was only 16 years old when she met her untimely death and some say she is still seen wondering around the old linen mill. Some say her footsteps can be heard echoing around the old derelict rooms and some even claim to have recorded her ghost on a webcam! However some parts of this story are also claimed to be false. The truth, it seems, has been integrated with fantasy to create a bigger mystery than the one that already existed. True reports of ghostly activity have indeed been reported in the old mill, but the ghost of Helena Blunden is thought to be made up. Why anyone would create this lie and purposely deceive the public is beyond me, but it leaves behind one of the most famous ghosts tales of Northern Ireland.

Onwards to Londonderry via a very long bus ride through Co Antrim passing places such as Mussenden Temple Library where a patch of blood is said to appear and then disappear only a few minutes later, and Ballygally Castle right in the northeast corner of Ireland, which was built in 1625 and is haunted by Lady Isobel Shaw. We arrived in Londonderry (eventually) and made our way to our hotel. Most of this weekend was taken up with my judo commitments so I will leave this section as it is, as I couldn't really explore this wonderfully haunted place properly. One day I will inevitably return to finish off what I have began in Northern Ireland.

TATTERSHALL CASTLE, LINCOLNSHIRE

Tattershall Castle is located in Tattershall near Sleaford in Lincolnshire and was built in 1434 on the site of a much older fortress. It is a magnificent 100 foot towering edifice and has six floors for visitors to explore. I visited Tattershall a while back and was simply in awe of the place and how well preserved the tower actually is. It also helps to be in shape if you visit Tattershall, as there are many stone stairs to climb in order to see all levels of the wonderful old building. By the time you reach the top you could well be out of breath!

It is cared for by the National Trust and when chatting with the guide during my visit I asked about any resident ghosts the castle may have and was informed that odd occurrences do happen on occasion such as the sudden sense of presence often being felt although no one else is around. Footfalls shuffling up the stone stairwells have been heard, again, when no one is there to account for them, and the ghost of a lady wearing medieval style clothing has been seen drifting down the stairwell. No one knows who she is or why she may haunt the place.

SIZERGH CASTLE, NEAR KENDALL, CUMBRIA

I spent the day at Sizergh Castle during some time away in the Lake District a few years ago. It was built in the fourteenth century as a stronghold and its walls are 9 feet thick. It is home to the Strickland family and has been for nearly 800 years. The great hall was added to this magnificent castle in 1450 and in 1770 it was enlarged and redecorated in Georgian style. Part of the great hall now, is the present day visitor's entrance. The National Trust looks after it and it was a total joy to visit the castle and its wonderful gardens.

On enquiring about any resident ghosts I was informed there is indeed a ghost legend that tells the story of a jealous husband who locked his wife up in one of the rooms in the castle, subsequently starving her to death. It is her tormented ghost that is heard screaming from time to time.

CALGARTH HALL, WINDERMERE, CUMBRIA

During some time on a trip away to Lake Windermere, I stayed in a bed and break-fast that overlooked the lake and commanded spectacular views of the distant Lakeland fells. Windermere is a beauty spot and tourist attraction that is second to none and although it appears to be serene, tranquil, and a place of calm, there are a number of reported 'paranormal' goings on that would send chills down the spines of the most hardened sceptics. Out of many stories I was told during my stay here, there is one that I would like to tell you now, and that is of the cursed skulls of Calgarth Hall.

Calgarth Hall stands on the shores of Lake Windermere and is one of the oldest known buildings in Windermere. It is said that this manor is cursed by what is known as 'The Calgarth Skulls'. After an alleged theft of silver cutlery at the manor house many years ago it is said that the accused, a man and his wife called Kraster and Dorothy Cook upon their arrest, pointed to Myles Philipson, the owner of the manor house and cursed him for framing them. They knew Philipson wanted the land the Cook's owned for his greedy self and thus plotted against them to rid them out of the way. The Cooks threatened to haunt Philipson to the end of his days in revenge for his brutal act and selfishness.

It was not long after the Cooks were hanged when two skulls were found in the premises of Calgarth Hall. They had eyeless sockets and both skulls were baring evil grins. Philipson was horrified and ordered these skulls to be destroyed, but to no avail as the skulls were found back in the house after being destroyed time and time again. The hall, night after night, was then disturbed by howls, shrieks and terrible screams. Philipson knew the Cooks had indeed come back to haunt him with a vengeance, and they did so for many years after. The skulls remained in Calgarth Hall, staring at Philipson with their evil grins every time he walked past and never again did he get a good night's rest. It was a reminder of the evil deed he so unjustly carried out – until his dying day. A guide on the Windermere cruise relayed this great tale to me as we sailed past and viewed Calgarth Hall from the lake.

FOUNTAIN'S ABBEY, RIPON, NORTH YORKSHIRE

I have visited Fountain's Abbey on many occasions now and I never get tired or bored of meandering through the magnificent ruined stone shell, which is one of the finest and largest examples of a ruined monastic abbey in the whole of the UK. It is situated at the bottom of a wooded valley and stands next to the river Skell. This 822-acre beauty spot, of which the abbey is the main attraction, also has over 10 other historic buildings and is festooned with chic ornamental lakes, a wonderful deer park, and many other fabulous attractions well worth exploring.

But it is the abbey itself I wish to talk about, and many a time I have sauntered through these magnificent ruins and cloisters of this ancient monastic building, (which was incidentally founded in 1132 by 13 Benedictine monks who later became part of the Cistercian order) and wondered if some of those monks still reside here in spirit.

One would expect that there may be if first impressions are to go by as it certainly looks like the stereotypical haunted locale with long passageways and dark corners where any resident ghosts could almost certainly be lurking. As you leave one area and walk into the next you can't help but wonder who, or what may be waiting for you as you step into the next stone room. I have heard that on occasion, dark hooded figures have indeed been seen lingering around the place along with the faint sound of a male choir that is thought to be chanting monks being heard from time to time.

My last visit was in autumn a few years ago and I saw the abbey and the other attractions in the park, lit up with floodlights on a splendid, but dark evening's drive through. It was an unforgettable experience.

Whitby Abbey, North Yorkshire Coast

Whitby Abbey stands perched on the cliff tops overlooking the old wonderful haunted whaling town of Whitby. It is associated with Bram Stokers *Dracula* and those brave enough (or fit enough) to venture up the 199 stone stairs to the top will be rewarded with glorious views of the little old town beneath their feet, and of course the splendid ruin that is the abbey itself. The abbey was founded sometime between AD 650 and 660 on the site of what some people believe to be a Roman building and of course is famous for the formidable 'St Hilda' who was a Northumbrian princess. She too, has become part of the legend and folklore in her own right at Whitby, as it is said that she ridded the town of snakes by severing their heads with a magical and mysterious whip! More common legends, however, concern the ghosts that are said to haunt the old abbey.

St Hilda herself is said to be one of the resident spectres that is seen in one of the upper windows of the ruin, wrapped in a shroud. Another more famous apparition is that of a phantom hearse style coach and horses that is seen and heard thundering across the graveyard, complete with coffin, before tumbling over the cliffs into the ice-cold North Sea. It is driven by a headless driver, and the four horses that pull it along are also reported to be headless. The ghost of another woman is also said to haunt the Abbey. Believed to be a former nun who broke her vows she was subsequently bricked up alive in the dungeons at Whitby. Her ghost has allegedly been seen pleading for mercy on a stone flight of stairs that once led to the dungeons.

Colchester Castle – Essex

I visited Colchester Castle as part of, and during my weekend visit to Borley in Essex. It is a magnificent example of a Norman castle and was built in the same style as the 'white tower' at the Tower of London. The castle is now a grade one listed building and many an edifice has been previously built upon this site. William the Conqueror built a fort here and when Colchester was the first capital of Roman Britain, the temple of Claudius stood on this spot.

On the day we visited, it was blisteringly hot and the sky was a beautiful dark blue and from the outside of the castle it seemed so hospitable. Yet as you enter through the main gateway into the castle grounds a sudden chill comes over you and you don't feel so welcome anymore. It is not surprising when you find out that the castle was once used as a prison and held witches, heretics, and all sorts of low life. Death and torture took place there and was truly a place of torment and anguish. For the last 150 years or so the castle has housed a terrific museum and of course they have a ghost.

A guide informed me that their ghost is quite a famous one. It is a sad tale but very typical of traditional ghost lore. Legend has it that in the 1600s, a prisoner and Quaker martyr called James Parnell was forced to endure very physically demanding and tough tasks so that he could eat. He is said to have fallen to his death during one of these tasks and is said to haunt the dungeons in which he was held captive. His groans of torment are still said to be heard on occasion to this day.

SWANTON MORLEY VILLAGE – NORFOLK

Swanton Morley is a beautiful little Norfolk village about 12 miles from the market town of Swaffham, which is featured earlier in this book. On my second visit to Norfolk, I stayed nearby Swanton Morley at the 'Robertson Army barracks' home of the light dragoons, which at one time was an RAF base. The village lies half a mile down the country lane and has a wonderful church named 'All Saints Church', two public houses (Darby's and The Angel Inn), a village hall and some wonderful old historic looking buildings, one of which caught my eye and looked like a deserted rectory or old church hall. I wasn't in town long enough to do some real nosing around but I did get a chance to quickly chat with one or two of the locals and follow up with some research.

It is alleged that one of the former RAF servicemen that was based at what is now the army barracks, has been seen on a number of occasions dressed in full 1940s uniform around the village of Swanton Morley. He then, I was told, disappears without a trace. No one knows who he is. Another wonderful ghost story concerns an alleged phantom plane with engines that are heard, but not seen, chugging overhead above the trees and fields as though whatever is in the air is in trouble. The noises, no sooner do they begin, cease, leaving those who heard them wondering what on earth it was. Although this is an interesting ghost story one wonders if there is anything that may back up an old potential wartime plane crash in this area. This may account for any phantom plane engines one might hear when in this area. Having said that, haven't all RAF bases got their resident ghost planes and phantom airmen?

TYNEDALE FARM, PENDLE HILL, LANCASHIRE

This ruined and disused shell of an old farmhouse stands in the shadow of Pendle Hill in the Lancashire countryside. I visited the site on my way to another investigation that I was undertaking in the north-west area. Tyndale Farm has become world famous after Living TV's *Most Haunted* team carried out a live investigation at Pendle Hill on Halloween 2004 and a terrifying night was had by all. But before *Most Haunted* was there to investigate, ghosts and apparitions seemed to centre on this farmhouse that was built in around the mid-1700s.

An apparition of a monk has been seen around the area of the farm and a hooded figure has been seen kneeling on the lonely desolate dirt road that leads to the farmhouse. People have often reported strange occurrences and heard strange noises and laughter from inside the empty farmhouse and it was believed to be the ghosts of the Pendle witches.

To this day descendants of the Nutter family (who played a large part in the pendle witch trials) own Tynedale Farm and it was allegedly used as the Pendle witch's coven. From here, the Pendle witchcraft murders stemmed, which led to the famous trials and consequent deaths of 17 people due to the alleged evil witchcraft in the Pendle area. Ten of the witches including Alison Device, Elizabeth Device, Anne Whittle or 'Chattox' as she was known, and Alice Nutter were hanged at Lancaster castle on 20 August 1612 for their part in these murders and after confessing to witchcraft. The Pendle witch trial is the most famous witch trial ever held in English history.

INVERLOCHY CASTLE AND HOTEL, FORT WILLIAM, SCOTLAND

Many years ago I visited this wonderful castle that sits nicely at the base of Ben Nevis on the west coast of Scotland. The original thirteenth century castle is now a ruin but the hotel that now stands on this land (Inverlochy Hotel) was built in 1863 by the first Lord Abinger and was used as a private residence until 1969 when it was transformed into one of Scotland's luxurious hostelries. I have visited Scotland many times as a child on family holidays, and as an adult for one reason or another, and I have to say with all honesty that this area is one of the most beautiful areas of Scotland I have ever seen. The backdrop that is Ben Nevis literally blows you away. Queen Victoria once said "I have never seen a lovelier or more romantic spot" and I must say I have to agree with her.

In regards to the ghosts here, well, if I have to be honest there doesn't seem to be any reports of any hauntings whatsoever. So why have I included Inverlochy Castle and Hotel in this book? Well, I think the place speaks volumes, it is rich in history, it exudes magnificence and grandeur and one would think that there is indeed a ghost or two there. If there are no ghosts there (which I think is unlikely) I really think it deserves one, and a friendly one at that!

DOVER CASTLE, KENT

Dover Castle is situated on the south-east tip of the British Isles and I visited the castle many years ago on my way to Dieppe in France. We stopped off at the castle for a few hours before boarding the ferry and setting sail, leaving those wonderful white cliffs behind us. Inside those cliffs is a hidden world, a labyrinth and network of tunnels, which lead to and from Dover Castle. Some were dug as early as the Napoleonic wars and as they were built so well, and with such a high quality, they were used right up until the twentieth century. Many ghosts are said to walk these old passageways including phantom servicemen from the Second World War, complete with full uniform and they are as solid as you or I.

The castle itself is one of the largest castles in the country and is located on the shortest crossing point from the UK to mainland Europe and has seen action from the Iron Age to the Second World War, and to the present day. It is known, as the 'gateway to England' and is literally a time capsule, therefore it is not surprising that there are ghosts reputed to haunt there. It is alleged to have around six active spirits including the spectre of a woman who has been seen on the stairs in the keep, a phantom pair of legs has been seen in the King's bedroom, (a similar apparition to that of The Black Swan in York) there have been cold spots and doors opening and closing on their own around the castle, and of course there is the famous phantom headless drummer boy that is said to haunt the battlements. Killed for his large sum of money by two greedy soldiers that were stationed at the castle.

CHAPTER THIRTY

GHOST HUNTING TOOLS OF THE TRADE

Contrary to what most people think, on paranormal investigations and ghost hunts a ghost will not appear before your very eyes and walk straight through a wall unless you are very fortunate indeed. More often than not I return from an overnight investigation and acquaintances and colleagues will ask, "Well, did you see a ghost, then?" and the vast majority of the time I have to be honest and say no. Ghosts and spirits are not like trained dogs, and in that respect I mean they do not appear on demand, and they certainly do not jump through hoops just because you are there to see them. Ultimately we would all like to see the full-blown apparition or ghost, and even more so, we would like to capture its movements on video camera or 35mm camera film.

Other than that, there are some other tell-tale signs that shades of the other world are not too far away and it is these signs we try to record and document in order to at least gather some sort of viable evidence in the hope that one day, we can prove the existence of ghosts. A ghost hunter's kit can be as large or as small as one wishes. It can have simple, low-cost items contained within or it can have more expensive modern day hi-tech gadgets. Some people believe that the best tools of the trade are our five senses; sight, sound, taste, touch and smell but one must bear in mind that although a lot of people do indeed use nothing but their senses on investigations, it has to be noted that this psychic testimony carries little or no weight whatsoever in regards to scientific and objective evidence which is ultimately, what we are all seeking. I prefer to use both scientific methodologies as well as using psychics testimonies too. They can indeed go hand in hand.

In regards to using the hi-tech gadgetry and our other tools of the trade it also must be specified that all the equipment outlined herein are used hypothetically in regards to finding ghosts. An EMF meter is not a ghost detector; beam barriers and motion sensors are not really meant to trip ghosts, and infra red night vision video cameras were not built to film ghostly forms in pitch-black rooms. Ghost detecting is all about monitoring the environment, as past experiences have told us that when a ghost is seen, or when a spirit manifests itself to us in some way, subtle environmental changes occur and it is these subtle changes in the environment that we monitor and document to help support the theory that ghosts may indeed walk among us.

During the course of an investigation we gather what objective evidence and scientific data we can in the form of room temperatures, humidity readings, the electromagnetic field analysis, sound recordings, ultrasound and infrasound readings and so on and so forth to see if any odd patterns emerge from the investigations. When patterns do emerge we then have some sort of viable scientific objective data to say at least something out of the ordinary or strange within the environment has occurred which can be labelled as 'anomalous'. In effect we are looking at, and recording the small details, building up a compilation of scientific data in an attempt to see or at least piece together the bigger picture. I will now outline some tools of the trade and explain the hypothetical reasons why they are used.

The Baseline Test

Prior to any of these techniques being applied on an investigation, a baseline test must be carried out on the venue, which is to be investigated. These tests will include temperature readings, along with EMF sweeps, so to determine the normal baseline readings of the rooms and locations.

Should any anomalies be traced and picked up on the investigation itself, we will have a detailed account and record of these readings to compare with so we can determine what is normal and what is paranormal. During a baseline test we also seek out creaky floorboards, draughty rooms and corridors, faulty doors, which may close on their own and other common, natural occurrences that are often mistaken for paranormal activity.

Notepad, Pen, and a Watch

These are probably the most important of an investigator's tools simply because we need to take a detailed and accurate account of any anomalies recorded and events witnessed throughout the duration of the investigation. In order to compile a thorough investigation report this is of the utmost importance. To note down the times of occurrences and events as and when they happen is much preferable to jotting down notes after the investigation at the risk of forgetting important details and even subconscious elaboration of the incidents in question.

TORCHES AND FLASHLIGHTS

Needless to say on overnight investigations whether they be indoors or outdoors, the environment we are investigating can sometimes be very dark indeed. As well as the health and safety issues that come with overnight paranormal investigations (as we need to be able to find our way around in the dark without hurting ourselves or others), we also need a torch or flashlight in order to compile our investigation notes. Unless you are using a dictation device it is always sensible to take two torches along on your vigil just in case something should go wrong with one. Spiritual battery drainage may zap one of your torches if something gets too close. At least you will have torch two to resort to, unless you lose the power in that one too! Failing that, snaplights are perfect for the job.

BATTERIES (AND SPARES)

This is where your spare batteries will come in handy. It is normally the case just as something interesting is about to happen you can guarantee you will lose power in your battery operated device ultimately diminishing your chances to capture some good evidence. Just about all the equipment we use on investigations take batteries and without them they are useless. You would be surprised how many investigators forget to bring spare batteries on investigations or even purposely not bring them thinking that they will get through the investigation without having to change them. Wrong! Batteries cost very little and having a handful in your pocket ready to change them when required could be the best thing you do on an investigation.

WALKIE-TALKIES OR A MOBILE PHONE

Communication devices such as your mobile phone or walkie-talkies are imperative on investigations for a number of reasons. First, health and safety issues. If you are investigating an area in which there are only two in the group and one of you takes a tumble and gets injured, walkie-talkies can be used to radio for first-aid without leaving the casualty on his or her own. I would recommend that if walkie-talkies or mobile phones are not available (which is unlikely) do not place less than three people in a unit to investigate. At least then one person can go for help while someone else can stay with the injured party.

     On an investigative note, walkie-talkies can prove invaluable in the respect that someone could be experiencing phenomena in one location (for example footsteps are being heard in an overhead passageway) and can subsequently radio other units to verify where everyone is. If everyone is in his or her respective vigil locations the rational explanation can be ruled out and other explanations can then be sought.

THE COMPASS

The compass is one of the easiest tools to use and can be acquired very cheaply, making it one of the best and most basic tools. The principal is simple. Ordinarily, the compass needle points north, so if a ghost or spirit is trying to manifest near you or in the same area you are located, it is likely the needle will go haywire simply because an external energy force or magnetic field is interfering with the magnetic field of your compass. You are in effect detecting another electric or electromagnetic field.

THE FLOUR TRAY

One of my favourite ghost hunting tools, simply because we have ascertained some of the best results with it. You cannot get any more basic than a large flat plastic tub filled with flour. Simply flatten the flour and place in it, objects of relevance to the alleged ghosts or spirits that are said to reside where you leave the tray. If the objects have been interacted with you should find the flour has been disturbed. It is the same principal as the trigger object and should be locked off in a controlled room in order to prevent trickery.

Having said that to mess about with the flour tray in order to fool people can leave you with egg on your face as the flour gets everywhere and it is not hard to determine who has been touching it simply because your clothes do indeed get covered. This has been determined while setting up the experiment in the first place. Some investigators use the same principal with the flour and place a light coating of flour on a surface such as a floor or a door handle to see if they can capture ghost footprints or handprints in the flour. It is a common method called 'dusting' which has had some amazing results.

INFRASOUND METERS

Infrasound is a noise on a frequency, which cannot be detected with the human ear and it has long been suggested it could be the cause for a lot of reports of paranormal activity. The study of these sounds is sometimes called infrasonics and it is believed that natural occurring events and phenomena such as avalanches, the ocean waves, volcanoes, earthquakes, and tornadoes to name a few could produce this low frequency sound. It has also been suggested that creatures such as whales, dolphins, elephants and alligators use the infrasound waves to communicate: even migrating birds are thought to use naturally generated infrasound as a means of navigation.

Since it is not consciously perceived, it is said that when humans are exposed to certain amounts of it, they may begin to feel nauseas, dizzy, uneasy and frightened for what they believe 'is for no apparent reason'. Indeed, past tests have shown that certain amounts of exposure to infrasound waves does increase levels of anxiety and fear (which is so often reported at haunted locations) giving the sceptics and the non-believers the ammunition to use against the theories that do support the idea of ghosts. They simply say that haunted houses and spooky places must be subject to infrasound

Having said that infrasound only effects humans in the way of feelings (nerves, fear etc) and it does not account for other classic phenomena, like moving furniture, which could be witnessed in these haunted locations. A device to detect infrasound waves would be invaluable on ghost investigations during a baseline reading simply because if infrasound was detected, and it was proven to heighten fear and anxiety, you could so easily monitor the location with audio and visual recording equipment and simply disregard the human testimony. If you catch a ghost on film, you cannot blame infrasound.

ELECTRO-MAGNETIC FIELD (EMF) METERS

These devices are used normally for measuring the natural electro-magnetic field emissions within houses, offices, etc. It is known that televisions, clock radios, refrigerators and other electrical appliances such as computers emit what are known as EMFs. If one is subjected to these EMFs over a long period of time it can prove fatal as research shows they can, in extreme cases, cause cancer. The EMF-meter was designed to detect how much actual EMF pollution these appliances give off and gives advice on where to put these appliances in the home so to create as little risk as possible from potential exposure.

It is believed by psychics and ghost hunters alike that when a ghost or spirit tries to move something (perhaps a bunch of keys or an item of furniture), or to materialise (show itself in its full ghostly form), it needs to draw energy from somewhere in order for this to be achieved. The electro-magnetic field is said to be the primary and most favourable choice and when this happens there is an alleged fluctuation or distortion within the natural electro-magnetic field.

On investigations we sometimes find perfectly good working cameras and torches suddenly go dead on us and it literally leaves us in the dark. When we leave the location the torch or camera somehow restores its power and works fine once more. Nevertheless brand new batteries are required as there may have been a total power loss. It is thought a close-by entity may be responsible for this and is commonly known as 'drainage'. The EMF meter is used to detect any anomalies within this electro magnetic field.

DIGITAL THERMOMETERS AND TEMPERATURE READING DEVICES

It is said that when a ghost or spectre is close by the surrounding air and atmosphere tends to go ice-cold. This is called a temperature drop and these thermometers and temperature-reading devices are used in order to trace and record these temperature anomalies.

NIGHT VISION VIDEO CAMERAS

Ghosts are said to be afraid of natural light but I do not believe this at all. Most ghost sightings tend to be when they are least expected and more often than not they are during the day. The theory goes that by using night vision video cameras / infra-red night vision cameras the device can pick up anomalies and see things the human eye cannot in these pitch-black vigil conditions. On our investigations they have proved quite invaluable and quite often we may record what is now known as an Electronic Voice Phenomenon (EVP).

DICTATION MACHINES AND EVP

A dictation machine is used in order to try and record voices from beyond or ghostly auditory phenomena. These are usually locked in a room where people have heard ghostly voices or experienced loud bumps, or knocks that cannot be explained by any natural means. As mentioned earlier with the video cameras these too can often pick up unexplained noises that are not normally heard at the time of recording. This modern day device is now known as an EVP recorder. An EVP recorder is a digital dictation machine and both electronic and audiocassette machines are used on investigations. They are also great for taking notes and it is a lot more preferable than jotting down scribbles on paper in the pitch darkness.

MOTION SENSORS AND BEAM BARRIERS

Motion sensors and beam barriers are used to detect motion in a locked-off room or passage where a ghost is alleged to walk. When beam barriers are placed down either side of a corridor or a stairwell an infra-red beam acts as a tripwire so to speak and if anyone or anything breaks the beam, an alarm is tripped thus indicating someone – or something – has maybe walked past. Motion sensors do more-or-less the same thing, only they cover more of the room and act like a room alarm – indeed, this is what they are! Like the beam barriers, if anything breaks the beam within the room an alarm will sound indicating this. The reason they are locked off is simply because the investigators have a good idea that nobody or anything of this world should be able to trip the beam. The same principle for sound recording can apply to the dictation machines, EVP and video-recording equipment too.

DIGITAL AND STANDARD 35MM CAMERAS

Both of these types of cameras are used on our investigations. Digital cameras are good in that you can view your photographs almost immediately and delete any unwanted photos from the memory card and save any decent photos one might acquire. The only downfall with digital photography is that the cameras are prone to pick up reflections of dust particles, which are often mistaken for orbs or light anomalies. With a normal 35mm camera the dust reflections are somewhat reduced to the point of non-existence, and any good photographs acquired on an investigation will have a negative. What is on the photo should be on the negative. The negative can then be examined.

It is sad but true that, with the use of digital photography and modern photographic software on computers, it is all to easy to fix, manipulate or fake good ghostly photos, and experts have not got anything to examine in order to prove authenticity – like a negative which a 35mm camera would have. Although I do use a digital camera on investigations, I prefer to use my 35mm Nikon SLR in which you can use cable release or time exposure for taking shots in the dark without the use of a flash mechanism, which essentially rules out light reflections should one acquire any light anomalies or orbs.

THE TRIGGER OBJECT

Invented by the pioneer of modern ghost hunting, Harry Price, the trigger object was used in the case of Borley Rectory in Essex, England between 1929 and 1939 and other cases he documented. Objects would move around on their own and would often be thrown violently across the rooms, so objects such as ornaments on the mantelpiece and window-sills would be chalked around and left locked off in an empty room. If the ghosts and spirits, or psychic energy (wherever it comes from) moved any of these objects they would obviously be moved from the chalked lines, thus indicating paranormal activity. The use of this simple but effective technique is still used to this day, as mischievous ghosts still like to move things around.

We often use this method with good results. It is normal procedure to train a video camera on the trigger object so should it be moved it would be caught on film. Trigger objects vary these days from coins to keys and even rubber ducks. Certain types of ghosts may interact with a certain type of trigger object, for example a spirit of a small boy may want to play with a trigger object of a toy car, or a ghostly smuggler or contraband thief may interact with old coins or jewellery. The trigger objects vary from investigation to investigation. In a poltergeist case, anything can be used.

DOWSING RODS AND CRYSTAL PENDULUMS

It is believed by some that spirit contact can be made by using dowsing rods and crystal pendulums. The theory goes that a spirit can use its energies to manipulate the crystal or rods in certain directions in order to answer questions put to it by the dowser. This technique I feel is controversial as subconscious movements of the dowser may be responsible for the movement of the rods or the crystal. However, in some cases unorthodox movement of the crystal cannot so easily be explained away, for example the crystal may move violently in a triangular motion, and sometimes it has been pulled out of the dowsers hand. Dowsing has been proven to work with water, and minerals so why can't it be used to dowse for spirit? For this hypothetical reason we use them on the team.

DATA LOGGERS

A data logger is a fabulous device that sits on a small tripod that can be situated anywhere and it simply monitors the whole environment. When you leave the logger recording it can take measurements of the room temperature and humidity every 10 seconds or so and stores all data on a small chip situated within it. If the room is vacated when the data logger is in use, nothing will be missed if anything untoward happens and there are subtle changes within the environment.

Data loggers such as the one a ghost-hunting colleague of mine uses on his investigations are ideal for sitting in the centre of séances. If anyone feels cold, or suggests that there is a temperature drop, the data logger will record it. If the data logger does not record a temperature drop when someone suggests there is one, we can determine that this person just thinks he or she is going cold. It is a fabulous device to ascertain objective evidence in regards to environmental anomalies.

LAPTOP COMPUTERS

A lot of paranormal investigators use laptop computers on investigations simply as a means to scrutinise and examine any potential anomalous photographs that may be taken on the night with digital cameras. The above-mentioned device (the data logger) also has a lead that connects to the laptop so the data it has collated can be transferred to the laptop for immediate analysis. Graphs and charts can be produced almost in an instant giving the researchers something to work on. EVPs and strange sound recordings can also be transferred to the laptop and examined with sound enhancement software. It is indeed a wonderful piece of apparatus in which without it any good evidence ascertained might not be discovered until the following day. In my opinion, discovering and confirming good phenomena on the night of the investigation could prove crucial in deciding how to go forward with the investigation in order to perhaps increase the chance of seeing or ascertaining the ultimate proof.

THE SÉANCE

The séance is not so much equipment but a technique used on some investigations as a means to communicate with the deceased. Without going into too much detail, a circle is formed by the holding of hands either while standing up or seated around a table. A designated investigator, usually a spirit medium or a psychic, will lead the proceedings. However it has been known for a non-mediumistic person to lead the séance but this only happens on our investigations when a medium or psychic is present to supervise. Spirit contact would then be attempted by asking the spirits to acknowledge their presence in the forms of knocks, bumps, and so on and so forth. It is also requested politely that they may attempt to show themselves to us.

Although I have felt, heard seen and sensed phenomena through controlled séances, I have yet to see a clear apparition of a ghost as a result of the psychic energy that is built up within the séance circle. Séances can be very physically and emotionally demanding for the sitters so care must be taken at all times. I must now stress that séances are very dangerous indeed, physically and mentally, if they are not undertaken in the correct manner, or under the correct supervision of a medium or psychic. I would recommend if you are interested in this form of spirit communication you should visit your local spiritualist church and under no circumstances try them out for yourself.

AFTERWORD

It gives me great pleasure to pen the afterword for Darren W. Ritson's latest book, *In Search of Ghosts*. That being said, I must now explain why.

Years ago, I inherited a fading, yellowed newspaper cutting from a good friend. It was dated 1923, and told the story of a Scottish crofter's house that was haunted by the spirit of an old shepherd. The cutting was incredibly brief, and simply mentioned the name of the village, the name of the crofter and the appearance of the old man in his living room. Pretty much par for the course in ghost-hunting circles, of course, but there was something about this particular tale that intrigued me. I began to dig, and uncovered a wealth of information that allowed me to breathe fresh life into the story and write it up as a newspaper feature. The life of a story is in the detail, for it allows the reader to visualise what occurred much more accurately. It also sets the context and can reanimate a dried-out old legend for the benefit of a whole new generation, which may never have heard it before.

Darren W. Ritson understands this principle all too well, and in this book *In Search of Ghosts* he has taken a host of tales (some ancient, others brand new) and waved his magic wand over them. He sets the scene, relates the history and then plunges the reader into a world of ghosts and wraiths. This is not a world found within the pages of a work of fiction; it is all too real, and as you now know.

Darren is not just an experienced and meticulous investigator. He is also a master true storyteller. In this book he has given us the best of both disciplines, and we should thank him for it.

Some investigators like to number-crunch; take measurements, readings and calculations by the score in an effort to determine whether anything truly paranormal is occurring. Good for them, I say, but it isn't my greatest forte. I prefer the experience. I like true ghost tales to tickle my senses, toy with my emotions and tighten my stomach muscles. *In Search of Ghosts* did that wonderfully for me, but its artistry in no way detracts from its value as a good handbook for investigators.

When Darren penned his first book, I warned him that the writing bug would infect him henceforth and that there was no cure for it. He now writes prolifically, and I'm glad to say that he'll find it irresistible to pen further works on ghosts and ghost-hunting in the future. If I'm wrong, don't worry; I'll force him to write more at gunpoint if I have too. The world of paranormal research would be the less without them.

Mike Hallowell
West Boldon, 2007

GLOSSARY/TERMINOLOGY

Apparition: The lifelike appearance of a soul or deceased person showing themselves after physical death. (See *ghost*).

Anomaly, anomalous: Something that deviates from the general rule, an inconsistency.

Apport: A solid object that seemingly appears from nowhere. They usually occur in poltergeist cases. They are often teleported from another location.

Astral Body: The image of a body while on an astral journey; some say the soul.

Astral Plane: Believed by some to be another level of existence where the souls move on to after their bodies expire.

Astral Projection: a self-induced out of body experience while in a trance-like state.

Baseline reading: The recording of data such as temperature, electro magnetic fields and humidity etc, prior to an investigation for comparison during an investigation.

Beam Barriers: An infrared beam device with an alarm used in ghost hunting to monitor empty rooms and corridors.

Crisis Apparition: A form of an apparition or astral image projected by a person at a time of crisis, i.e. an accident or at death. A loved one, or close friend usually sees this apparition.

Cold Spot: An area in a haunted location, in which the air temperature measures considerably colder than the surrounding air.

Calling out: To call out to the atmosphere, or any alleged spirits in the location, in the hope they will respond to your request and produce phenomena in order to document.

Control: (To control a vigil location). A course of action undertaken to ensure that the experiments that are being carried out are of the highest possible eminence, therefore ensuring any results established have not been jeopardised by any external influences.

Correlation: An association between two independent witnesses that have experienced the same phenomena, sometimes on different occasions.

Data Logger: See 'chapter 27'

Dematerialise: To disappear without trace thereby ceasing to have any material existence.

Disembodied: Lacking a body or freed from any attachment to a body.

Electro-Magnetic Field Meter (EMF): A device in which the natural electromagnetic fields can be measured and monitored.

Electronic Voice Phenomenon (EVP): The recordings of voices and auditory phenomena believed to be from beyond the grave.

Ectoplasm: Believed to be the substance ghosts are made from after being excreted from a mediums body.

Ethereal Body: What the spirit body is said to be made of while on an astral journey or out of body experience.

Ghost: The spirit or soul of a dead person showing themselves after physical death. (See *apparition* and *spectre*).

Harbinger: A spirit or ghost that is said to be a foreteller of doom or death, often dogs or animals.

Haunt: A ghost that returns to the same place is said to haunt it.

Laptop Computer: See 'chapter 27'

Lock off: A term used in ghost hunting to describe a locked but monitored area or room. Locked to prevent human intervention. Cameras, Dictaphones and trigger objects are normally used.

Medium: A person who claims to be able to communicate with the dead, and relay messages to the living.

Orbs: believed by psychics and mediums to be the first stages in ghost materialisation. Round balls of light said to be spiritual energy.

Paranormal: Beyond Normality. Para = Beyond. Above the normal understanding of the natural order.

Psychokinesis: The ability to move objects with the human mind. Recurring spontaneous Psychokinesis (RSPK), is to move objects with the human mind, only being unaware of doing so.

Poltergeist: An old German term for noisy ghost, now termed as Ein Spuk. Nowadays considered being the psychokinetic mind of a troubled or disturbed young individual lashing out frustration without being aware. (RSPK) A psychic temper tantrum.

Pareidolia: Parapsychologists term meaning to find pattern in randomness, i.e. faces in wallpaper, clouds or anomalous mists.

Psychic Breeze: A cold rush of air felt on investigations believed to be spirits passing by.

Possessed: Terms used by mediums indicating their bodies have been taken over by a spirit during attempted communication.

Pick Up: To sense a spirit, to be given a name or a message from a deceased person or from a building.

Residual Energy: The essence of a person left over from bygone days. Energy left over as residue. Apparitions or place memory ghosts are usually residual energy.

Rap-rapping: To Knock or bang on something in order to communicate. Used by spirits during séances and often in poltergeist cases.

Subjective Experience: a paranormal experience that is not corroborated by any objective means. For example photographic or environmental monitoring equipment, or by other witnesses.

Subjective Verified Experience: a paranormal experience that is observed by two or more witnesses but not verified by any other means. For example photographic or environmental monitoring equipment.

Spirit: The soul of a dead person or a spectral being with free will, and has the ability to move, and communicate.

Spectre: Another term or word for an apparition or ghost.

Sensory Deprivation: A technique or experiment in ghost investigations where one of the senses is deprived in order to enhance the others.

Séance: A method used in an attempt to communicate with the spirit world. The sitters hold hands in a circle around a table and call out to the alleged spirits in order to make contact. It is not recommend unless a trained psychic or medium is present.

Table Tilting: A ghost hunting technique used in Victorian times to communicate with the spirits. Similar to a séance only the spirits lift and tilt up the table in response to questions.

Vortex: A doorway or spirit path into our physical world. Used by spirits to get from one place to another.

Vigil: A designated period of time in a haunted location.

Whole Real Experience: a paranormal experience that is observed by any number of witnesses that are verified by objective means. For example with photographic or environmental monitoring equipment.

THE NORTH EAST GHOST RESEARCH TEAM

MICHAEL HALLOWELL – TEAM PATRON

Mike Hallowell was born in South Shields, Tyne & Wear, England, in 1957. He has been married to his wife Jackie for 30 years and has three sons. Mike is a freelance writer and broadcaster and runs his own media business. He specialises in writing about the paranormal and Native American culture and spirituality – he has Indian heritage in his family. Mike has had a number of books published. His first – *Herbal Healing* – was released in 1985. His latest book, based on the South Shields poltergeist case, was co-authored with Darren W. Ritson.

Mike contributes regularly to a number of journals and newspapers. He has penned his BIZARRE column for the *Shields Gazette* for nearly a decade. It is the longest running weekly paranormal column in a provincial newspaper in the UK. Mike has also starred in a number of documentaries about the paranormal, including the *Ghost Detectives*, *Uninvited Guests* and *Anatomy of a Haunting*. He regularly appears on BBC radio and other channels both here and abroad.

During his decades of paranormal investigation, Mike has interviewed numerous personalities, including David Wells, Colin Fry, Uri Geller, Tony Stockwell, Cliff Crook, Larry Warren, Richard Freeman, Stephen Holbrook, Jon Downes, Derek Acorah and Nick Redfern. Mike has worked closely with Darren W. Ritson on a number of intriguing cases and the two investigators run the WraithScape paranormal investigation site between them. Mike is a regular columnist with *Vision Magazine*, and contributes to numerous other publications such as *Paranormal Magazine*, *Cosmic Connections* and *Magonia*.

Mike is currently the patron of The North East Ghost Research Team and has been for the last three years.

"I was honoured to be asked by Darren to patron his team and I duly obliged as I feel Darren is one very few investigators out there with a real sense of passion and drive. There are a lot of people out there who claim to research the paranormal but I find very few 'investigators' with the ambition, tenacity, the knowledge, and the will to succeed in this particular chosen field, and Darren is certainly one of those."

Suzanne Hitchinson (Nee McKay)

I was born in 1982. I live in Northumberland with my fiancé Gavin and we have been together since 2002. I have lived in Northumberland all my life and was brought up in a little village community with my three brothers and my parents. I am an animal lover and I proudly support the Royal Society for the Prevention of Cruelty to Animals (RSPCA). I have been into the paranormal and unexplained phenomena since I was a young girl and I had my first encounter at the age of eleven when I saw my deceased grandmother at the side of my bed only three weeks after she had passed away. It encouraged me on to become involved with investigating and find answers not just for personal reasons, but also revealing the truth. I have also been a developing psychic for many years as well as investigating for many years having done no less that fifty investigations to date.

My path throughout the past few years has led me to my spiritual guides. My first being a spirit man called Hashimoko from Japan, who taught me to stop doubting myself. He also granted me protection whenever I felt uneasy. My new guide, I have yet to meet but I know he or she is there waiting for the right time to step forward and make him or herself known. I await this with excitement and anticipation. I am hoping to find some answers in the paranormal field including the answers that I think everyone craves for, to either oppose or support an afterlife. My other interests include movies, music, astronomy, crystals, reading, crafts and creative writing such as poetry.

Darren Olley

I was born in 1984 in Newcastle; I lived in Fawdon until I was about 13 years old then I moved to Dinnington village with my family. When I was younger I used to love hearing old ghost stories and hearing of experiences that people have had, especially my family members as this meant that they were first hand accounts and not just hearsay or simply rumour. My interests evidently include the paranormal and I also enjoy playing guitar. I am also interested in martial arts; as I have previously studied Judo, Karate, Thai Boxing, Tai Chi and Wing Chun. I am currently undertaking a course in criminology and I am planning to do a course in psychology in the near future. I am fascinated with how the human mind works and what effect it can have on people when in alleged haunted locations and how people perceive ghosts and the paranormal experiences they claim to have. Derren Brown is a big influence in the way of my thinking and this is, to a degree, why I am quite sceptical. However I am indeed open to the idea of an afterlife.

I have been a member of The North East Ghost Research Team more or less since the beginning and I have always found the subject of paranormal activity fascinating but never really did anything other than read about it. Then I met Darren through a friend at work. He started me on the path of ghost hunting and paranormal research. After attending a few ghost hunts with Darren and a couple of other people, I was asked to become a member of the group. I guess my role was defined from the outset – that of the person who knows there *might* be something out there, but tries to find a logical explanation for the things that we see and hear on the investigations. I guess I am the team's open-minded sceptic. Of course the rest of the team look for the rational explanations too and do not jump to hasty conclusions, any good team wouldn't, it's just that I am more sceptical than the others and I think I will take more convincing.

There are, however, some incidences I have experienced on these investigations that I couldn't explain or work out what was going on! The experiences I have had whilst being a member of this amazing team have allowed me to indulge in a passion that I find fascinating. It has also enabled me to go to many historical and interesting venues, and see parts of these wonderful places, which are often closed to the public. To spend the night at some of these wonderful locales is indeed an honour and a privilege. Someday I hope to add to the list of experiences one which I will never forget – that of solid proof of the afterlife. My thanks go to the founder, Darren W. Ritson for asking me to join his team and give me these wonderful opportunities to investigate ghosts, hauntings and the paranormal.

GLENN HALL

I was born in 1973 and lived in Middlesbrough for 22 years with my parents and my older sister Mel. I then moved to Stockton where I currently live with my partner Claire Smith and our daughter Caitlin. My interests include reading, relaxation and I am a huge fan of Middlesbrough FC. During my time living in Middlesbrough I often used to explore the disused mines in Cleveland Hills, which is thought to be a UFO 'hotspot'. I have been into the paranormal for a long time listening to my father's stories about big foot and alien abduction, but nothing engrossed me more than the ghost stories and hauntings of our local area. I had always taken a back seat in the paranormal, until I started to develop my sixth sense in 2003 and since then the paranormal has intrigued me so much to a point I wanted to join this team! I met Darren during my time with another local based team in which Darren was also a key member.

When I heard he was also running his own team, I hoped he would like another enthusiastic and dedicated investigator on board. I asked him about this opportunity and after attending a few investigations with him and his team, he accepted me as a team member and I have never looked back! I have been in several teams during my development and during my work with these groups I have seen and experienced a lot of strange things, which are hard to understand. In all honesty working with Darren and being on his team has really made me realise my potential as a developing psychic and an investigator in general and I endeavour (like the rest of the team) to seek out proof of ghosts and it is the quest for the answers that drives us on. So far I have done dozens of investigations and I am hopeful for a lot more to come. I am in no doubt that in time; this team will reach almost every corner of the UK and investigate some of Britain's most haunted and historic locations in the quest for the truth. I am so proud to be in a team such as this.

CLAIRE SMITH

I was born in Sunderland in 1984. I currently live in Stockton-on-Tees with my partner Glenn and our beautiful daughter Caitlin. I lived in Washington for 21 years with my mum, dad and brother Andrew, who is also interested in the paranormal and unexplained. I attended St Robert of Newminster Roman Catholic School and during my time there I had a couple of visits to the Washington Arts Centre, which is believed to be a haunted location. I was unaware of this at the time but found myself intrigued by the place and always longing for a return visit. I also used to visit Washington Old Hall and Newcastle Keep during the day for days out and enjoyed wondering around them taking photographs and generally soaking up the atmosphere. I was always looking for new and interesting places to visit and I enjoyed learning the history of a location as well as hearing the ghost stories. I first became interested in the actual ghost research after a visit to the famous Schooner Hotel in Alnmouth, Northumberland where I met a few members of different Investigation teams based in the north-east of England. I started off a bit sceptical but there has always been a believer in me, which was soon to be brought out.

My first official Investigation was at Beamish Hall in County Durham and it was a good positive experience. I was unfamiliar with the history of this particular location and any past experiences people had encountered there, so it was easy to relax and take in the general atmosphere and feelings that the building had to offer. Since my first Investigation I have been fully addicted and I am lucky enough to have been accepted into The North East Ghost Research Team. I love the fact that every Investigation has a different feel to it even if you have been to the same location more than once. Things do indeed change and you cannot always logically explain every occurrence. The most exciting experience I have had was during an investigation at an anonymous location at Gateshead. We were guests of another well respected northeast based research team and it was during this investigation when I saw an apparition of a man kneeling down during the early hours of the morning. I saw this gentleman as clearly as I saw my fellow investigators and after the initial shock, I was thrilled and I wanted to share the experience with everyone. This sighting had a profound effect on me and it literally reduced me to tears. The experience was fairly recent and it is something I did not expect in the least and it is something I will never forget. Ghost research and the paranormal is my passion and the places we get to visit and stay overnight are remarkable and it is indeed an honour to able to do this.

JULIE OLLEY

I was born in 1978, and I grew up in Newcastle with my mum, dad, two sisters and brother. I attended Fawdon primary school and Kenton comprehensive. When I left school, I attended The John Marley Centre and have completed, and now hold an NVQ level 2 in childcare and education. I work as an activities coordinator and play worker at a child care setting in Gosforth and have been working there for nearly 10 years. I moved from Fawdon in 1997 and now live in Dinnington Village. My hobbies and interests include cycling, art, astrology and archaeology. I enjoy socialising, listening to music, reading, going on family days out and spending time with my family. I am also a big animal lover. I am a very down to earth and honest person and enjoy meeting new people and having fun.

I have been a member of The North East Ghost Research Team for over two years now. I have always been interested in the paranormal, when I was younger I always loved to hear of other peoples experiences and read up on the subject. I was introduced to Darren W. Ritson through my brother who is also on the team. I would say I am quite sceptical and try to find logical explanations for everything I have experienced, but on a few occasions I have been unable to do so. After attending a couple of investigations as a guest investigator, I was hooked and the experience of spending time in haunted locations inspired me to start reading the Paranormal Magazines and through them I discovered MAPIT. I have now completed the British Investigators Training Course in Anomalous Phenomena and Parapsychology unit B1 and I now hold a certificate of distinction in the field of Paranormal Investigations. I am currently in the middle of the advanced course and hope to, in the future go on to do the professional level in this subject. I was thrilled when I was asked to join this amazing team and my thanks go to the founder, Darren W. Ritson, who has enabled me to be part of a field which I have always been interested in and for giving me the opportunity to experience phenomena for myself instead of just reading about it.

Mark Winter

I was born in 1976 in Ashington, Northumberland, I am married to Paula and we have one child, Aaron, and another now on the way. I love science fiction films and horror films; I also have a keen interest in music. My favourite films include *Star Wars*, *The Exorcist*, *The Sixth Sense* and *Halloween*. I also DJ when I can. I joined the team in 2004 after a life-long interest in ghosts and the paranormal. I have always had a keen interest in the paranormal due to my parents and grandparents telling me stories of their experiences, I always remember a story I was told, my mother and grandparents were awoken one night by a banging noise coming from downstairs in their home, my mother went halfway down the stairs to investigate and saw the cupboards in the kitchen opening and closing by themselves, and on further investigations my grandfather found that the food from the cupboards had been emptied onto the benches and floor.

My interest became more prominent when I awoke one night to get a drink of water and as I was getting back into bed I saw the ghost of a small girl with long dark hair standing at the end of my bed, she was wearing wire framed glasses and a black duffle coat and she was standing there clear as day. In passing I got chatting to Darren and found out that he did psychical research on a regular basis and asked if I could go along to an investigation with him and since then I have been hooked. I find the feeling of being scared very exhilarating and really enjoy visiting different locations and hearing the stories connected with these locations. I also would like to learn more about my own psychic abilities. Hopefully being a member of The North East Ghost Research Team will enable me to realise my dreams.

ABOUT THE AUTHOR

Darren W. Ritson is a civil servant and lives in North Tyneside with his long-term partner Jayne Watson and their daughter Abbey. He has had an interest in the paranormal for most of his life due to some unexplained happenings he experienced as a child growing up. He founded The North East Ghost In-Spectres research team in May 2003 after a lifelong long interest in the subject of ghosts. The team, now called The North East Ghost Research Team is a non-profit making organization dedicated to trying to find out the truth behind ghosts and hauntings. As well as once being a team member in just about every research team in the north-east of England, he is also a founding member of the Ghost and Hauntings Overnight Surveillance Team.

Ever since he was a small boy he was fascinated with the thought of ghosts existing, and after experiencing poltergeist activity at the age of thirteen in France in 1986, his path was set and he decided to try to learn more. Over the next 20 years he built up a library of books, magazines and literature on the paranormal including the works of the late Harry Price (1881–1948) Peter Underwood FRSA, and Guy Lyon Playfair, of which these three prolific ghost researchers and writers are his main influences. It was then he formed his research team and their goals and objectives are simple. To collate data, signed witness testimonies and to gather evidence from their investigations in order to attempt to piece this intangible supernatural puzzle together. They try to take a scientific, objective and professional approach to each investigation they undertake, and although they believe in ghosts, each investigation is looked at sceptically.

Evidence collated is viewed and looked at objectively and a process of elimination is carried out before producing our findings in a full investigation report. Any good evidence is usually sent for further analysis. He is immensely proud of the team he runs, and the work they have carried out, and they will continue to investigate, write, and interview witnesses in their endless quest for the truth. In addition to him travelling the country and ghost hunting wherever possible, he also writes articles and features for nationwide publications and has featured in magazines such as *Paranormal* and *Vision Magazine*.

Over the years Darren has worked with who he considers to be some of the best paranormal investigators in the country today. He is a good friend of Michael Hallowell and Tony Liddell who have both authored books on the paranormal, he has met and worked with Mark Webb from ITV's *Haunted Homes* on a number of occasions, television medium Marion Goodfellow, Diana Jarvis – the editor of *Vision Magazine*, Ralph Keeton – who is Britain's number one exorcist, and *Most Haunted's* spirit medium David Wells along with many others. The North East Ghost Research Team have also worked with many ghost-hunting teams across the UK including The British Paranormal Alliance, and Dave Wood and Nicky Sewell of PSI. He also regularly corresponds with veteran ghost hunter Peter Underwood FRSA who is the president of the Ghost Club Society, and Guy Lyon Playfair who co-investigated the famous Enfield Poltergeist with the late Maurice Grosse.

After becoming a member of The Incorporated Society for Psychical Research (SPR) in May 2006 he hopes to continue his ghost hunting and paranormal research in addition to meeting new people and working with them in order to try to prove the existence of ghosts.

THE SPECTRAL MONK

A Poem
By Darren W. Ritson

Swinging lights, slamming doors,
This prospect is quite daunting.
A ruined Abbey, or an old public house,
The scene of a gruesome haunting.

Footsteps echo, in an old dark room
A disembodied voice, that foretells your doom,
An EVP that will chill the blood
There stands a monk, robed, with a hood.

He glides towards you as you root to the spot
The sweat pours down you, you're frightened, but not!
As the spectre draws closer, you shake with fear
Just wait for a moment, and watch him disappear!

An empty room, it is now once more
You take your chance, and run for the door
Your pulse is racing, and your heart has sunk
For you have just witnessed, the spectral monk!

"Enough!" You say, as you leave in the morning
It's now getting brighter, as the day is dawning
The vigil over, you have finished your search
As you've just spent the night, in a haunted church.

This Spectral Monk, a harbinger of death
The time is upon you, to draw your last breath
A prediction fulfilled, to turn grey, your hairs,
For the monk won't be seen now, for a 100 more years.